The Socratic Method Today

This exciting new textbook provides a sophisticated examination of the Socratic method for teaching political science students in higher education. It shows how the Socratic method is employed in the Platonic dialogs, compares its transformative approach to other student-centered teaching philosophies, and addresses the challenges of adopting the Socratic method in the contemporary classroom.

The book is divided into three sections that integrate these practical aspects on the Socratic method with the theoretical considerations of Socratic philosophy while also addressing contemporary concerns about teaching and learning in higher education.

- Section One explores how the Socratic method is portrayed by Socrates in Plato's dialogs.
- Section Two compares the Socratic method with modern and contemporary accounts of teaching and learning.
- Section Three examines some of the contemporary challenges of practicing the Socratic method in the university classroom today and how teachers can overcome them.

Written in a clear and engaging style, this timely intervention is essential reading for upper undergraduate students enrolled in courses that specialize in pedagogical techniques, political theory, Socratic philosophy, and law.

Lee Trepanier is Professor of Political Science at Saginaw Valley State University, USA; editor of Lexington Books' Politics, Literature, and Film series; and author and editor of numerous books, the latest being *Why the Humanities Matter Today: In Defense of Liberal Education* (2017).

This is a unique and important volume on the timeless Socratic Method and its importance to education. Its publication is timely, as many institutions of higher education are struggling to engage students in an active form of pedagogy. The essays in this volume are brilliant, insightful, and are sure to illuminate the path back to the timeless method pioneered by Socrates, the greatest teacher of liberal education who ever lived.

Khalil Habib, Associate Professor of Philosophy,
Salve Regina University, USA

The Socratic Method Today
Student-Centered and Transformative
Teaching in Political Science

Edited by Lee Trepanier

NEW YORK AND LONDON

First published 2018
by Routledge
711 Third Avenue, New York, NY 10017

and by Routledge
2 Park Square, Milton Park, Abingdon, Oxon, OX14 4RN

Routledge is an imprint of the Taylor & Francis Group, an informa business

© 2018 Taylor & Francis

The right of Lee Trepanier to be identified as the author of the editorial material, and of the authors for their individual chapters, has been asserted in accordance with sections 77 and 78 of the Copyright, Designs and Patents Act 1988.

All rights reserved. No part of this book may be reprinted or reproduced or utilized in any form or by any electronic, mechanical, or other means, now known or hereafter invented, including photocopying and recording, or in any information storage or retrieval system, without permission in writing from the publishers.

Trademark notice: Product or corporate names may be trademarks or registered trademarks, and are used only for identification and explanation without intent to infringe.

Library of Congress Cataloging-in-Publication Data
A catalog record for this title has been requested

ISBN: 978-0-8153-7188-5 (hbk)
ISBN: 978-0-8153-7190-8 (pbk)
ISBN: 978-1-351-24582-1 (ebk)

Typeset in Times New Roman
by Sunrise Setting Ltd., Brixham, UK

For my teachers who taught in the spirit of Socrates

Contents

List of Contributors	ix
Introduction: The Socratic Method Today LEE TREPANIER	1

PART I
The Socratic Method in Plato's Dialogs   7

1 Poetic Questions in the Socratic Method MARLENE K. SOKOLON	9
2 Socratic Method and Existence BARRY COOPER	22
3 Guiding *Eros* Toward Wisdom in *Alcibiades I* VANESSA JANSCHE	35
4 Skepticism and Recollection in Socrates ANN WARD	47

PART II
The Socratic Method and Other Approaches   57

5 The Socratic Method in Plato and Kant STEVEN F. MCGUIRE	59
6 The Americanization of the Socratic Method ANDREW BIBBY	70
7 The Socratic Method and John Dewey DAVID W. LIVINGSTONE	81
8 The Courage of the Socratic Method JORDON B. BARKALOW	94

PART III
The Socratic Method in the Classroom   113

9   "No Guru, No Method, No Teacher"   115
      SEAN STEEL

10   Is Socrates Culturally Imperialistic?   125
      REBECCA LEMOINE

11   The Socratic Method in Today's University   138
      PAUL COREY

12   The Socratic Method's Search for Standards   152
      RAMONA JUNE GREY

Appendix to Chapter 8: Discussion Questions for Plato's Laches   164
Index   166

Contributors

Jordon B. Barkalow is an Associate Professor of Political Science at Bridgewater State University.

Andrew Bibby is the Director of the Center for Constitutional Studies at Utah Valley University and author of *Montesquieu's Political Economy* (Palgrave Macmillan, 2015).

Barry Cooper is a Professor of Political Science at the University of Calgary. He is the author, editor, and translator of over thirty books, with the latest being *Consciousness and Politics: From Analysis to Meditation in the late Work of Eric Voegelin* (St. Augustine Press, 2016).

Paul Corey is the Program Coordinator and Professor of Liberal Studies at Humber Institute of Technology and Advanced Learning, and author of *Messiahs and Machiavellians: Depicting Evil in Modern Theatre* (University of Notre Dame Press, 2008).

Ramona June Grey is a Professor of Political Science at the University of Montana.

Vanessa Jansche is an Assistant Lecturer of Philosophy at St. Gallen University.

Rebecca LeMoine is an Assistant Professor of Political Science at Florida Atlantic University and is author of the forthcoming book, *Plato's Caves: The Liberating Sting of Cultural Diversity*.

David W. Livingstone is University College Professor of Liberal Studies and Political Science at Vancouver Island University and editor of *Liberal Education, Civic Education, and the Canadian Regime: Past Principles and Present Challenges* (McGill-Queen's University Press, 2015).

Steven F. McGuire is Thomas W. Smith Fellow at the Matthew J. Ryan Center at Villanova University and co-editor of *Subjectivity: Ancient and Modern* (Lexington Books, 2016) and *Eric Voegelin and the Continental Tradition* (University of Missouri, 2008).

Marlene K. Sokolon is Chair and Associate Professor of Political Science at Concordia University and author of *Political Emotions: Aristotle on the Symphony of Reason and Emotion* (Northern Illinois Press, 2006) and co-editor of *Fertile Ground: Production in Canada* (McGill-Queen's University Press, 2014).

Sean Steel is Lecturer at Ambrose University College and author of *The Pursuit of Wisdom and Happiness in Education: Historical Sources and Contemplative Practices* (SUNY Press, 2014).

Lee Trepanier is a Professor of Political Science at Saginaw Valley State University; editor of Lexington Books' Politics, Literature, and Film series; and author and editor of numerous books, the latest being *Why the Humanities Matter Today: In Defense of Liberal Education* (Lexington Books, 2017).

Ann Ward is an Associate Professor of Political Science at Campion College, University of Regina; author of *Contemplating Friendship: Aristotle's Ethics* (SUNY Press, 2016), *Herodotus and the Philosophy of Empire* (Baylor University Press, 2008); and editor of several books, the latest being *Socrates and Dionysus: Philosophy and Art in Dialogue* (Cambridge Scholar Publishing, 2013).

Introduction

The Socratic Method Today[1]

Lee Trepanier

There has been a renewed interest in pedagogy, teaching, and student learning in political science, with a focus on topics like flipping the classroom and active learning.[2] Surprisingly absent in this discussion is the Socratic method, one of the oldest ways whereby teachers educate students. This book remedies this situation. It examines how the Socratic method is employed in the Platonic dialogs, how it is similar and different from contemporary pedagogical accounts, and how it can be adopted in today's classroom. Although aimed primarily for those in political science, this collection has broad appeal to anyone interested in the Socratic method.

When looking at previous works on the Socratic method, we encounter two types of books: 1) how-to manuals that are written for secondary school teachers; and 2) highly technical works of political philosophy where the Socratic method is secondary to the broader concerns of the authors. Examples of the first type are Nelson's *Socratic Method and Critical Philosophy*; Gower and Stokes' *Socratic Questions*; Seeskin's *Dialogue and Discovery*; Nehamas' *The Art of Living*; Valla's *Socratic Citizenship*; Eisele's *Bitter Knowledge*; Jenks' *How Plato's Theory of Truth Explains the Socratic Method*; Schlosser's *What Would Socrates Do?*; and Sebell's *The Socratic Turn*.[3] There are also works where the Socratic method is the main subject of inquiry but they fail to show how the ideas can be translated into the classroom, such as Scott's *Does Socrates Have a Method?*; Cain's *The Socratic Method*; and Sintonen's *The Socratic Tradition*.[4]

The second type of works about the Socratic method is entirely practical, devoid of any philosophical consideration, and aimed at secondary school teachers: Whipple Jr.'s *Socratic Method and Writing Instruction*; Saran and Neisser's *Enquiring Minds*; and Kreeft's *Socratic Logic*.[5] Other books in this category that focus on fostering group discussion are Gross' *Socrates' Way*; Copeland's *Socratic Circles*; and Wilberding's *Teach Like Socrates*.[6] And with respect to the study of law, the emphasis is on the Socratic method's effectiveness (or lack thereof) as a pedagogical technique.[7] The works in this group lack any theoretical grounding of the Socratic method and thereby neglect the larger philosophical and pedagogical debates that surround it.

Providing a fresh, scholarly, and practical account of the Socratic method, this book synthesizes the strengths of the previous literature by integrating the theoretical considerations of the Socratic method with the practical aspects of teaching in the classroom. In this work, we have invited a mixture of established and rising scholars to provide a broad perspective of the Socratic method. We have organized the volume into three sections: 1) The Socratic Method in Plato's Dialogs; 2) The Socratic Method and Other Approaches; and 3) The Socratic Method in the Classroom.

In the first chapter of the first section, Marlene K. Sokolon shows how Socrates employs a mixture of stories, appeals, and argumentation to persuade his interlocutors, whereas in "Socratic Method and Existence" Barry Cooper investigates how *elenchus* is understood in both the *Apology* and the *Euthyphro* as a type of transformative learning. In "Guiding *Eros* Toward Wisdom in *Alcibiades I*," Vanessa Jansche looks at how the Socratic method requires a realignment of one's *eros* toward philosophy. Ann Ward concludes this section by reconciling different aspects of the Socratic method from the *Apology* and the *Meno*. What we discover from these chapters is that the

Socratic method is more than a technique: it requires a range of devices to access the motivations of students so they can become active learners.

For the second section, the Socratic method is compared with other philosophical and pedagogical approaches of teaching and learning. Steven F. McGuire compares Socrates' and Kant's understandings of recollection and the role it plays in their educational philosophies. In "The Americanization of the Socratic Method," Andrew Bibby shows that the Socratic method adopted at the time of the American Founding was transformed into a mode of individual critical *thinking* and self-expression. David W. Livingstone explains in "The Socratic Method and John Dewey" how the Socratic method is sometimes incorrectly equated to Dewey's discovery of learning. Finally, Jordon B. Barkalow investigates the Socratic method as an alternative to student-centered learning in his chapter, "The Courage of the Socratic Method."

The final section explores some of the practical concerns and challenges of teaching the Socratic method in the classroom. In "No Guru, No Method, No Teacher" Sean Steel argues that the Socratic method as a technique is indistinguishable from that of the sophists and that the real difference lies in the motivations of the teacher. Rebecca LeMoine examines whether the Socratic method is culturally imperialistic, particularly in multicultural classrooms in her chapter, "Is Socrates Culturally Imperialistic?" Paul Corey in "The Socratic Method in Today's University" discusses the obstacles teachers confront that make the Socratic method difficult to teach in today's universities; and Ramona June Grey closes the volume on whether a set of standards can be discovered in the Socratic method.

What we can conclude from all these chapters is that the Socratic method is both a technique and a transformative experience where the student's soul is turned away from the realm of opinion toward a search for truth (*Republic*, 515e).[8] Although the teacher can employ an array of techniques, enchantments, and appeals to the student, the love for wisdom ultimately lies outside the control of the instructor. Like love and friendship, the Socratic method is like a prayer rooted in hope that this fragile enterprise we undertake will yield something good for us and our students – but only the gods know for sure.

Notes

1 I want to thank APSA, where these papers were presented at the 2017 Teaching and Learning Conference; the staff at Routledge, especially Natalja Mortensen and Maria Landschoot; and the referees for this project.
2 Some recent examples are Ken Bain, *What the Best College Teachers Do* (Cambridge: Harvard, 2004); Anne C. Martin and Ellen Schwartz, *Making Space for Active Learning: The Art and Practice of Teaching* (New York: Teacher College Press, 2014); Hal Blythe and Charlie Sweet, *It Works for Me, Flipping the Classroom: Shared Tips for Effective Teaching* (Stillwater: New Forum Press, 2015); Claire Howell Major and Michael S. Harris, *Teaching for Learning* (London: Routledge, 2015); Julee B. Waldrop and Melody A. Bowdon, *Best Practices for Flipping the Classroom* (London: Routledge, 2015).

With respect to political science, see Diana E. Hess, *Controversy in the Classroom* (London: Routledge, 2009); Paula McAvoy, *The Political Classroom: Evidence and Ethics in Democratic Education* (London: Routledge, 2015); Laure Paquette, *Teaching Political Science to Undergraduates* (Berlin: De Gruyter, 2015); Sule Yaylaci and Edana Beauvais, "The Role of Social Group Membership on Classroom Participation," *PS: Political Science & Politics* 50/2 (2017): 599–64.
3 Leonard Nelson, *Socratic Method and Critical Philosophy: Selected Essays* (Mineola: Dover, 1949); Barry S. Gower and Michael C. Stokes, *Socratic Questions* (London: Routledge, 1992); Kenneth Seeskin, *Dialogue and Discovery: A Study in the Socratic Method* (Albany: SUNY Press, 1987); Alexander Nehamas, *The Art of Living: Socratic Reflections from Plato to Foucault* (Berkeley: University of California Press, 2000); Dana Valla, *Socratic Citizenship* (Princeton: Princeton University Press, 2001); Thomas D. Eisele, *Bitter Knowledge: Learning Socratic Lessons of Disillusion and Renewal* (South Bend: University of Notre Dame Press, 2009); Rod Jenks, *How Plato's Theory of Truth Explains Socratic Method* (Lewiston: Edwin Mellen Press, 2010); Joel Alden Schlosser, *What Would Socrates Do? Self-Examination, Civic Engagement, and the Politics of Philosophy* (Cambridge: Cambridge University Press, 2014); Dustin Sebell, *The Socratic Turn: Knowledge of Good and Evil in an Age of Science* (Philadelphia: University of Pennsylvania, 2016).

Other, similar works are Gregory Vlastos, "The Socratic Elenchus," in *Oxford Studies in Ancient Philosophy*, Julia Annas, ed. (Oxford: Oxford University Press, 1983), 27–58; Leo Strauss, *The City and the Man* (Chicago: Rand McNally, 1964); Seth Bernardete, *Second Sailing: On Plato's Republic* (Chicago: University of Chicago Press, 1989); Jill Gordon, *Turning toward Philosophy: Literary Device and Dramatic Structure in Plato's Dialogues* (University Park: Pennsylvania State University Press, 1999); Gregory Vlastos, *Socrates: Ironist and Moral Philosopher* (Ithaca: Cornell University Press, 1991); Diskin Clay, *Platonic Questions: Dialogues with the Silent Philosopher* (University Park: Pennsylvania State University Press, 2000); Melissa Lane, *Plato's Progeny: How Plato and Socrates Still Capture the Modern Mind* (London: Bristol Classical Press, 2001); Iakovos Vassiliou, *Aiming for Virtue in Plato* (Cambridge: Cambridge University Press, 2008).

4 Gary Alan Scott, *Does Socrates Have a Method? Rethinking Elenchus in Plato's Dialogue and Beyond* (University Park: Pennsylvania State University, 2002); Rebecca Bensen Cain, *The Socratic Method: Plato's Use of Philosophical Drama* (London: Continuum, 2007); Matt Sintonen, *The Socratic Tradition: Questioning as Philosophy and as a Method* (London: College Publications, 2009).

5 Robert D. Whipple Jr., *Socratic Method and Writing Instruction* (Lanham: University Press of America, 1997); Rene Saran and Barbara Neisser, *Enquiring Minds: Socratic Dialogue in Education* (Stoke-on-Trent: Trentham Books, 2004); Peter Kreeft, *Socratic Logic: A Logic Text Using Socratic Method, Platonic Questions, and Aristotelian Principles* (South Bend: St. Augustine's Press, 2005).

6 Ronald Gross, *Socrates' Way: Seven Master Keys to Using Your Mind to the Utmost* (New York: TarcherPerigee, 2002); Matt Copeland, *Socratic Circles: Fostering Critical and Creative Thinking in Middle and High School* (Portland, ME: Stenhouse Press, 2005); Erick Wilberding, *Teach Like Socrates: Guiding Socratic Dialogues and Discussion in the Classroom* (Austin: Prufrock Press, 2014); also see Tziporah Kasachkoff, *In the Socratic Tradition: Essays on Teaching Philosophy* (Lanham: Rowman & Littlefield, 1998).

7 Frank Guliuzza III, "In-Class Debating in Public Law Classes as a Complement to the Socratic Method," *PS: Political Science & Politics* 24/4 (1991): 703–5; Steven Friedland, "How We Teach: A Survey of Teaching Techniques in American Law Schools." *Seattle University Law Review* 20/1 (1996): 1–44; Lani Guinier, Michelle Fine and Jane Balin, *Becoming Gentlewomen: Women, Law School, and Institution Change* (Boston: Beacon, 1997); Cynthia G. Hawkins-León, "The Socratic Method-Problem Method Dichotomy: The Debate over Teaching Method Continues." *Brigham Young University Education and Law Journal* 1 (1998): 1–18; Orin S. Kerr, "The Decline of the Socratic Method at Harvard," *Nebraska Law Review* 78 (1999): 113–34; Sara Lawrence-Lightfoot, "Inside the Classroom of Harvard Law School Professor David Wilkins," *Journal of Blacks in Higher Education* 25 (1999): 113–19; Peter M. Cicchino, "Love and the Socratic Method," *American University Law Review* 50 (2001): 533–50; Avi Mintz, "From Grade School to Law School: Socrates' Legacy in Education," in *A Companion to Socrates*, Sara Ahbel-Rappe and Rachana Kamtekar, eds. (London: Blackwell, 2006), 476–92; Carrie-Ann Biondi, "Socratic Teaching: Beyond *The Paper Chase*," *Teaching Philosophy* 31/2 (2008): 119–40; Benjamin V. Madison III, "The Elephant in Law School Classrooms: Overuse of the Socratic Method as an Obstacle to Teaching Modern Students," *University of Detroit Mercy Law Review* 85 (2008): 293–346; Joseph A. Dickinson, "Understanding the Socratic Method in Law School Teaching after the Carnegie Foundation's Educating Lawyers," *Western New England Law Review* 31/1 (2009): 97–113; Evan Peterson, "Teaching to Think: Applying the Socratic Method Outside the Law School Setting," *Journal of College Teaching & Learning* 6/5 (2009): 83–7; Christie A. Linskens Christie, "What Critiques Have Been Made of the Socratic Method in Legal Education? The Socratic Method in Legal Education: Uses, Abuses, and Beyond," *European Journal of Law Reform* 12/3–4 (2010): 340–55; Michael Hunter Schwartz, Gerald F. Hess and Sophie M. Sparrow, *What the Best Law Teachers Do* (Cambridge: Harvard University Press, 2013); Jamie R. Abrams, "Reframing the Socratic Method," *Journal of Legal Education* 64/4 (2015): 562–85; Charles Szypszak, "Socratic Method for the Right Reasons and in the Right Way: Lessons from Teaching Legal Analysis Beyond the American Law School," *Journal of Political Science Education* 11 (2015): 358–69.

8 Alan Bloom, *The Republic of Plato* (New York: Basic Books, 1991).

Bibliography

Abrams, Jamie R. 2015. "Reframing the Socratic Method." *Journal of Legal Education* 64/4: 562–85.
Bain, Ken. 2004. *What the Best College Teachers Do*. Cambridge: Harvard University Press.
Bernardete, Seth. 1989. *Second Sailing: On Plato's Republic*. Chicago: University of Chicago Press.
Biondi, Carrie-Ann. 2008. "Socratic Teaching: Beyond *The Paper Chase*." *Teaching Philosophy* 31/2: 119–40.
Bloom, Alan. 1991. *The Republic of Plato*. New York: Basic Books.

Blythe, Hal and Charlie Sweet. 2015. *It Works for Me, Flipping the Classroom: Shared Tips for Effective Teaching*. Stillwater: New Forum Press.
Cain, Rebecca B. 2007. *The Socratic Method: Plato's Use of Philosophical Drama*. London: Continuum.
Christie, Christie A. Linskens. 2010. "What Critiques Have Been Made of the Socratic Method in Legal Education? The Socratic Method in Legal Education: Uses, Abuses, and Beyond." *European Journal of Law Reform* 12/3–4: 340–55.
Cicchino, Peter M. 2001. "Love and the Socratic Method." *American University Law Review* 50: 533–50.
Clay, Diskin. 2000. *Platonic Questions: Dialogues with the Silent Philosopher*. University Park: Pennsylvania State University Press.
Copeland, Matt. 2005. *Socratic Circles: Fostering Critical and Creative Thinking in Middle and High School*. Portland: Stenhouse Press.
Dickinson, Joseph A. 2009. "Understanding the Socratic Method in Law School Teaching after the Carnegie Foundation's Educating Lawyers." *Western New England Law Review* 31/1: 97–113.
Eisele, Thomas D. 2009. *Bitter Knowledge: Learning Socratic Lessons of Disillusion and Renewal*. South Bend: University of Notre Dame Press.
Friedland, Steven. 1996. "How We Teach: A Survey of Teaching Techniques in American Law Schools." *Seattle University Law Review* 20/1: 1–44.
Gordon, Jill. 1999. *Turning toward Philosophy: Literary Device and Dramatic Structure in Plato's Dialogues*. University Park: Pennsylvania State University Press.
Gower, Barry S. and Michael C. Stokes. 1992. *Socratic Questions*. London: Routledge.
Gross, Ronald. 2002. *Socrates' Way: Seven Master Keys to Using Your Mind to the Utmost*. New York: TarcherPerigee.
Guinier, Lani, Michelle Fine and Jane Balin. 1997. *Becoming Gentlewomen: Women, Law School, and Institution Change*. Boston: Beacon.
Guliuzza III, Frank. 1991. "In-Class Debating in Public Law Classes as a Complement to the Socratic Method." *PS: Political Science & Politics* 24/4: 703–5.
Hawkins-León, Cynthia G. 1998. "The Socratic Method-Problem Method Dichotomy: The Debate over Teaching Method Continues." *Brigham Young University Education and Law Journal* 1: 1–18.
Hess, Diana E. 2009. *Controversy in the Classroom*. London: Routledge.
Jenks, Rod. 2010. *How Plato's Theory of Truth Explains Socratic Method*. Lewiston: Edwin Mellen Press.
Kasachkoff, Tziporah. 1998. *In the Socratic Tradition: Essays on Teaching Philosophy*. Lanham: Rowman & Littlefield.
Kerr, Orin S. 1999. "The Decline of the Socratic Method at Harvard." *Nebraska Law Review* 78: 113–34.
Kreeft, Peter. 2005. *Socratic Logic: A Logic Text Using Socratic Method, Platonic Questions, and Aristotelian Principles*. South Bend: St. Augustine's Press.
Lane, Melissa. 2001. *Plato's Progeny: How Plato and Socrates Still Capture the Modern Mind*. London: Bristol Classical Press.
Lawrence-Lightfoot, Sara. 1999. "Inside the Classroom of Harvard Law School Professor David Wilkins." *Journal of Blacks in Higher Education* 25: 113–19.
Madison III, Benjamin V. 2008. "The Elephant in Law School Classrooms: Overuse of the Socratic Method as an Obstacle to Teaching Modern Students." *University of Detroit Mercy Law Review* 85: 293–346.
Major, Claire H. and Michael S. Harris. 2015. *Teaching for Learning*. London: Routledge.
Martin, Anne C. and Ellen Schwartz. 2014. *Making Space for Active Learning: The Art and Practice of Teaching*. New York: Teacher College Press.
McAvoy, Paula. 2015. *The Political Classroom: Evidence and Ethics in Democratic Education*. London: Routledge.
Mintz, Avi. 2006. "From Grade School to Law School: Socrates' Legacy in Education." In *A Companion to Socrates*. Sara Ahbel-Rappe and Rachana Kamtekar eds. London: Blackwell: 476–92.
Nehamas, Alexander. 2000. *The Art of Living: Socratic Reflections from Plato to Foucault*. Berkeley: University of California Press.
Nelson, Leonard. 1949. *Socratic Method and Critical Philosophy: Selected Essays*. Mineola: Dover.
Paquette, Laure. 2015. *Teaching Political Science to Undergraduates*. Berlin: De Gruyter.
Peterson, Evan. 2009. "Teaching to Think: Applying the Socratic Method Outside the Law School Setting." *Journal of College Teaching & Learning* 6/5: 83–7.

Saran, Rene and Barbara Neisser. 2004. *Enquiring Minds: Socratic Dialogue in Education.* Stoke-on-Trent: Trentham Books.

Schlosser, Joel A. 2014. *What Would Socrates Do? Self-Examination, Civic Engagement, and the Politics of Philosophy.* Cambridge: Cambridge University Press.

Schwartz, Michael H., Gerald F. Hess and Sophie M. Sparrow. 2013. *What the Best Law Teachers Do.* Cambridge: Harvard University Press.

Scott, Gary A. 2002. *Does Socrates Have a Method? Rethinking Elenchus in Plato's Dialogue and Beyond.* University Park: Pennsylvania State University.

Sebell, Dustin. 2016. *The Socratic Turn: Knowledge of Good and Evil in an Age of Science.* Philadelphia: University of Pennsylvania.

Seeskin, Kenneth. 1987. *Dialogue and Discovery: A Study in the Socratic Method.* Albany: SUNY Press.

Sintonen, Matt. 2009. *The Socratic Tradition: Questioning as Philosophy and as a Method.* London: College Publications.

Strauss, Leo. 1964. *The City and the Man.* Chicago: Rand McNally.

Szypszak, Charles. 2015. "Socratic Method for the Right Reasons and in the Right Way: Lessons from Teaching Legal Analysis Beyond the American Law School." *Journal of Political Science Education* 11: 358–69.

Valla, Dana. 2001. *Socratic Citizenship.* Princeton: Princeton University Press.

Vassiliou, Iakovos. 2008. *Aiming for Virtue in Plato.* Cambridge: Cambridge University Press.

Vlastos, Gregory. 1983. "The Socratic Elenchus." In *Oxford Studies in Ancient Philosophy.* Julia Annas ed. Oxford: Oxford University Press: 27–58.

Vlastos, Gregory. 1991. *Socrates: Ironist and Moral Philosopher.* Ithaca: Cornell University Press.

Waldrop, Julee B. and Melody A. Bowdon. 2015. *Best Practices for Flipping the Classroom.* London: Routledge.

Whipple Jr., Robert D. 1997. *Socratic Method and Writing Instruction.* Lanham: University Press of America.

Wilberding, Erick. 2014. *Teach Like Socrates: Guiding Socratic Dialogues and Discussion in the Classroom.* Austin: Prufrock Press.

Yaylaci, Sule and Edana Beauvais. 2017. "The Role of Social Group Membership on Classroom Participation." *PS: Political Science & Politics* 50/2: 599–64.

Part I
The Socratic Method in Plato's Dialogs

1 Poetic Questions in the Socratic Method

Marlene K. Sokolon

On the first day of class, I noticed him. He sat at the back, with his cowboy hat covering his face and feet sprawled in front of him. He seemed rarely to pay attention and never took notes. He would answer questions when asked, but never volunteered his own opinions. His first assignment, outlining the argument of the various definitions of justice in Book One of the *Republic*, was competent, but formulaic. His second assignment, on Plato's censorship of the poets, offered typical critiques that it was authoritarian and violated freedom of expression. When he came to the required meeting to discuss his term paper, I expected very little.

"What topic are you thinking of writing on?" I asked.
"Maybe something to do with the education of the guardians."
"Okay," I replied, "what do you find interesting about this topic?"
"It seems to me that Socrates thinks that education should really change people," he said.

"I think he takes education way more seriously than we do today. It is not about training for a job or checking off what one learns. Most of my classes are about cramming all kinds of information in my head – like memorizing definitions from textbooks or stats about stuff. Or repeating to professors the opinions they want to hear. I don't think that kind of teaching could ever change anyone."

A bit surprised by his response, I follow up by asking, "So you think Plato shows us an example of a kind of education that could change people?"

"Sure," he said, "Plato is about how different types of people think and act. Some of the people Socrates talks with are jerks, like Thrasymachus. I have a friend like him, who is only interested in telling others what to think and not listening to what they think."

He went on to write the best undergraduate essay I have ever received.

This student, whom I nicknamed Cowboy Plato (a genuine cowboy who earned money to pay for college by breaking in horses), was enrolled in several courses I taught at a small university in the panhandle of Texas. In my current classes, I tell stories of this student and his questions and ideas about the assigned readings, sometimes as a "foil" to engage students in offering their ideas about the material, but more often as an approachable contemporary interlocutor of historical texts. In response, students tend to be more at liberty in offering their own ideas and personal stories and such narrations often become crucial to class discussion of course content. Despite what seems to be an obvious pedagogical approach to engage students in course material, many contemporary proponents of what is called the "Socratic method" focus on a rationalized method and pay little attention to the crucial role of storytelling in Plato's dialogs. This chapter, first, explores perspectives on the contemporary pedagogical "Socratic method," including elements typically deemed crucial for its use in the classroom. It then turns to the debate on what we can extract from Plato's example of the way in which Socrates "teaches." Finally, it turns to explore Plato's use of narrative in two examples from the *Republic*: the ship of state in Book Four and the allegory of the cave in Book Seven. As both examples highlight, Plato's use of narrative or "image-making" as part of the dialectical conversation, not only reinforces his logical argumentation but is a necessary component of these arguments and the soul's educational journey.

Socratic Method: The Contemporary Teaching Tool

Although widespread in contemporary pedagogy, there is no agreed upon definition of the "Socratic method" or the conditions or context of when it should be used in an educational setting.[1] At minimum, the method is understood as a pedagogical style employing a teacher-led question-and-answer format to foster student discussion and active learning; in the extreme, proponents require adherence to a formal structure in which the teacher systematically directs students through a series of steps that develop critical reasoning (often with expected learning outcomes). Proponents of the Socratic method are found in all educational levels from early elementary classrooms to doctoral tutorials. It is employed in virtually every discipline from the hard sciences and mathematics to the humanities, social sciences, and legal studies.

Introduced as a pedagogical approach by the German philosopher Leonard Nelson's 1922 seminal lecture entitled "The Socratic Method," it developed in response to two educational models of the twentieth century. First, the Socratic method challenges the overreliance on passive learning models, such as formal lecturing, and rote memorization of concepts and ideas. In contrast, by emphasizing a "self-directed," "learning-centered," or "human centered" process, the method engages students in active learning, because it requires them to "do [their] own thinking" or "actively construct their own understanding."[2] Second, the Socratic method counters the continuing preoccupation in higher education on training for vocational knowledge and marketplace skills. It was particularly influential on the Great Books movement as a way to interrogate texts by gaining deeper insight into the truth of philosophic questions. It continues to be championed as a strength of humanities and liberal art programs, which employ it to develop critical thinking skills and the pursuit of knowledge for its own sake.[3]

Because the approach to Socratic questioning is so broad, it is impossible to provide agreed upon criteria for the practice, except that it necessarily involves conversation, dialog, or "talk" directed to elicit understanding. Broadly speaking, the teacher should not tell students the answer, but function as a neutral facilitator who guides students with a series of questions which challenge original understandings and opinions.[4] Although the characteristics of the method are debated, many scholars approach it systematically.

Boghossian, for example, argues that the method involves five stages: wonder (the posing of a question); hypothesis (the student's original understanding or opinion); cross-examination and counterexamples (*elenchus*); acceptance or rejection of counterexamples to the hypothesis; and action on outcomes.[5] Others focus on three stages: *elenchus* (here understood as an acknowledgment of perplexity); mental midwifery (the activity of learning or "remembering"); tethering or binding new knowledge to previous knowledge.[6] Others still focus on outlining expectations of the participants: honesty in expressing convictions; articulation of ideas in clear, logical language; willingness to work with and understand others; and critical evaluation of one's own views.[7] Kreeft argues that the method requires honesty on the part of participants, rejection of extreme positions such as pure skepticism or dogmatism, and the overcoming of extreme attitudes, such as the fear of reason.[8] From this perspective, the Socratic method is a systematic approach to discussion-based learning intended to replace faulty thinking with deeper insight. It employs questioning for the sake of rigorous and sound reasoning intended to seek clarity and transparency on any discussion topic. What makes the method "Socratic" is not that discussion is expected to arrive at specific outcomes, but that "all opinions should be advanced with reasons."[9]

Other perspectives, especially those which emphasize the "Socratic" origin of teaching, understand the method not as a neutral tool to promote active learning, but emphasize the significance of the student as a "moral agent."[10] The use of the Socratic method can promote moral pedagogy in two ways. First, the Socratic discussion can focus directly on moral questions that require judgment of better or worse answers. This approach is promoted in the humanities and social sciences which use course content to develop and practice this kind of critical thinking and moral judgment.[11] In this case, the topic under Socratic discussion focuses on abstract moral principles or ontological analysis. By asking abstract philosophic questions, such as "what is justice," students want "to win knowledge about their own inner experience and develop insights into the truth concerning philosophical questions."[12] Although Nelson rejected the idea that ethical principles could be derived from observed facts, some teachers use the method to guide moral judgment by using practical examples of moral conundrums. For example, in lessons intended to develop adolescent character, children are asked to think through questions, such as whether they should buy a stolen bicycle.[13] It is through thinking and talking about real-world examples that children come to recognize and understand for themselves the difference between poor and better moral choices.

Second the Socratic method is also promoted as a form of moral pedagogy even if the content of discussion is not philosophic or ethical, because the method develops critical thinking skills considered essential to living together in a political community. Consequently, regardless of the topic of discussion or course content, Socratic questioning promotes "rational thinking, persistence, and pattern recognition"; the method can lead to improved self-reflection, autonomous and independent thinking, and an increased willingness to cooperate and work with others.[14] In the group format, often called "Socratic Circles," participants are expected to participate in open and honest discussion and strive for consensus.[15] By employing the method, students gain "greater clarity about what is and what is not in keeping with considered, thoughtful, and reasonable conduct."[16] The Socratic method is promoted because it provides a rich set of reasoning skills that either directly or indirectly helps students engage in the moral perplexity of the world. This goal of the method is not surprising. Nelson, for example, was extremely active in socialist politics and viewed his seminal work on the Socratic method as a way to rationally train activists and enrich the civic community.[17] From this perspective, the Socratic method is not simply a neutral pedagogical tool used in educational settings, but because it develops "reasoning abilities requisite to living a rational life," the student is central to broader political goals of living well in just communities.[18]

Thus, although the method is used broadly and in various contexts, goals of the Socratic method appear threefold. First, it is a pedagogical method intended to help students think about and discover for themselves factual or evidence-based knowledge in any discipline. Second, the Socratic method can directly ask students to engage in questions of moral and philosophic reasoning that allow students to reject self-deceptive thinking in favor of deeper understandings. Third, the very act of a question-and-answer format is argued to develop rational judgment required of any citizen in a democratic regime. The Socratic method, thus, becomes an essential element of not only understanding course material, but living well, and living with others in the political community. Although some proponents of the method make use of vivid analogy or dismiss pure rationalism, whether the method is simply a neutral teaching style or used to promote citizenship development, it adopts reflective, and objective thinking, rational articulation of ideas in unambiguous language, and the requirement that all opinions are advanced with reasoning. As Kreeft puts it: "reason is the common master."[19] The Socratic method in modern pedagogy emphasizes "confidence in reason" as the means to promoting greater understanding of philosophic truths and civic harmony.[20]

Socratic Method: Plato's Dialogs

Although the contemporary understanding of the Socratic method varies from a simple question-and-answer teaching style to a systematic technique directed toward engaging students in the search for philosophic truth, it is a source of debate whether such practices reflect either the historical Socrates or Socrates' characterization in extant dialogs, especially those by Plato. Contemporary scholars disagree as to whether the contemporary teaching method can be attributed to Socrates or even if Socrates can be called a teacher.[21] In the *Apology* (19e) Socrates emphatically denies he is a "teacher" of the young men inspired to follow his example of questioning their fellow citizens.[22] Socrates repeatedly asserts that he knows nothing; or, at most, if he possesses any wisdom, it is because he admits "human wisdom is worth little or nothing."[23] This denial may be the foremost case of Socratic irony, as he is shown to possess *some* knowledge of truths. In the classic case used by proponents of the Socratic method, Socrates in the *Meno* (82b–85c) guides, by means of directed questions, an uninformed slave boy to the correct answer of an abstract mathematical question (of which Socrates obviously has prior knowledge of the correct answer); or, as Jenks points out, Socrates does make "astonishing truth claims," such as in the *Gorgias* (472b) when he tells Polus that he cannot be dislodged from his possession of the truth.[24] Yet, as Socrates states in the *Apology*, he is ignorant concerning the highest or most important things, such as the meaning of virtue (*Meno*, 71b) or justice (*Republic*, 337e).

Importantly, Socrates' denial of teaching or possessing the truth regarding these most important things contrasts with his intellectual rivals: the sophists. At the heart of his dispute with the sophists was the fifth-century debate concerning whether virtue could be taught.[25] Unlike Socrates, these sophistic "wise men" claimed they could teach such things and demanded payment. In contrast, the context of Socrates' denial of being a teacher in the *Apology* (18c) is to counteract the poet Aristophanes' characterization of him in the *Clouds* as a sophist, who not only demanded payment, but also instructed young men to "making weaker arguments defeat the stronger."[26] In the same *Apology* context, Socrates elaborates the reason why he went about questioning his fellow citizens: to test the validity of the Delphic oracle's claim that "no one was wiser than Socrates" (21a). Hence, he questioned the truth of the opinions of politicians, poets like Aristophanes, and craftsmen with the conclusion that such men did not know what they claimed to know. Rich young men, who unsurprisingly enjoyed hearing such examinations, began to imitate him, and question their fellow citizens. Thus, what Socrates did that got him into trouble in the late fifth-century and which inspired Plato's (and Xenophon's) literary accounts in the dialogs was an unremitting questioning of what others claimed to know, especially about the highest things such as ethical truth.

Whether Plato's literary imitation of Socrates' mission of questioning his fellow citizens regarding their wisdom can provide us with a method in the contemporary sense as a systematic or established procedure remains controversial. On the one hand, in the dialogs, Socrates' questioning rarely is portrayed as organized, ordered, or systematic. Many dialogs end without reaching any consensus and often without a conclusion. Some scholars, such as Vlastos, questioned whether Socratic *elenchus* can lead to truth or only a consistent set of beliefs.[27] Others suggest that Socratic questioning is not an art (*technē*) because there is no evidence that the result of such questioning can or is intended to reach a conclusion (including the conclusion of *aporia* or recognition that one does not know): the questioning leads nowhere and does not "prove anything."[28] O'Connor similarly is skeptical that Socrates' way of conducting conversations includes any systematic or formal structuring necessary for "a method"; at best, Socrates is an exemplar of using "sound" or a conversational style of philosophy.[29] There is also nothing in the dialogs furthermore, suggesting participants approach the discussion with honesty, consistency, or openness to others' ideas.

On the other hand, many contemporary proponents, such as the method's progenitor Nelson, remain undeterred because, like the young men who followed Socrates, they are inspired by his "mission" of questioning the truth of fellow citizens' opinions regarding the most important things.[30] What is crucial is not whether Socrates claimed to teach about the highest things; whether *elenchus* is a craft that can result in understanding or uncovering truth; or whether Socratic questioning is or can be labeled a systematic "method." What is relevant is Socrates' example of "teaching ... the art of philosophizing" not with the intention of transmitting particular truths, but to "point out the path along which it might be found."[31] From this perspective, attempting to construct a modern "method" from Socrates' example is misguided.

However, this does not imply the discussions in the dialog are haphazard or simple random deductive exercises. Plato's dialogs are carefully constructed to mimic the dialectical activity of human reflection. This is especially relevant for reflecting on moral questions, which in its purest form, is a social activity requiring people coming together to discuss and examine opinions, regardless of outcomes.

If we are to mimic Socrates' example, it is significant that the interlocutor Socrates never directly addresses how to go about this kind of questioning. As Seeskin puts it: "our knowledge of elenchus is derived from watching Socrates in action."[32] From Seeskin's perspective, the action of the dialogs reveals not a method *per se*, but an approach to questioning that remains subject to rules of argumentation, such as not engaging in hypotheticals and remaining logically consistent, even if views change. The quality of the logic of the argument remains the crucial factor in the search for essences or questioning the truth of opinions.

In contrast, Cain takes the view of "Socrates in action" a step further by arguing that as a philosopher-dramatist-poet, Plato unavoidably incorporates poetic and dramatic elements into the fabric of his philosophic themes to educate the entire soul in the process of moral improvement.[33] Cain further argues Socrates never relies solely on straightforward deductive or inductive logic, but unlike the contemporary method that demands transparency and clarity, Socrates employs such techniques as intentional ambiguity, exaggerated speech, sophistic forensic style, or shameful examples to engage and challenge his interlocutors. Hence, the dramatic form is "exemplary Platonic philosophizing," in which the dramatic level or "internal frame" is central to understanding his philosophy.[34]

It is possible, however, to take the relevance of Plato as the philosopher-dramatist-poet a step further than Cain by drawing attention to the relevance of dramatic context. As has been noted many times, despite his critique of the poets in such dialogs as the *Republic*, Plato himself employs not just a poetic style in the craft of the dialog, but Socrates makes continual reference to poets and employs myth as part of his argument in the dialogs.[35] Socrates will resort to myth in cases in which human knowledge is impossible, such as afterlife myths found at the end of several dialogs (*Apology*, 40c–42a; *Gorgias*, 523a–27e; *Republic*, 613b–21c). In other examples, such as the myth of the metals in the *Republic* (414c–17b), Socrates provides a "how to" guide for crafting "useful" stories of political origin. In other cases, however, Socrates appears to use myth or stories as an elaboration on, or as part of, the logical content of the ongoing discussion. In this case, Socrates tells such stories as elaborate allegories or, as he calls them, "images" (*eikonos*) (*Republic*, 487e). Significantly the stories Socrates tells in this context are often the most memorable parts of his dialogs and the most easily recalled by students long after the details of his logical argument fade. As such, storytelling may prove to be the most essential aspect of mimicking Socrates' technique of questioning opinions, especially as part of the ongoing social activity of human conversation regarding the most important things.

Socratic Method: The Storytelling

The Pilot and the Sailors

As Plato has Socrates admit to his interlocutors, one of the most provocative arguments he makes in the *Republic* is his digression into the details of the city in speech in Book Five. The wealthy metic Polemarchus prods Adeimantus into demanding Socrates revisit his comment in Book Four (424a) that in a just city women and children will be held in common. The discussion of the city in speech began in the interlocutors' attempt to understand the origin of justice and injustice. Cities or political communities come into being because each of us is not self-sufficient, but in need of much (369b). Thus, because specialization creates finer work and each of us is not the same but differs in our nature, it seems (*dokei*) to Socrates, that justice is performing the function in the city best suited to one's nature (*physis*) and not being a "busybody" (*polupragmonein*) or interfering in the function of others (433a). Socrates resists the pressure to elaborate on the details of the city, because the details would unleash a "swarm" of troublesome arguments (450b) which are frightening and laughable (451a).

Nevertheless, in Book Four, the interlocutors press him forward to describe the three waves (*kuma*) of the city in speech: female guardians; community of women and children; and the philosopher-king. These details reveal that justice is not only about performing a function which contributes to the city, but also about not being a busybody by performing only that function and not interfering in the function of others. Similarly, injustice in cities arises from private pleasures and griefs, when individuals do not call the same things "my own," but separate and keep apart one's own things (like wives, children, and property). Finally, Socrates leads the discussion to the philosopher-king, who is that rare individual who loves that upon which knowledge depends and can grasp "what is always the same in all respects" (484b). The philosopher-king's function is to lead cities, because they can best guard the community's laws and practices. At this point, Socrates distinguishes the philosopher's knowledge from general opinion with complicated logical argument (from 475d–80b) that concludes that opinion stands in between knowledge and ignorance, or being, and not-being; furthermore, lovers of opinion do not seek the fair or justice, but only the many instances of justice. Thus, philosophers who seek "what is," should rule over those who know only instances and examples (or the particulars).

Students are often intrigued by Plato's version of gender equality in the first wave, usually alarmed by the second wave's elimination of the family, and dismissive of the philosopher-king as a blatant power-grab by the philosopher Socrates; yet, few students pay attention to or carefully work through the complicated logic of the *elenchus* between Glaucon and Socrates justifying the expertise or rationale for the philosopher-king as a distinction between knowledge and opinion. In the dialog, however, Adeimantus has clearly been paying attention as he rejects Glaucon's easy acceptance of the philosopher-king by interjecting: "how is the philosopher-king possible since philosophers are strange, vicious, or completely useless to cities" (487d). It is in this context, that Socrates admits the answer to such a question requires an "image" (*eikonon*). Adeimantus pokes fun, by pointing out that Socrates is unaccustomed to such image-making; but, Socrates admits he is "greedy" for images and will, on behalf of the hardships of decent men, bring together a "mixture" from many sources, similar to how painters make images of "goat-deer" (488a). Thus, begins his analogy of the pilot of a ship, which was first introduced in Book I (341b–3) during Socrates' exchange with Thrasymachus concerning who is a ruler in a precise sense. In that book, similar to doctors' ruling patients for their own good, Socrates claims the pilot possesses the necessary skill to rule over sailors for their own good.

In Book Four, Socrates tells us to see or have in one's mind (*noēson*) the following image of events happening on a ship (488b–90a). Although the tallest and strongest, the shipowner is deaf, nearsighted, and has no knowledge of how to pilot a ship. The sailors quarrel with each other, each thinking he should be the pilot, even though none of them have ever learned this art. In fact, they only agree on two things: there is no such art of piloting; and, even if piloting were an art, it is unteachable. All the sailors fawn over the shipowner, trying to win his favor. Failing at persuasion, violence erupts, and they kill each other and cast rivals overboard. The remaining sailors chain up the shipowner and take over, spending their time drinking, and feasting. The man who is most clever at figuring out how to persuade and subdue the shipowner is called "pilot" and they dismiss anyone without these skills of persuasion and violence as "useless." Yet, the sailors cannot recognize the true pilot: the man who knows that piloting a ship safely and to the intended destination requires careful attention to the seasons, the heavens, and the winds. Instead, the sailors dismiss such knowledge and call the one who knows such things a useless "stargazer."

It does not take much of a careful examination, Socrates further tells us, to see the *resemblance* of this situation to ruling in the city (489a–91d). Like our stargazer, philosophers are only considered "useless," because we do not recognize their value for political systems: instead of disregarding them, we should be begging such men who strive to learn "what is" to rule over us. Socrates' story ends here, but his "image" allows the reader to fill in what would happen to such sailors who are ruled by a pilot mainly interested in drinking and feasting. It is inevitable, is it not, that such a ship is doomed to run afoul of weather or treacherous rocks with all, including the poor "stargazer," going down to a watery grave.

For the most part, Socrates is correct that the analogy of the true pilot easily relates to political rule and to why philosophers are considered "useless." The analogy explains the reason why Socrates considers the philosopher-king a paradox, because even though such men should rule, the suggestion is met with laughter (473a). The philosopher is the city's "stargazer," who strives to understand what is truly necessary to rule or guide a city. For Socrates, although changing those who rule is a minor change (unlike female guardians or eliminating private families which are great disruptions), it is laughable because our political systems really do resemble the ship: no one possesses or believes that such knowledge of ruling exists.

In addition, the "image" or story of the pilot underscores the reason for the discussion of the city in speech in the first place: to see justice more clearly. The origin of communities was found in the need we have for each other and justice was contributing the function that best suited our natures and not being a "busybody" (*polupragmonein*). Thus, Socrates reveals injustice on the ship: the sailors' claim to rule when they know nothing of the art of piloting. They were busybodies or involved in a function of piloting. The sailors similarly rule not for the good of the ship (or even for their own good), but for the sake of the pleasures of drinking and feasting. The true pilot, as we learned in Book One, ruled not only because he had true knowledge of his function, but also because he ruled in the interest of the sailors.

Like all analogies, the analogy of the ship to the city is neither perfect nor exact. The ship analogy focuses on the third wave of the philosopher-king, but unlike cities, the sailors do not confront the issues raised by the other two waves: whether there are gender-specific functions or families should be eliminated from the city. Furthermore, although the sailors know nothing about the art of piloting, such as knowledge of winds and the stars, they also claim that no such knowledge exists. It is on this last point that careful students, such as Cowboy Plato, raise a challenge: at the end of Book Five, Glaucon readily agreed that philosopher-kings should guard the community's laws, because they seek the fair and justice itself, and not the many instances of the fair and just; yet, it is uncertain whether philosophical knowledge is akin to the pilot's knowledge of seasons, winds, and stars. If, for example, the true pilot needs knowledge of both the particulars (i.e., these rocks to avoid along that bend) and the universals (i.e., stargazing), how does the philosopher learn the particulars of ruling a city? Is the philosopher's seeking of "what is" sufficient for ruling our political communities which exist, like ships, in the world of coming into being and passing away?

There are, of course, many more lines of inquiry raised by Socrates' analogy of the ship of state. Importantly, the way in which analogies do not hold reveal the utility of this comparison for exposition and understanding. Like all metaphors, analogies are used to reveal both the meaning of hidden similarities and differences.[36] Yet, Socrates' story of the doomed voyage of this foolish shipowner and his crew is a vivid and relatable "image" which reflects his definition of justice in the city of speech and rule of the philosopher-king. The image also brings to the forefront assumptions at the heart of the dialog and allows readers to think more seriously about the significance of these assumptions. With the analogy of the sailors, Socrates presents an example of how such storytelling and literacy devices are essential to dialectical questioning. Most obviously, the analogy allows Socrates to further the discussion with Adeimantus who initially rejects the philosopher as "useless." For many readers, however, the "image" of the sailors focuses on unanswered and potentially unanswerable questions, such as is philosophy a necessary and sufficient education for this art of guiding the city? Hence, if we are looking for a "method" or even merely to imitate Socrates' example, it is equally important to pay attention not only to the logic of his argument, but how he is "greedy" for images and uses them to bring together a "mixture" of logic and storytelling.

Plato's Cave

The fact that Socrates uses the word "image" (*eikonos*) to describe his imaginary ship is significant as it is used again in his most famous analogy of all: the allegory of the cave. This allegory immediately follows one of the most difficult passages in the *Republic* (509e–11e): Socrates' first attempt to further explain his theory of the forms (*eidē*) in what is known as "the divided line." The complexity of this passage, perhaps significantly, often requires a diagram which is helpfully provided by most translators.[37] Socrates begins by asking Glaucon to see (*noēson*) a line between what is visible and what is intelligible. Below the line is the visible, which is further subdivided into those things which are "images" (*eikones*), such as shadows, or reflections in water, at the very bottom; above them, there are the things which are around us (or known to the senses), such as animals, and artifacts. Above the line, the intelligible is further divided into geometrical "objects"; and above those, finally are the forms or ideas (*eidē*). Socrates then develops a seemingly straightforward correspondence of the "affections" of our soul to each segment: intellection (*noesis*) to ideas (*eidē*); thought (*dianoia*) to geometry; proofs (*pistis*) to the physical world; and, imagination or image-making (*eikasia*) to "images." Although no student ever seems to easily comprehend this passage (and Cowboy Plato insisted it was impenetrable), Glaucon readily agrees that he understands the arrangement of "the forms."

At this point, Socrates introduces his famous image of the cave (514a–18d) which focuses the conversation of the dialog obviously on imagination or image-making (*eikasia*). First, Glaucon is asked to "see" (*ide*) human beings living since childhood in a long underground cave with light across the entire width. The necks and legs of each person are bound in such a way that they can only see the cave wall in front of them. Far above and behind them is a fire with a road in between and a partition separating the chained people from other human beings who project shadows of all sorts of artifacts on the cave wall in front of them. Because the chained people have never experienced anything different, they think that truth is nothing more than naming the shadows they see.

Next, Socrates asks us to consider what would happen if one of them is released and compelled to look back toward the firelight; such a man would be in pain and unable to see because of the brightness of the light; if he were asked to name the artifacts as they went by he would be at a loss and would think the shadows he saw before were more real and true. If this man were dragged out of the cave into the light of the real sun, he would become even more distressed and dazzled; eventually, however, his eyes would adjust and he would see shadows of real things and the human beings living outside the cave; then he would see the things and people themselves. Finally, he would be able to see the light of the heavens: stars, moon, and the sun. He would finally understand that the sun is the source of everything.

He would recognize that the honors given in his previous life to those who were best at making out the shadows lived only in opinions of things. Imagine again, Socrates says, the same man returning to the cave: he would have to adjust once again to the darkness and the people would laugh at him, if he tried to tell them that they saw only shadows of artificial things. And, the chained men would kill him or anyone who tried to release them and lead them to the light.

Socrates then explains this image as the soul's journey of a philosophic education from being chained and seeing only shadows to the knowledge of light of the sun (517a–18b). At first glance, the story of the cave "repeats" the sections of the divided line. Those things in the cave are likened to the bottom half of the visible world: the shadows are "images" (the lowest section of the line) of the sensible things or artifacts (second section of the line) which are manipulated by the puppet masters. The one dragged out of the cave can first make out reflections of real things (mathematical or geometrical thought (*dianoia*) in the third section of the line); then, he can see or understand the highest things in themselves (the highest section of the forms or *eidē*). Finally, by turning to the heavens, he can see the sun (or the Good) which is the source of all things. Men who experience such an education do not desire to turn back and "mind the business of human beings" (517a); they would appear ridiculous if compelled to contest the identity of the various shadows with those who never left the cave. Such an education, Socrates continues, is not like pouring knowledge into a soul that does not have it; instead, the educational journey is a "turning around" (*stpherein*) from that which is coming into being and passing away to look at and see that "which is" (518d).

On the one hand, Socrates overtly uses this "image" of the cave to explicate and further develop his description of the divided line by identifying corresponding images and inserting a sense of motion in the educational journey. Yet, on the other hand, as an explanation of the divided line, the allegory of the cave is not always helpful and raises many more subsidiary questions than it clarifies. Why, for example, are the material things of the visible world in the divided line – which included everything that grows – reduced in the human world of the cave to artifacts made of stone, wood, and material? What does Socrates mean by suggesting that the city is pure artifice and devoid of all other living things? Or, as Cowboy Plato pointed out, because the allegory is an "image" or a picture painted on our mind, is the act of thinking through or figuring out Plato's allegories akin to the contest of naming the shadows on the cave wall? If so, does this make Plato, and other philosophers puppet masters? Hence, like the analogy of the ship of state, the allegory of the cave both reinforces and elucidates his complex dialectic, while simultaneously introducing crucial questions that point in new directions.

These questions highlight the importance of storytelling or "picture-making" (*eikasia*) in how human beings think, talk, and relate to the world and each other. The allegory of the cave paints a picture of how Plato understands "images" within the uncomfortable and even potentially dangerous journey of human education. Importantly, this image-making is not confined to the "beginning" of education, like the image of "images" in the divided line. Socrates' discussion of the cave and divided line is part of a broader discussion of the imaginary city in speech. And this discussion of an imaginary city, because the interlocutor Socrates is narrating the conversation in the *Republic*, is essentially a story of what was said the previous night to an unnamed, imaginary individual. Of course, the entire dialog form is an "image"; it is Plato's "picture-making" of an imaginary conversation which took place at least forty years before he wrote it, on the night of a festival of Bendis around 421 BCE.

Therefore, although Socrates places imagination at the bottom of the divided line or at the beginning of the educational journey, he uses image-making consistently throughout his dialogic conversations. As with the dismissive comments about poetry or storytelling noted earlier, Socrates' presentation of images, and image-making may be a further example of Socratic irony.[38] From the perspective that the dialog presents "Socrates in action," his storytelling or image-making is not simply a "step" in the journey that is overcome with the capacity for rational abstraction; similarly, image-making is not dichotomous, or separate from, but part of, and essential to, his use of rational, and abstract logic. Platonic images appear in those moments of blindness as we adjust to innovative ways of thinking that challenge cherished opinions of what we believe to be true, but have never examined. Stories also appear essential, as is found in the image of ship of state, as the "connective tissue" that mediates human understanding between the philosopher's abstraction of "what is" and the pilot's knowledge of the world of coming into being and passing away. Importantly, Socrates employs "image-making" or stories in the manner suggested in the analogy of the ship of state (488a–b): his dialogical conversations bring together many things as a "mixture," like painters who make "goat-deer" or other half-creatures. Perhaps Plato's integral relatedness of storytelling and reason is less surprising when it is recalled that the Greek term *logos*, although usually translated by political theorists as "reason" or "rationality," has a broader meaning in Greek as "word," a "telling," or "story." Rather than understanding the divided line as a "ladder" with steps that lead one higher and higher away from image-making, the embeddedness of allegories, images, and stories are essential to human language and understanding.

Interestingly, Plato's use of storytelling as part of his dialogs reflects contemporary research on how human beings behave in small group discussions. In one-on-one or small group discussions, research has shown that participants do not rely on facts and logical argumentation; instead, they tend to engage more in the context of the discussion by telling stories about themselves, their families, or events on the news.[39] This study also indicates that during debate, participants use narrative that agrees with some aspect of their interlocutor's position to minimize conflict or disagreement. Other studies reveal how social decision-making is often a product of comparing new narratives to previous relevant stories.[40] Research also reveals that narrative accompanies rational discourse, because it tends to be more persuasive in engaging participants in new ideas or contrasting perspectives.[41] Similar to Plato's use of image-making, storytelling is not simply entertainment, an embellishment, or secondary support for rational discussion, but is an essential aspect of the way human beings converse with and learn from each other.

Conclusion

To return to our contemporary classrooms and the debate on whether a method can be derived from the dialogs, Plato's "stories" of Socrates offer little support for a contemporary systematic educational method with predetermined steps or specific learning objectives. Instead, Plato's account is more of an inspirational model of a pedagogical journey that embeds image-making as part of dialogical encounters. Again, this is not to suggest that reasoned argument and factual evidence are not important in Plato's dialogs or our modern classrooms. It only suggests that a Socratic "method" of teaching involves more than engaging students in "active" learning through a question-and-answer format.

A teaching style inspired by Socrates must also engage students' imagination through stories that foster understanding by identifying connections and dissonances. It would be misguided to look for, or expect, a methodological procedure for how often or when to tell pedagogical stories. As we also learn from Plato and from our own experience in classrooms, we should not speak the same way or say the same things to everyone: a story that works in one section of a class or with one student, falls on deaf ears with another.[42] At times, pedagogical stories are simply practical examples that reiterate or reinforce challenging course material; yet, at other times, like Socrates' complicated allegories, stories can be highly abstract and mediate beyond and between the logic of inductive and deductive argumentation. The easiest way to start incorporating stories in the classroom is to think of your own Cowboy Plato and tell stories of how that student struggled, but figured out how to make sense of difficult course material.

Finally, if Plato presents Socrates as a pedagogical "image" worth imitating, this "mixture" of logic and storytelling may be most crucial to how human beings learn and think through moral questions, such as the best way to live and live together. Considering the emphasis that ancient Greece and other cultural traditions placed on narrative as essential to moral education (such as found in Aesop's *Fables*), Plato's use of narrative as part of moral discussions should not be undervalued. The dialog form, therefore, represents Plato's potential answer to fifth-century debate with the sophists on whether morality can be taught. If it can be taught, it is through a social activity of engaging with others by asking and answering questions, and telling stories which engage us to think about the limitations of our opinions and what might be the best way to live. Such an inquiry may never be complete, but as Plato's metaphor suggests: education is not a method, it is a journey.

Notes

1 For discussion see Rene Saran and Barbara Neisser, "Introduction," in *Enquiring Minds: Socratic Dialogue in Education*, Rene Saran and Barbara Neisser, eds. (Sterling: Trentham Books, 2004), 1–8; Jack Schneider, "Socrates and the Madness of Method," *Kappan* 94/1 (2012): 26–9; Robert D. Whipple, Jr., *Socratic Method and Writing Instruction* (Lanham: University Press of America, 1997), 1–17.
2 Leonard Nelson, *Socratic Method and Critical Philosophy*, Thomas K. Brown III, trans. (New York: Dover, 1949), 11; Wilbert McKeachie, *Mckeachie's Teaching Tips* (New York: Houghton Mifflin, 1999), 52.
3 Martha Nussbaum, *Not for Profit* (Princeton: Princeton University Press, 2012), 1–10, 102.
4 Schneider, "Socrates and the Madness of Method," 27–9.
5 Peter Boghossian, "Socratic Pedagogy," *Educational Philosophy and Theory* 44/7 (2012): 710–20.
6 Jamie Linz et al., "Socrates Was a Bad Teacher," *Independent School* 60/1 (2000): 84–7.
7 Dieter Birnbacher and Dieter Krohn, "Socratic Dialogue and Self-Directed Learning," in *Enquiring Minds: Socratic Dialogue in Education*, Rene Saran and Barbara Neisser, eds. (Sterling: Trentham, 2004), 23–4.
8 Peter Kreeft, *Socratic Logic* (South Bend: St. Augustine's Press, 2005), 348–50.
9 Schneider, "Socrates and the Madness of Method," 29.
10 See for example, Saran and Neisser, "Introduction," 4–5; Rebecca Bensen Cain, *The Socratic Method* (London: Continuum, 2007), 8–10.
11 Richard Paul and Linda Elder, *Thinkers Guide to Socratic Questioning* (Tomales: Foundation for Critical Thinking Press, 2016), 16, 18–19; Nussbaum, *Not for Profit*, 81–102.
12 Saran and Neisser, "Introduction," 1.
13 Nelson, *Socratic Method and Critical Philosophy*, 16; see also David H. Elkind and Freddy Sweet, "The Socratic Approach to Character Education," *Educational Leadership* 54/8 (1997): 59.
14 Linda B. Nilson, *Teaching at Its Best* (New York: Jossey-Bass, 2010), 138. See also Saran and Neisser, "Introduction," 1–4.
15 Haris Delic and Senad Becirovic, "Socratic Method as an Approach to Teaching," *European Researcher* 111/10 (2016): 511–17; see also Birnbacher and Krohn, "Socratic Dialogue and Self-Directed Learning," 11–13.
16 Saran and Neisser, "Introduction," 3.
17 *Ibid.*, 10.
18 Paul and Elder, *Thinkers Guide to Socratic Questioning*, 71.
19 Kreeft, *Socratic Logic*, 348.
20 Paul and Elder, *Thinkers Guide to Socratic Questioning*, 69.
21 Cf. Kenneth Seeskin, *Dialogue and Discovery* (Albany: State University of New York Press, 1987), 5–7, 37–8, 149; Whipple, *Socratic Method and Writing Instruction*, 1–17; Gary Alan Scott, "Introduction," in *Does Socrates Have a Method?*, Gary Alan Scott, ed. (University Park: Pennsylvania State University, 2002), 1–18; Cain, *The Socratic Method*, 3–10; Thomas C. Brickhouse and Nicholas D. Smith, "Socratic Teaching and Socratic Method," in *The Oxford Handbook of Philosophy of Education*, Harvey Siegel, ed. (Oxford: Oxford University Press, 2009), 177–94; E. Moustsopoulos, "Moderation and Kairos in the Philosophy of Socrates," in *The Socratic Tradition: Questioning as Philosophy and Method*, Matti Sintonen, ed. (London: College Publications, 2009), 89–93; Rod Jenks, *How Plato's Theory of Truth Explains Socratic Method* (Lewiston: The Edwin Mellen Press, 2010), 1–25; David O'Connor, "Socrates as Educator," in *A Companion to Ancient Education*, W. Martin Bloomer, ed. (Malden: Wiley Blackwell, 2015), 77–89.
22 Plato, *The Apology*, Harold North Fowler, trans. (Cambridge: Harvard, 2005). All subsequent citations will be taken from this edition; unless otherwise noted, all translations are the authors from the Greek text of this edition.
23 See Plato, *Apology*, 23a, 21a; Plato, *Meno*, W.R.M. Lamb, trans. (Cambridge: Harvard, 1924), 71b; Plato, *The Gorgias*, W.R.M. Lamb, trans. (Cambridge: Harvard, 1925), 509a; Plato, *The Republic*, Paul Shorey, trans. (Cambridge: Harvard, 1925), 337e; Plato, *Euthydemus*, W.R.M. Lamb, trans. (Cambridge: Harvard, 1924), 293a. All subsequent citations will be taken from these editions; unless otherwise noted, all translations are the authors from the Greek text of these editions.
24 Jenks, *How Plato's Theory of Truth Explains Socratic Method*, 8; see also Gregory Vlastos, "The Socratic Elenchus," in *Oxford Studies in Ancient Philosophy*, Julia Annas, ed. (Oxford: Oxford University Press, 1983), 27–58.
25 Jacqueline de Romilly, *The Great Sophists in Periclean Athens*, Janet Lloyd, trans. (Oxford: Clarendon Press, 1992), 5–30.

20 *Marlene K. Sokolon*

26 Aristophanes, *Clouds*, Jeffrey Henderson, trans. (Cambridge: Harvard University Press, 1999), 889–1112.
27 Vlastos, "The Socratic Elenchus," 27–58.
28 Brickhouse and Smith, "Socratic Teaching and Socratic Method," 177–94.
29 O'Connor, "Socrates as Educator," 77–89.
30 Nelson, *Socratic Method and Critical Philosophy*, 4–6, 15–17; Seeskin, *Dialogue and Discovery*, 8–9, 37–53.
31 Nelson, *Socratic Method and Critical Philosophy*, 1–5.
32 Seeskin, *Dialogue and Discovery*, 37.
33 Cain, *The Socratic Method*, 1–31; See also Ian Kidd, "Socratic Questions," in *Socratic Questions*, Barry S. Gower and Michael C. Stokes, eds. (London: Routledge, 1992), 82–92.
34 Kidd, "Socratic Questions," 91.
35 See recent examples, Ramona A. Naddaff, *Exiling the Poets* (Chicago: University of Chicago Press, 2002) 1–10; 21–34; Lawrence J. Hatab, "Writing Knowledge on the Soul," *Epoche* 11/2 (2007): 319–32; Pierre Destree and Fritz-Gregor Herrmann, eds. *Plato and the Poets* (Leiden: Brill, 2011).
36 James Geary, *I Is an Other* (New York: Harper, 2011), 1–16.
37 See, for example, Bloom's translation. Plato, *The Republic of Plato*. Allan Bloom, trans. (New York: Basic Books, 1968), fn39, 464.
38 Naddaff, *Exiling the Poets*, 1–36; see also Julius A. Elias, *Plato's Defense of Poetry* (Albany: State University of New York, 1984), 209–39; Glenn W. Most, "What Ancient Quarrel between Philosophy and Poetry," in *Plato and the Poets*, Paul Destree and Fritz-Gregor Herrmann, eds. (Leiden: Brill, 2011), 1–20.
39 David M. Ryfe, "Narrative and Deliberation in Small Group Forums," *Journal of Applied Communication Research* 34/1 (2006): 72–93.
40 Philip Mazzocco, Melaine Green and Timothy C. Brock, "The Effects of a Prior Story-Bank on the Processing of Related Narrative," *Media Psychology* 10 (2007): 64–90.
41 Daniel C. Fouke, "Democratic Deliberation and Moral Awareness," *Journal of Public Deliberation* 5/1 (2009): 10–17; Melanie C. Green, "Research Challenges in Narrative Persuasion," *Information Design Journal*, 16/1 (2008): 47–52.
42 Plato's comments are part of his critique of writing; in this example, the written word does not know when to speak or when to remain silent. Plato, *The Phaedrus*, Harold North Fowler, trans. (Cambridge: Harvard, 2005), 275c–d.

Bibliography

Aristophanes. 1999. *Clouds*. Jeffrey Henderson trans. Cambridge: Harvard University Press.
Birnbacher, Dieter and Dieter Krohn. 2004. "Socratic Dialogue and Self-Directed Learning." In *Enquiring Minds: Socratic Dialogue in Education*. Rene Saran and Barbara Neisser eds. Sterling: Trentham Books: 9–24.
Boghossian, Peter. 2012. "Socratic Pedagogy." *Educational Philosophy and Theory* 44/7: 710–20.
Brickhouse, Thomas C. and Nicholas D. Smith. 2009. "Socratic Teaching and Socratic Method." In *The Oxford Handbook of Philosophy of Education*. Harvey Siegel ed. Oxford: Oxford University Press: 177–94.
Cain, Rebecca B. 2007. *The Socratic Method*. London: Continuum.
de Romilly, Jacqueline. 1992. *The Great Sophists in Periclean Athens*. Janet Lloyd trans. Oxford: Clarendon Press.
Delic, Haris and Senad Becirovic. 2016. "Socratic Method as an Approach to Teaching." *European Researcher* 111/10: 511–17.
Destree, Pierre and Fritz-Gregor Herrmann eds. 2011. *Plato and the Poets*. Leiden: Brill.
Elias, Julius A. 1984. *Plato's Defense of Poetry*. Albany: State University of New York.
Elkind, David H. and Freddy Sweet. 1997. "The Socratic Approach to Character Education." *Educational Leadership* 54/8: 56–9.
Fouke, Daniel C. 2009. "Democratic Deliberation and Moral Awareness." *Journal of Public Deliberation* 5/1: 1–32.
Geary, James. 2011. *I Is an Other*. New York: Harper.
Green, Melanie C. 2008. "Research Challenges in Narrative Persuasion." *Information Design Journal* 16/1: 47–52.
Hatab, Lawrence J. 2007. "Writing Knowledge on the Soul." *Epoche* 11/2: 319–32.

Jenks, Rod. 2010. *How Plato's Theory of Truth Explains Socratic Method*. Lewiston: The Edwin Mellen Press.

Kidd, Ian. 1992. "Socratic Questions." In *Socratic Questions*. Barry S. Gower and Michael C. Stokes eds. London: Routledge: 82–92.

Kreeft, Peter. 2005. *Socratic Logic*. South Bend: St. Augustine's Press.

Linz, Jamie *et al.* 2000. "Socrates Was a Bad Teacher." *Independent School* 60/1: 84–7.

Mazzocco, Philip, Melaine Green and Timothy C. Brock. 2007. "The Effects of a Prior Story-Bank on the Processing of Related Narrative." *Media Psychology* 10: 64–90.

McKeachie, Wilbert. 1999. *Mckeachie's Teaching Tips, 10th Edition*. New York: Houghton Mifflin.

Most, Glenn W. 2011. "What Ancient Quarrel between Philosophy and Poetry." In *Plato and the Poets*. Paul Destree and Fritz-Gregor Herrmann eds. Leiden: Brill: 1–20.

Moustsopoulos, E. 2009. "Moderation and Kairos in the Philosophy of Socrates." In *The Socratic Tradition: Questioning as Philosophy and Method*. Matti Sintonen ed. London: College Publications: 89–93.

Naddaff, Ramona A. 2002. *Exiling the Poets*. Chicago: University of Chicago Press.

Nelson, Leonard. 1949. *Socratic Method and Critical Philosophy*. Thomas K. Brown III trans. New York: Dover Publications.

Nilson, Linda B. 2010. *Teaching at Its Best*. New York: Jossey-Bass.

Nussbaum, Martha. 2012. *Not for Profit*. Princeton: Princeton University Press.

O'Connor, David. 2015. "Socrates as Educator." In *A Companion to Ancient Education*. W. Martin Bloomer ed. Malden: Wiley Blackwell: 77–89.

Paul, Richard and Linda Elder. 2016. *Thinkers Guide to Socratic Questioning*. Tomales: Foundation for Critical Thinking Press.

Plato. 1924a. *Euthydemus*. W.R.M. Lamb trans. Cambridge: Harvard University Press.

Plato. 1924b. *Meno*. W.R.M. Lamb trans. Cambridge: Harvard University Press.

Plato. 1925a. *The Gorgias*. W.R.M. Lamb trans. Cambridge: Harvard University Press.

Plato. 1925b. *Republic*. Paul Shorey trans. Cambridge: Harvard University Press.

Plato. 1968. *The Republic of Plato*. Allan Bloom trans. New York: Basic Books.

Plato. 2005a. *The Apology*. Harold North Fowler trans. Cambridge: Harvard University Press.

Plato. 2005b. *Phaedrus*. Harold North Fowler trans. Cambridge: Harvard University Press.

Ryfe, David M. 2006. "Narrative and Deliberation in Small Group Forums." *Journal of Applied Communication Research* 34/1: 72–93.

Saran, Rene and Barbara Neisser. 2004. "Introduction." In *Enquiring Minds: Socratic Dialogue in Education*. Rene Saran and Barbara Neisser eds. Sterling: Trentham Books: 1–8.

Schneider, Jack. 2012. "Socrates and the Madness of Method." *Kappan* 94/1: 26–9.

Scott, Gary A. 2002. "Introduction." In *Does Socrates Have a Method?* Gary Alan Scott ed. University Park: The Pennsylvania State University Press: 1–18.

Seeskin, Kenneth. 1987. *Dialogue and Discovery*. Albany: State University of New York Press.

Vlastos, Gregory. 1983. "The Socratic Elenchus." In *Oxford Studies in Ancient Philosophy*. Julia Annas ed. Oxford: Oxford University Press: 27–58.

Whipple Jr., Robert D. 1997. *Socratic Method and Writing Instruction*. Lanham: University Press of America.

2 Socratic Method and Existence

Barry Cooper

The most popular understanding of Socratic method, portrayed in the 1973 movie, *The Paper Chase*, amounts to sophistic intimidation and the abuse of authority. A gentler version, often called Socratic seminars or circles, enables students to query one another. In the hands of a skilled teacher, this method provides students with questions to ponder rather than answers to memorize. One can make a case that this understanding originated with Plato's nephew and successor at the Academy, Speusippus.[1] This "Neopythagorean" approach to Plato has been succeeded over the centuries down to what is often called today a doctrinal, dogmatic, or analytical approach to the text.

Here the focus is almost exclusively on the argument.[2] The notion of Socratic method, however, contains the notion of a "way" (*hodos*), present as well in the *epanodos,* the rough, steep "way up" of the cave image (*Republic*, 515e). The point of Plato's use of "way" in such passages points to a second, and to my mind more important, understanding of philosophy as a "way" of life. This understanding of method is indicated by the term "Socratic existence" in my title. Characteristically such a starting point leads one to understand the dialogs not primarily as arguments but as "philosophical dramas."[3] Using such an approach, the drama appears through the argument, which makes the argument the occasion for the drama, or "action," as Strauss called it.[4] But what kind of drama?

To answer that question we must be more specific. For many years, I have taught the *Euthyphro* and the *Apology* as part of an introductory course in political theory.[5] The chief reason for assigning the *Apology* in an undergraduate course is that, like the Athenian jury, undergraduates know little about philosophy.[6] A second reason is that the *Euthyphro* is deeply ironical and often comical, which is a clear pedagogical aid. Indeed Euthyphro's very name is a joke. *Eu/the/phron* is "an agglomeration of syllables" that sounds like "the good god's judgment" or "good as god's judgment" among others.[7] This raises an interesting hermeneutical question: does the obvious comedy of the *Euthyphro* and its connection to the *Apology* indicate that the latter dialog is also comedic?

Such a possibility contradicts such respectable interpretations as that of Brickhouse and Smith for whom Socrates' defense was "sincere and effective," to say nothing of Hegel's famous proclamation that the *Apology* was tragic.[8] Even so, there are several persuasive studies of the parodic features of Socrates' address to the jury, though few go so far as to suggest that his being on trial for his life is in any way funny. Yet philological evidence indicates the literary origin of the Socratic dialog lies in "habitually comic" Syracusian and Attic mimes and in Attic comedy;[9] a few commentaries hint at comic elements in Socrates' speeches.[10]

A more interesting interpretive question concerns the affinity of comedy and philosophy. Externally, Socrates' "look," his ugliness, his peculiar gait, bug-eyes, baldness, and pot belly, all are indices of a comic persona.[11] In the *Philebus* (48a–50c) Socrates and Protarchus discuss the experiences associated with tragedy and comedy and the occasions in which they occur. The ridiculous or laughable (*gelion*) involves the opposite to the Delphic inscription, "know thyself." Accordingly, when humans think they are wealthier, handsomer, wiser, or more virtuous than they are, this conceit is either hateful, if the individual is strong, or laughable if weak. Either way, the individual is ignorant (*asthenes*). Exposing such ignorance, Socrates remarked, is "not unpleasant" (*Apology*, 33c). Indeed, unmasking pretentions is the heart of comedy.[12] Or as Bergson, put it: "the specific remedy for vanity is laughter, and the one failing that is essentially laughable is vanity."[13]

To be even more specific, in the *Apology* Socrates transforms the meaning of shame, (*aidos*), away from its social context, which modern philosophers identify with the blush (Nietzsche) and the gaze (Foucault), to the soul, to that part of human existence that is indifferent to shame. The great problem, as Zeus declared in the *Protagoras* (322d), is that he who is without *aidos* is a disease to the city, no matter how just he may be. Just as comic poets expose all pretentions and vanities on stage, so "for Socrates nothing is too sacred to escape thrusting it forward for observation and examination."[14] That is one meaning of the examined life. Equally important, Socrates accomplishes his transformation of *aidos* by mockery, jokes, and irony – by comedy.

When Socrates exposes the ignorant as ignorant they are ashamed as well as mocked. In contrast, Socrates is not ashamed of his ignorance. His questioning of others aims to prove even the god of the Oracle ignorant and so even to shame the god. Socrates, however, is proud of his ignorance and proud that, "in truth" (23b) his wisdom is worth nothing, which also explains his poverty. Thus does Socrates flaunt both his ignorance and his poverty, "apparent failings that most others would wish to hide" out of shame. In short, Socrates "mocks what causes them shame" and teaches the young men to be shameless as well. "For this Socrates will be executed."[15]

As has often been noted, like the execution of Jesus, the execution of Socrates was a historic event.[16] But Plato's *Apology*, as is true of the perhaps more subtle account of Xenophon, is not a transcription of the trial record.[17] All we have are the reports of Socrates' defenders, Plato and Xenophon: who knows what inculpatory evidence they may have suppressed? What counts, then, is the dramatic and philosophical question of the relationship of the philosopher to the non-philosophical Athenians and, by extension, to the non-philosophical (or not-yet-philosophical) undergraduates. And "the meeting of the philosophers and the non-philosophers" Strauss said, "is the natural theme of comedy."[18] Interpreting the *Apology* as a comedic drama means highlighting and then explaining Socrates' many jokes. Strauss once referred to such an interpretive activity as a "loathsome business."[19] Since I am pretty confident I did not find all Socrates' jokes, the result could have been even more loathsome.

The *Apology*

The first impressions most students experience upon reading the *Apology* are variations on indignation. If Plato's intent were also comic, however, here is another: Socrates claims to be innocent but was found guilty, sentenced, and executed. Clearly his life was a failure. He spent his life looking for wisdom and, for his pains, was killed. He cannot even answer the one question he said matters: what is virtue? He did not even make a start in answering that question. All he knows is that he is ignorant. What a disappointment! What a loser![20]

Turning to the text, Socrates' first speech to the jury dismisses the accusers as liars. The most outrageous of their lies is that Socrates is a clever speaker.[21] Soon enough they will be refuted when, by his actual speech, Socrates will be revealed as a simple truth-teller. This is Socrates' opening joke – Question: how do you refute the accusations by a clever liar that you are a clever liar? Answer: by showing you are not a clever liar. But if the accusers were right, plain speaking when accused of being a clever speaker would just show how clever you really were. Maybe Socrates and his accusers were both clever liars. How can you tell?

Socrates says that he tells the truth, the whole truth, and that doing so is just. Or rather, Socrates trusts (*pisteuein*) it is just to tell the whole truth, which raises the obvious question: whom do you trust, Socrates or his accusers? Then, as if to put his appeal to trust him to the test, he says it would be unseemly for an old man to use rhetorical devices, that is, to speak cleverly. Who could imagine

Socrates doing something unseemly? The most comic aspect of this parody of rhetorical cleverness occurs when Socrates claims this is the first time he has come before the court.[22] Literally, Socrates indicated he has never been in court as a defendant, but in the context of his claimed inability to use forensic rhetoric and comparing this inability to that of a foreigner speaking a non-Attic dialect, Socrates' actual suggestion is that he has never been in court, which is a lie, as he later indicates (32a ff.). That is, his *suggestio falsi* is a demonstration of the rhetorical skill that his actual words deny. How clever is that?

After having thus indicated the spirit in which he will speak, Socrates outlines his defense. He does not initially deal with the accusations against him, namely that he does not acknowledge or worship the gods of the city and that he corrupts the young, but with the accusers, especially the old (and mostly dead) accusers. Thus, he increased the number of accusers beyond the present accusers, Meletus, Anytus, and Lycon. Then he adds another charge that he is a thinker (*phrontistes*) on, or worrier about, things aloft, but one who, "having investigated all things under the earth," which presumably would include Hades, also makes the weaker argument the stronger (18b–c). By adding the things aloft and the things under, Socrates not only increases the accusations, he makes them more serious because, for the jury, thinking about the heavenly bodies and the underworld, rather than simply acknowledging them, looks like atheism, as Socrates promptly points out. One conclusion: Socrates is not mounting a dubious defense; he is not making a defense at all. As Brann said, Socrates quickly turned his defense into an offense: he charges his accusers of being liars.[23]

His next words, a defense against the old accusers, are clearly inept. He reminds them of Aristophanes' *Clouds* and implies that the present accusers' slander is equally comic. He denies any knowledge of the heavens. Though in fact around the time the *Clouds* was produced he was interested in such things (*Phaedo*, 96a ff.). He denies he is a sophist but says that if what they promised were true it would be wonderful. But then, one of the jury might ask, if you are not a sophist, what is your business (*pragma*)? And more important, where did he get his bad reputation? Before answering, he notes that some in the jury might think he is joking (20d). But he is telling the whole truth, which makes the problem of the origin of his bad reputation even more intractable (cf. *Gorgias*, 515c–19d).

He gained his bad reputation, he says, by possessing a certain kind of wisdom – not sophistic wisdom, which would be superhuman, but human wisdom. At this point evidently the jury starts shouting.[24] Socrates then tells the jury to shut up and listen to a witness for the defense, the god at Delphi. Or rather, listen to a story told by Chaerophon – or, since he is dead, listen to Chaerophon's brother.[25] Because Chaerophon's brother didn't take the stand and didn't get along with Chaerophon anyhow (*Memorabilia*, II: 3), Socrates alone attests to the bizarre tale according to which Chaerophon asked the Oracle if anyone (human or divine) was wiser than Socrates. Chaerophon's motive for so doing is never explained, but the Pythia replied that no one was wiser.[26] Socrates interpreted the words to mean that he was the wisest but also that the god's words were a riddle, and so true but not in a manner that was immediately evident.[27] The uproar by the jury is not just an expression of their view that Socrates is boasting but a reaction to Socrates' mockery. It was as if he said: "if you believed those unfounded rumors of the old accusers, here is another rumor to consider; why not believe it?"[28] It seems to me, therefore, that the entire Oracle story was a joke and the jury didn't like it one bit.[29]

By conversing (*dialogomenos*) and examining or considering (*diaskopon*, which can also mean to see through), Socrates discovered that those reputed to be wise, starting with the political men (*politikoi*), were not. Since neither the *politikoi* nor their followers enjoyed being examined by Socrates, they grew to envy and hate him (21d) because the sons of the wealthy enjoyed listening to Socrates examine those reputed to be wise, and enjoyed trying their own hand at it as well. Socrates, then, is perfectly well aware why the jury is prejudiced against him. His impiety was not that he did not worship the gods of the city, which is never proved in any event, but that he (along with the sophists) undermined another element of the *civic cultus* equally protected by the gods of the city, namely the daily association, *sunousia*, of father and son, younger and older generations, by which familial, tribal, and civic traditions and conventions were transmitted. Such "corruption" of an institution could easily enough appear as impiety.[30] Pointing this out to the jury is designed to win him additional opprobrium.

The cross-examination of Meletus, "this fool of a prosecutor," is filled with jokes.[31] Socrates begins by saying Meletus is joking and then starts punning on his name.[32] He then changed the charge from not worshiping the gods of the city to introducing new *daimonia*, which might be translated as "new divinities."[33] It is a relatively easy argument to show that, on his own premises, Meletus contradicts himself, which says nothing about Socrates' premises.[34] By making fun of Meletus in this way, with an argument "as logical as it is ludicrous,"[35] Socrates also insults him and, to the extent that Meletus represents the city, insults all the jurors, and all the Athenians. Socrates demonstrates he has no concern at all for the opinions of the many (cf. 24d–25b), which is why again he has to tell them to quit shouting (27b).

The following section, usually called "Socrates' Mission" or even "Socrates' Business" (*pragma*) (28a–34b) is replete with insults to the jury and to the Athenians. If the hostility of the first accusers was accounted for by the amazing Delphi story, the hostility of the second and present accusers, whom Socrates treats "as if they were" different (24b), is accounted for by his "mission."[36]

He begins by comparing himself to Achilles, the most renowned Greek hero. To the jury, this comparison would be entirely inappropriate,[37] and so is yet another insulting joke. In the process he misquotes the *Iliad* and distinguishes between himself, an *aner agathos*, a good "real" man,[38] and an *anthropos*, a mere life-loving human being, and says that, like a good soldier, he will refuse to run away and will follow his orders, which come from the god, "to examine myself and others" (28e). Moreover, if he were granted a conditional discharge, namely that he could go free provided he did not continue to philosophize, he would refuse the offer, even if he were to die many deaths (30c). At this remark the jury again erupts in shouting and Socrates again tells them to be quiet.

The sequel is equally provocative: Socrates claims he is the greatest benefactor of the city because he does not follow the ways of life most Athenians favor, a clear rejection of a major component of traditional *aidos*. The implication is clear: Socrates' defense speech is not about defending himself or his "business," but about defending the Athenians so they do not do wrong and reject a divine gift, namely Socrates, by condemning him (30e). Here Socrates makes another joke. What looked to be his business, namely cross-examining his fellow citizens, is now said to be exhorting them to virtue. The good hombre and updated Achilles now sounds like a Boy Scout: "have you done a good deed today?" He follows this reduction in his offensiveness with another: he is like a horsefly or a "gadfly" and the Athenians are like a drowsy big horse. The image is not entirely far-fetched because it is possible we are meant to think of the six outbursts of the jury as having resulted from Socrates' "bites." That is, whereas we can reasonably infer that the cross-examining was what gained Socrates whatever hatred he experienced, now he is saying his "business" was "boy scout" exhortation. Exhortation, however, is unlikely to engender hatred so much as ridicule. And whereas the parasitic gadfly needs the horse, Socrates wants the Athenians to think that they need him, a gift of the gods.

In the sequel, Socrates combines exalted exhortation with less exalted horsefly themes when he says that he minds everybody else's business (*polypragmosyne*) in private but does not mind the business of the community, that is, he does not take part in politics, because of the warning issued by his *daimonion*. Unlike the Delphic utterance, which urges him to act, the *daimonion* restrains him. To the superstitious jurors this *daimonion* might mean that Socrates thinks he is especially favored by the gods and that the *daimonion* is precisely the "new divinity" that Meletus accused Socrates of introducing to the Athenians. He further insults the Athenians by pointing out that when he did take part in politics he endangered his life both under the democracy and under the Thirty: an honest man such as he cannot survive if he were to participate in Athenian politics, whatever the regime.

And when at last the *daimonion* did not restrain him from acting on the Delphic "riddle," he was by then an old man so that staying alive to interrogate the Athenians was less important because his business would soon be over anyhow – a fact that Socrates pointed out several times.

He also makes a joke of the corruption charge. Granted, Socrates says, "it is not unpleasant" for young men to spend time listening to Socrates "examine" persons who think they are wise but are not, but it would be easy to prove that such pleasures are not corrupting (33c–d). Just ask the young men! There are several such persons in the audience who, had he corrupted them, would be happy to testify against him. Socrates names them. Supposing that Socrates had corrupted them, would they or their families be likely to display their dirty laundry in public? Particularly where the corruption (*diaphthora*) involved might include pederasty?

Abruptly he says "that is all I have to say in my defence," but then adds a few more insults (34b–35d). First, he reminds them that, even though he has a family, he never dragged them onstage to weep and beg and carry on and that "someone among you"[39] might be angry at him for failing to provide such entertainment. He refused this option because it would reflect badly on the reputation of the Athenians as much as on his own (34c–e). But here too Socrates jokes. At the same time as he said he would never do something so disgraceful "he offers a sketch in speech of his own family, even numbering his children and giving their ages" (34d).[40] By so doing, he echoes Aristophanes' *Wasps* (562–70).[41]

His final remarks are equally insulting. These "piteous or mournful dramas" say something ridiculous about the city because acquittal on the basis of weeping and begging is a sign the jury did not do its job. Had Socrates taken that path, he would have connived in perjury and, because the jurors had sworn an oath, he would have implicitly taught that there were no gods.

> But that is far from true. For I acknowledge or worship (*nomizo*) them, men (*andres*) of Athens as none of my accusers does. And I hand over to you and to the god to judge me in whatever way it is going to be best for me and for you (35d).

Nowhere in his final remarks before receiving the verdict does Socrates mention the gods of the city.

In terms of the divisions of the *Apology* provided by Plato rather than his various editors, Socrates' counter-proposal (35e–38c) is the central and arguably the most dramatically important part of the dialog. He begins by saying he is not indignant or displeased (*aganaktein*) at the result in part because it was "not unexpected" (*anelpiston*) or "not unhoped-for." If the latter meaning was intended, Socrates is suggesting that the verdict was the one he hoped for. He was, however, surprised at how close the vote was.

Meletus proposed death as what Socrates deserved so Socrates, by law, has to propose a deserved alternative. In doing so, he ignores the fact that he had been found guilty of impiety and mentions only that he did not desire the things most Athenians sought, which any remaining jurors in the audience are likely to construe either as bragging or as a rejection of civic traditions. So what, in truth, does Socrates deserve by impoverishing and endangering himself in order to be a benefactor for the Athenians?

Even more than an Olympic victor in a chariot race, he says, he deserves to be kept at public expense in the Prytaneum. Because the Prytaneum was not a public restaurant but a sacred precinct to which one convicted of impiety would not likely be admitted, "Socrates is making what the court would consider a monstrous claim."[42] What makes it comic as well is that Socrates says that truthfulness requires him to make such a proposal. He caps this joke with another: he deserves to be maintained at the Prytaneum because, unlike the Olympic victors who only seem to make the Athenians happy, Socrates really does make them happy. Right: he makes the Athenians so happy they kill him.[43] And he coyly adds: "perhaps you think I am speaking provocatively" (37a). Perhaps? Socrates knows it is improper to propose a reward after he was found guilty. And if Burnet is correct in his speculation that the accusers proposed the death penalty in the hope that Socrates would choose exile, they were disappointed.[44] Eventually he proposes a fine that his friends might pay, which he could have proposed at the outset.

Socrates' remarks after sentencing, though not particularly comical, do put some of his previous statements in a different light. His opening words here (38c–e) make it evident that he was familiar with court procedures, thus indicating he was lying in his initial opening remarks to the jury (17d). When he delivers his oracular remarks to his condemners, he says he will be avenged by his younger and harsher followers (39d), which contrasts with what he said earlier (30e), when he remarked that if the Athenians got rid of him they would have trouble finding another. Now they won't.

Turning to the men who voted for his acquittal, whom he calls judges, he says he would be pleased to converse with them about what has happened, but there is no time. Nothing, however, prevents him from telling stories about how things turned out. Specifically, Socrates says that his *daimonion*, which even in small things opposed him if he were about to do something improper, did not oppose him concerning this action, so at this time, his dying must be a good thing. In the second half of this speech to the acquitters, Socrates remarks that, independent of the *daimonion*, there are stories, which he proceeds to recount, that give us great hope that death is good. And more specifically it is clear to Socrates now that it is better for him to be dead and "released from troubles" (41d). That is, now, when Socrates is already old, the effect of the Oracle, which earlier in his life – though how much earlier is not clear – had endangered Socrates, is now in harmony with the restraining effect of the *daimonion*.

His parting words to those who voted to convict him, men who had probably left the court anyway, is both a parting joke and an insult. They made a mistake by trying to harm Socrates and deserve to be condemned, which is a straightforward insult. Then, however, he names his condemners as his spiritual heirs, begging them to punish and pain his sons as Socrates had pained the Athenians if they seem to care for money or anything else more than virtue or if they gain a reputation for something when they are worth nothing. "If you do these things," Socrates says, "both I and my sons will have been treated justly by you" (42a). That is, Socrates seems to praise the Athenians by expecting them to improve his sons by paining them the way he has improved the Athenians by paining them. And we know how well that has worked.[45] His final words repeat an argument made previously, that it is unreasonable to fear death: "Now it is time to go away, I to die, you to live. Which of us goes to a better business is unclear to everyone but the god." And how would the jury have received that?

Conclusion

One conclusion from the foregoing analysis seems clear: "The *Apology*, though dealing with a very serious situation, strikes constantly the note of comedy." Even more: if comedy focuses chiefly on the exposure of vanity and pretention, when undertaken "at the behest of a god: surely this is piety! The unpopularity of Socrates arises from the fact that the public has no sense of humor."[46] Such a conclusion raises an obvious question. Granted that the text shows how Socrates makes fun of, and thereby offends, the Athenians, the big question remains: why? The answer to this problem may require a perspective beyond the text.

In this context, consider an argument of Voegelin. For him the conflict between the philosopher and the non-philosophers was a particular expression of the "tension of order and passion" that in Athens had once been mastered by the public cult of tragedy. The conflict between Socrates and the Athenians, however, made that cult

> senseless because from now on tragedy had only one subject matter, the fate of Socrates. Insofar as the Platonic dialog was animated by the tension between Socrates and Athens, it was in the history of Hellenic symbolic forms the successor to Aeschylean tragedy under new political conditions.[47]

By this argument, the dialog is the continuation of the public cult of tragedy and Plato is the spiritual successor of Aeschylus. Socrates' failure, attested by his trial and execution, thus raised an additional question: to whom is the symbolic form of dialog addressed if the jury and the citizens do not wish to listen?

Because "the law of the dialog cannot be enforced," the order of Athens could not be restored by Socrates or Plato. "Socrates had to die in the attempt. And *Dike* achieved no victory. Is the dialog a futile gesture after all?" Plato's answer, according to Voegelin, is that the dialog is continued in postexistence and is evoked by the myths of judgment in *Gorgias* and *Republic*. Moreover the *Apology* is "itself a mythical judgment." The Socrates of the *Apology* leaves his judges in no doubt that others will ask the questions that they tried to escape by sentencing him to death. The "others" have come. And the dialog is the continuation of the "trials" starting in the Academy and continuing to the present.[48]

Granted that the symbolic form of the dialog including its mythical dimension, was the successor to the symbolic form of tragedy, what is the place of comedy in this complex? Voegelin did not address this question directly though something of an answer can be constructed from his remarks on fifth-century Athenian spirituality. Let us start from an observation of Strauss: "The Aristophanean comedy certainly presupposes tragedy; it builds on tragedy; in this sense, at any rate, it is higher than tragedy."[49] This remark does not enable us to conclude that, if philosophical dialog builds on comedy, as we have argued it does, comedy is closer to philosophy than is tragedy. But it does mean that (to use Voegelinian language) the differentiation of philosophy makes a recovery of comedy, and *a fortiori* of tragedy, impossible. Once the insight afforded by philosophy has been gained, it cannot be un-learned, though the non-philosophers are under no compulsion to share it.

From a Voegelinian perspective, here is where matters become more complex. In the *Frogs*, for example, Aristophanes is able to represent the tragic dramas of Aeschylus and Euripides in a "naturalistic" way as representatives of the Athenians rise to greatness during the Persian Wars and decline into sophistic fraud and effeminate indulgence. As Voegelin observed, such an attitude is akin to reading Mann's *Magic Mountain* as a story about life in a sanatorium. The point, however, is that Aristophanes can take the "naturalistic" attitude of the audience for granted.[50] A generation later, with Aristotle's *Poetics*, tragedy and comedy are simply literary genres with the former being more complex because it achieves catharsis through the vicarious experiences of pity and fear. When drama is reduced to a kind of psychotherapy, however, it is clear its spirit has fled.[51] By this reading, philosophy expressed in the symbolic form of dialog is indeed obedience to the god who survived the death of the Olympians.

In practice, Socrates abandoned the conventions of *aidos*, shame, and practiced the comedic exposure of its inadequacies everywhere, in public and in private, by exercising the free speech (*parrhesia*) for which the Athenians were famous. The "examined" life that Socrates pursues is "a life dedicated to uncovering, to searching for a truth that lies behind the veils of customs, behind the public and private facades, behind the hierarchies established only by tradition."[52] The Socratic practice of *parrhesia* dissolves privacy and undermines the unexamined life that he says is not worth living for a human being even though such a life is the life of a conventionally pious human being. Such a human being, it needs hardly be said, would consider his or her life quite worth living, perhaps even worth living it as long as possible.

The deployment of *parrhesia* against *aidos* would be irresponsible and unjust if the philosophers had nothing with which to replace conventional *aidos*. Among other things, this is a problem explored in the *Protagoras*. There Protagoras argued that *aidos* complemented the art of politics thus enabling human beings to live together. In contrast, Socrates argued that *aidos* would limit wisdom and so had to be excluded from his famous discussion of the unity of the virtues, which named separately, include: wisdom, moderation, courage, justice, and holiness (*Protagoras*, 349b). As Saxonhouse noted, moderation has replaced shame for philosophers because, unlike shame, moderation is not limited by tradition and convention and thus by the gaze and opinions of others.

Unlike shame, moderation exists by nature and takes the form of an idea (*eidē*).[53] For a philosophically inclined statesman, it would surely be an exercise in moderation to permit the non-philosophers to retain their emotional attachments to whatever form or variety of *aidos* served public order, perhaps merely the reverential attitude to the past that today is associated with patriotism.

What, then, of holiness and piety? It is clear from both the *Euthyphro* and the cross-examination of Meletus that the Athenians have no knowledge of these things. But neither, it would seem, does Socrates. Francesco Gonzales has argued that Socrates deals with their problem by showing "he cares about piety and goodness" and that such care paradoxically "constitutes whatever piety and goodness humans are capable of."[54] Or, there is the problem of the Oracle story, which Socrates can neither accept at face value nor challenge directly, though questioning the Oracle is an indication of his care for piety. Examined piety, however, entails another paradox:

> Socrates disbelieves the oracle because he is aware of his own ignorance, but it is only through being aware of his own ignorance that he obeys the oracle. Furthermore, it is only through questioning what the god says that Socrates' life becomes a service to the god.[55]

Such dramatic, even existential reading of Socrates' Mission indicates that his "questioning is inconceivable without humility before, and the constant aspiration to, the divine. If it was concluded above that questioning is essential to Socratic piety, it must be concluded here that piety is essential to Socratic questioning."[56] Likewise human virtue and goodness consist of caring for one's goodness and virtue, which involves continual examination and discussion of goodness and virtue and not the possession of either. In this light, neither the Athenians nor Meletus care about those things, and that is their error and their fault. Socrates' discussion of this problem with them is necessarily ironical because philosophy is ironical. It is a way of life that is good and just but never possesses goodness or justice; it is a happy way of life that never attains satisfaction. Such ambivalence expressed as irony and, indeed, as comedy, is essential to Socratic existence.[57]

Notes

1 See Leonardo Taran, *Speusippus of Athens: A Critical Study with a Collection of the Related Texts and Commentary* (Leiden: Brill, 1982) and John Dillon, *The Heirs of Plato: A Study of the Old Academy* (Oxford: Clarendon, 2003).

2 For similar distinctions see: Gerald A. Press, "Introduction" to *Plato's Dialogues: New Studies and Interpretations*, Gerald A. Press, ed. (Lanham: Rowman and Littlefield, 1993), 7; Rosamund Kent Sprague, "Some Platonic Recollections," in *Plato's Dialogues*, 251, on her experience of listening to Gilbert Ryle discuss the Sophist; Jill Gordon, *Turning Toward Philosophy: Literary Device and Dramatic Structure in Plato's Dialogues*, (University Park: The Pennsylvania State University Press, 1999), 1–13.

3 Diskin Clay, *Platonic Questions: Dialogues with the Silent Philosopher* (University Park: Pennsylvania State University Press, 2000), ix; Dorothy Tarrant, "Plato as Dramatist," *The Journal of Hellenic Studies* 75 (1955): 82–9. For a "dramatic" criticism of an "argumentative" approach, see Clay's review of Gregory Vlastos' *Platonic Studies*, "Platonic Studies and the Study of Plato," *Arion: A Journal of Humanities and the Classics* 2 (1975): 116–32; Ruby Blondell, *The Play of Character in Plato's Dialogues* (Cambridge: Cambridge University Press, 2002), chapter 1, "Drama and Dialogue," 1–52, especially pp. 31–4 on comedy; William H. Johnson, "Dramatic Frame and Philosophic Idea in Plato," *The American Journal of Philology* 119 (1998): 577–98; Louis Dyer, "Plato as Playwright," *Harvard Studies in Classical Philology* 12 (1901): 165–80.

4 Most notably in Leo Strauss, *The Argument and the Action of Plato's Laws* (Chicago: University of Chicago Press, 1975).

5 I use *Four Texts on Socrates: Plato and Aristophanes*, Thomas G. West and Grace Starry West, trans. (Ithaca: Cornell University Press, 1998). For the Greek text I used *Plato's "Euthyphro," "Apology of Socrates" and "Crito,"* John Burnet, ed. (Oxford: Clarendon, 1970).

6 Catherine Zuckert, *Plato's Philosophers: The Coherence of the Dialogues* (Chicago: University of Chicago Press, 2009), 205.
7 Gene Fendt, "Five Readings of 'Euthyphro,'" *Philosophy and Literature* 38 (2014): 496. The title of Fendt's article is itself an indication of a joke: five ways of reading the dialog, not just one, the right way, which the author provides? Likewise, Patterson argues "Euthyphro . . . appears comic all around." Richard Patterson, "The Platonic Art of Comedy and Tragedy," *Philosophy and Literature* 6 (1982): 82.
8 Thomas C. Brickhouse and Nicholas D. Smith, "Socrates' First Remarks to the Jury in Plato's 'Apology of Socrates,'" *The Classical Journal* 81/4 (1986): 289–98; and their *Socrates on Trial*, (Princeton: Princeton University Press, 1989), 38. See also Jacob Howland, "Plato's 'Apology' as Tragedy," *The Review of Politics* 70 (2008): 519–46.
9 William Chase Greene, "The Spirit of Comedy in Plato," *Harvard Studies in Classical Philology* 31 (1920): 63; Diskin Clay, "The Tragic and Comic Poets of the 'Symposium,'" *Arion: A Journal of Humanities and the Classics* 2 (1975): 252; Diskin Clay, "The Origins of the Socratic Dialogue," in *The Socratic Movement*, Paul A. Vander Waerdt, ed. (Ithaca: Cornell University Press, 1994), 23–47. The ancient source for this information is Diogenes Laertius: see Charles H. Kahn, "Did Plato Write Socratic Dialogues," *The Classical Quarterly* 31 (1981): 305–20.
10 Notably David Leibowitz, *The Ironic Defense of Socrates: Plato's "Apology"* (Cambridge: Cambridge University Press, 2010) and Strauss, upon whom Leibowitz in some respects relies. Leo Strauss' "The Problem of Socrates," in *The Rebirth of Classical Rationalism,* Thomas L. Pangle, ed. (Chicago: University of Chicago Press, 1989), 103–83, "On Plato's 'Apology of Socrates' and 'Crito,'" in *Studies in Platonic Political Philosophy,* Thomas L. Pangle, ed. (Chicago: University of Chicago Press, 1983), 38–66, and the transcript of his class on the *Apology* given in the fall of 1966. Available at: https://leostrausscenter.uchicago.edu/sites/default/files/Plato%27s%20Apology%20%26%20Crito%20%281966%29_0.pdf. In his *Plato's "Apology of Socrates:" An Interpretation with a New Translation* (Ithaca: Cornell University Press, 1979), Thomas G. West remarks on the "almost tragic" figure of Socrates (p. 77) but also notes several allusions to jokes and comedy (pp. 74, 76, 100, 104, 145, 147–8, 177, 202, 220–1, 223, 225).
11 Ann N. Michelini, "Socrates Plays the Buffoon: Cautionary Protreptic in the 'Euthydemus,'" *The American Journal of Philology* 121 (2000): 514.
12 Roger Brock, "Plato and Comedy," in *"Owls to Athens": Essays on Classical Subjects Presented to Sir Kenneth Dover*, E.M. Craik, ed. (Oxford: Clarendon, 1990), 40; Greene, "The Spirit of Comedy in Plato," 67, 72, 123.
13 Henri Bergson, *Le Rire: Essai sur la Signification du Comique*, in *Oeuvres complètes de Henri Bergson,* vol. 3, (Genève: Skira, 1945), 110.
14 Arlene Saxonhouse, *Free Speech and Democracy in Ancient Athens* (Cambridge: Cambridge University Press, 2006), 110.
15 Saxonhouse, *Free Speech and Democracy*, 116–7; 82. Drew E. Griffin "Socrates' Poverty: Virtue and Money in Plato's 'Apology of Socrates,'" *Ancient Philosophy* 15 (1995): 1 points out that Socrates drew attention to his conventionally shameful poverty three times (*Apology*, 23b–c; 31c; 36d).
16 For "historical" accounts, see M.I. Finley, "Socrates and Athens," in his *Aspects of Antiquity: Discoveries and Controversies* (New York: Viking, 1968), 58–72; Paul Millett, "The Trial of Socrates Revisited," *European Review of History* 12 (2005): 23–62.
17 On Xenophon's subtlety see Leo Strauss, "The Problem of Socrates," 127 ff., 136; Thomas L. Pangle's account, which emphasizes Xenophon's "characteristic deftness," "The Political Defense of Socratic Philosophy: A Study of Xenophon's 'Apology of Socrates,'" *Polity* 18 (1985): 98–114; Kazutaka Kondo, "Reputation and Virtue: The Political Achievement of Socrates in Xenophon's 'Apology,'" *Interpretation* 42 (2015): 31–50; V.J. Gray, "Xenophon's Defence of Socrates: The Rhetorical Background to the Socratic Problem," *The Classical Quarterly* 39 (1989): 136–40.
18 Strauss, "The Problem of Socrates," 106. For anecdotes concerning Plato and Socrates, see Alice Swift Riginos, *Platonica: The Anecdotes Concerning the Life and Writings of Plato* (Leiden: Brill, 1976), 52–60.
19 Strauss, *On Tyranny*; Victor Gourevitch and Michael S. Roth, eds. (Chicago: University of Chicago Press, 2000), 28.
20 This is a paraphrase of Leibowitz, *The Ironic Defense*, 3. It is also a joke.
21 Leon Craig pointed out to me that *deinos* means "clever" only when modifying an art or skill; its primary meaning is "terrible" in the sense of terrifying. Thus when Socrates indicated that he is a *deinos* speaker he also means that he is a terrifying speaker because he speaks the truth about the received or conventional stories that constitute the foundation of the *polis* and that are expressed by the poets. And regarding the poets, the only time Socrates says he is ashamed (*aischynomai*) is when he claims to tell the truth about them: they do not make their poetry on the basis of wisdom but, rather like Euthyphro, on the basis of

divination (*Apology*, 22b–c). The point, therefore, is that the foundations of the *polis* are entirely conventional. Given the importance of *aidos* as discussed below, Socrates' profession of shame is also a joke.
22 See in general R.E. Allen, *Socrates and Legal Obligation* (Minneapolis: University of Minnesota Press, 1981). Douglas D. Feaver and John E. Hare argue that "every section of Socrates' main speech is in fact a parody, using the traditional [rhetorical] form with the reverse of the function traditionally attributed to it." "The *Apology* as an Inverted Parody of Rhetoric," *Arethusa* 14 (1981): 205. Kenneth Seeskin, "Is the 'Apology of Socrates' a Parody?" *Philosophy and Literature* 6 (1982): 94–105, argues convincingly that the *Apology* is directly modeled on, and is a parody of, Gorgias' *Apology of Palamedes*. Socrates happens to compare himself to Palamedes at *Apology* 41b.
23 Eva Brann, "The Offence of Socrates: A Re-reading of Plato's 'Apology,'" *Interpretation* 7/2 (1978): 6. See also Michael Zuckert, "Rationalism and Political Responsibility: Just Speech and Just Deed in the 'Clouds' and the 'Apology of Socrates,'" *Polity* 17 (1984): 297.
24 The jury raises a ruckus (*thorubos*) six times (*Apology*, 20d, 20e, 21a, 27b, 30c, and 31e) usually because Socrates deliberately says something that he knows will look to the jury as if he is boasting of his own superiority. Socrates discusses the *thorubos* of assemblies, theaters, encampments, and juries in *Republic* (492b–c). On *thorubos* more generally, see Victor Bers, "Dikastic *Thorubos*," *History of Political Thought* 6 (1985): 1–15. Unfortunately, Bers does not discuss the *Apology* because Plato is a "tainted witness." Although Xenophon does not say so explicitly, it is fair to say that the outbursts of the jury are responses to Socrates' "big talk" (*megalegoria*) mentioned three times in the first five sentences of his *Apology*.
25 In the *Charmides* 153b2 Chaerophon is called *manikos*, a crazy person. In Aristophanes' *Clouds*, 104, 144, 504 he is miserable, unhappy, and half-dead; in *Birds* 1296 his squeaky voice earns him the nickname "the bat."
26 James Riddell considered the Oracle story "unhistoric." *The "Apology of Plato"* (Oxford: Clarendon, 1867), xvi. Burnet, *"Euthyphro," "Apology" and "Crito"* disagrees, 91–2. Hugh Bowden, *Classical Athens and the Delphic Oracle: Divination and Democracy* (Cambridge: Cambridge University Press, 2005), 82, said, "it is difficult to be certain whether this story is evidence of a genuine consultation of the oracle." The historical question is in any event separate from the dramatic one.
27 David D. Corey, "Socratic Citizenship: Delphic Oracle and Divine Sign," *The Review of Politics* 67 (2005): 212.
28 George Gregory, "Of Socrates, Aristophanes and Rumors," in *Re-examining Socrates in the "Apology"*, Patricia Fagan and John Russon, eds. (Evanston: Northwestern University Press, 2009), 57.
29 Leibowitz, *The Ironic Defense*, 102, agrees.
30 Kevin Rabb, "Asebeia and Sunousia: The Issue behind the Indictment of Socrates," In *Plato's Dialogues*, Gerald A. Press, ed., 77–106; Saxonhouse, *Free Speech and Democracy*, 101 ff.
31 Feaver and Hare, "The 'Apology' as an Inverted Parody of Rhetoric," 211.
32 Socrates repeats the remark first made at *Apology* (24c) that Meletus is joking, three additional times (*Apology*, 26e, 27a, d). The pun is on Meletus and *melete*, care, and leads to such witticisms as "Mr. Care doesn't care," and so on.
33 Burnet, *Plato's "Euthyphro," "Apology of Socrates" and "Crito,"* 105.
34 Meletus thinks that *daimonia* are the offspring of gods and humans (*Apology*, 27b–e). In the *Symposium* (202d–e) Socrates argues that *daimonia* are intermediaries between gods and humans and that they cannot be offspring of gods and humans because those two kinds of beings do not have contact with one another.
35 Brann, "The Offence of Socrates," 10. The analogy Socrates uses, comparing half-gods (*hemitheoi*) to half-asses (*hemionoi*) "has so offended modern sensibilities that it does not appear in the Greek text in some editions of the *Apology* and is thus missing from some translations." Clay, *Platonic Questions*, 47; Clay, "Socrates' Mulishness and Heroism," *Phronesis* 17 (1972): 53–60. The analogy also suggests that, if gods were like big horses and *daimones* were like mules, then humans were asses, small comical caricatures of horses.
36 The qualification, that Socrates treats the present accusers "as if they were" different from the old accusers arguably indicates that Socrates did not see them as different at all. Both sets of accusers were simply prejudiced against him.
37 Robert Metcalfe, "Socrates and Achilles," in *Re-examining Socrates*, Fagan and Russon, eds., 62–84.
38 Strauss sometimes translates *aner* as "hombre" which certainly captures Socrates' *megalegoria*.
39 When Socrates uses the indefinite pronoun, *tis*, it almost invariably refers to the life-loving *anthropos* not a real man, *aner*. That is, the reference is itself insulting. See *Apology* 20c, 28b, 29c, 34d and *Gorgias*, 511a–b, 522c.
40 Maria L. Talero, "Just Speaking, Just Listening: Performance and Contradiction in Socrates' 'Apology,'" in *Re-examining Socrates*, Fagan and Russon, eds., 27.
41 Edith Hall, "Law Court Dramas: The Power of Performance in Greek Forensic Oratory," *Bulletin in the Institute of Classical Studies* 40 (1995): 39–58.

42 Burnet, *Plato's "Euthyphro," "Apology" and "Crito,"* 151. On Socrates' inadmissibility, see Douglas M. MacDowell, *The Law in Classical Athens* (Ithaca: Cornell University Press, 1978), 73–4.
43 Leibowitz, *The Ironic Defense*, 35, 161.
44 Burnet, *Plato's "Euthyphro," "Apology" and "Crito,"* 150.
45 Aristotle (*Rhetoric*, 1390b31) says the sons of Socrates were stupid (*abeleria*), something that Socrates would have known. Saxonhouse said that justice would be done "when the city becomes a surrogate father to Socrates' sons as Socrates has been to the city of Athens" ("The Philosophy of the Particular," 296), which may be true but is also an infinitely remote possibility and so evidence of a joke.
46 Greene, "The Spirit of Comedy," 71–2.
47 Eric Voegelin, *Order and History (Volume III): Plato and Aristotle,* Vol 16 of *The Collected Works of Eric Voegelin*, Dante Germino, ed. (Columbia: University of Missouri Press, 2000), 65. Compare Voegelin's argument with that of Nietzsche, *Birth of Tragedy*, 12–13.
48 Voegelin, *Plato and Aristotle*, 67.
49 Strauss, *Socrates and Aristophanes* (New York: Basic Books, 1966), 312.
50 See Eric Voegelin's *Order and History (Volume II): The World of the Polis, The Collected Works of Eric Voegelin*, Athanasios Moulakis, ed. (Columbia: University of Missouri Press, 2000), Vol. 15, 319.
51 In *Order and History (Volume V): In Search of Order. The Collected Works of Eric Voegelin*, Ellis Sandoz, ed. (Columbia: University of Missouri Press, 2000), Vol. 18, 84, Voegelin refers to Hegel's discussion in *Phänomenologie des Geistes*, J. Hoffmeister, ed. (Hamburg: Meiner, 1952), 517–20, 523, of Aristophanes and of the "happy consciousness" of comedy for which everything of significance is lost, a state of consciousness that finds expression "in the pityless words, god has died" *Gott gestorben ist*.
52 Saxonhouse, *Free Speech and Democracy*, 110.
53 *Ibid.*, 203.
54 Francesco J. Gonzales, "Caring and Conversing about Virtue Every Day: Human Piety and Goodness in Plato's 'Apology,'" in *Re-examining Socrates*, Fagan and Russon, eds., 118.
55 Gonzales, "Caring and Conversation," 127–9.
56 *Ibid.*, 134.
57 I would like to thank Ed Andrew, Leon Craig, Tom Darby, Tilo Schabert and John von Heyking for their comments on an earlier version of this paper.

Bibliography

Allen, R.E. 1981. *Socrates and Legal Obligation*. Minneapolis: University of Minnesota Press.
Bergson, Henri. 1945. *Le Rire: Essai sur la Signification du Comique. Oeuvres complètes de Henri Bergson*, Vol. 3. Genève: Skira.
Bers, Victor. 1985. "Dikastic Thorubos." *History of Political Thought* 6: 1–15.
Blondell, Ruby. 2002. *The Play of Character in Plato's Dialogues*. Cambridge: Cambridge University Press.
Bowden, Hugh. 2005. *Classical Athens and the Delphic Oracle: Divination and Democracy*. Cambridge: Cambridge University Press.
Brann, Eva. 1978. "The Offence of Socrates: A Re-reading of Plato's 'Apology.'" *Interpretation* 7/2: 1–21.
Brickhouse, Thomas C. and Nicholas D. Smith. 1986. "Socrates' First Remarks to the Jury in Plato's 'Apology of Socrates.'" *The Classical Journal* 81/4: 289–98.
———. 1989. *Socrates on Trial*. Princeton: Princeton University Press.
Brock, Roger. 1990. "Plato and Comedy." In *"Owls to Athens": Essays on Classical Subjects Presented to Sir Kenneth Dover*. E.M. Craik ed. Oxford: Clarendon: 39–49.
Burnet, John ed. 1970. *Plato's "Euthyphro," "Apology of Socrates" and "Crito."* Oxford: Clarendon.
Clay, Diskin. 1972. "Socrates' Mulishness and Heroism." *Phronesis* 17: 53–60.
———. 1975a. "Platonic Studies and the Study of Plato." *Arion: A Journal of Humanities and the Classics* 2/1: 116–32.
———. 1975b. "The Tragic and Comic Poets of the 'Symposium.'" *Arion: A Journal of Humanities and the Classics* 2/2: 238–61.
———. 1994. "The Origins of the Socratic Dialogue." In *The Socratic Movement*. Paul A. Vander Waerdt ed. Ithaca: Cornell University Press: 23–47.
———. 2000. *Platonic Questions: Dialogues with the Silent Philosopher*. University Park: Pennsylvania State University Press.

Corey, David D. 2005. "Socratic Citizenship: Delphic Oracle and Divine Sign." *The Review of Politics* 67/2: 201–28.
Craig, Leon. 1994. *The War-Lover: A Study of Plato's Republic.* Toronto: University of Toronto Press.
Dillon, John. 2003. *The Heirs of Plato: A Study of the Old Academy.* Oxford: Clarendon.
Dodds, E.R. 1956. *The Greeks and the Irrational.* Berkeley: University of California Press.
Dyer, Louis. 1901. "Plato as Playwright." *Harvard Studies in Classical Philology* 12: 165–80.
Feaver, Douglas D. and John E. Hare. 1981. "The 'Apology' as an Inverted Parody of Rhetoric." *Arethusa* 14: 205–16.
Fendt, Gene. 2014. "Five Readings of 'Euthyphro.'" *Philosophy and Literature* 38/2: 495–509.
Finley, M.I. 1968. *Aspects of Antiquity: Discoveries and Controversies.* New York: Viking.
Gonzales, Francesco J. 2009. "Caring and Conversing about Virtue Every Day: Human Piety and Goodness in Plato's 'Apology.'" In *Re-examining Socrates in the "Apology."* Patricia Fagan and John Russon eds. Evanston: Northwestern University Press: 117–67.
Gordon, Jill. 1999. *Turning Toward Philosophy: Literary Device and Dramatic Structure in Plato's Dialogues.* University Park: The Pennsylvania State University Press.
Gray, V.J. 1989. "Xenophon's Defence of Socrates: The Rhetorical Background to the Socratic Problem." *The Classical Quarterly* 39/1: 136–40.
Greene, William C. 1920. "The Spirit of Comedy in Plato." *Harvard Studies in Classical Philology* 31: 63–123.
Gregory, George. 2009. "Of Socrates, Aristophanes and Rumors." In *Re-examining Socrates in the "Apology."* Patricia Fagan and John Russon eds. Evanston: Northwestern University Press: 35–61.
Griffin, Drew E. 1995. "Socrates' Poverty: Virtue and Money in Plato's 'Apology of Socrates.'" *Ancient Philosophy* 15/1: 1–16.
Hall, Edith. 1995. "Law Court Dramas: The Power of Performance in Greek Forensic Oratory." *Bulletin in the Institute of Classical Studies* 40: 39–58.
Hegel, Georg Wilhelm Friedrich. 1952. *Phänomenologie des Geistes.* J. Hoffmeister ed. Hamburg: Meiner.
Howland, Jacob. 2008. "Plato's 'Apology' as Tragedy." *The Review of Politics* 70/4: 519–46.
Jaeger, Werner. 1943. *In Search of the Divine Centre. Paideia: The Ideals of Greek Culture,* Vol. 2. New York: Oxford University Press.
Johnson, William H. 1998. "Dramatic Frame and Philosophic Idea in Plato." *The American Journal of Philology* 119/4: 577–98.
Kahn, Charles H. 1981. "Did Plato Write Socratic Dialogues." *The Classical Quarterly* 31/2: 305–20.
Kondo, Kazutaka. 2015. "Reputation and Virtue: The Political Achievement of Socrates in Xenophon's 'Apology.'" *Interpretation* 42/1: 31–50.
Leibowitz, David. 2010. *The Ironic Defense of Socrates: Plato's "Apology."* Cambridge: Cambridge University Press.
MacDowell, Douglas M. 1978. *The Law in Classical Athens.* Ithaca: Cornell University Press.
Metcalfe, Robert. 2009. "Socrates and Achilles." In *Re-examining Socrates in the "Apology."* Patricia Fagan and John Russon eds. Evanston: Northwestern University Press: 62–84.
Michelini, Ann N. 2000. "Socrates Plays the Buffoon: Cautionary Protreptic in the 'Euthydemus.'" *American Journal of Philology* 121/4: 509–535.
Millett, Paul. 2005. "The Trial of Socrates Revisited." *European Review of History* 12/1: 23–62.
North, Helen. 1966. *Sophrosyne: Self-Knowledge and Self-Restraint in Greek Literature.* Ithaca: Cornell University Press.
Pangle, Thomas L. 1985. "The Political Defense of Socratic Philosophy: A Study of Xenophon's 'Apology of Socrates.'" *Polity* 18/1: 98–114.
Patterson, Richard. 1982. "The Platonic Art of Comedy and Tragedy." *Philosophy and Literature* 6/1–2: 76–93.
Press, Gerald A. 1993. "Introduction." In *Plato's Dialogues: New Studies and Interpretations.* Gerald A. Press ed. Lanham: Rowman and Littlefield: 1–14.
Rabb, Kevin. 1993. "Asebeia and Sunousia: The Issue behind the Indictment of Socrates." In *Plato's Dialogues: New Studies and Interpretations.* Gerald A. Press ed. Lanham: Rowman and Littlefield: 77–106.
Riddell, James. 1867. *The "Apology of Plato."* Oxford: Clarendon.
Saxonhouse, Arlene W. 1988. "The Philosophy of the Particular and the Universality of the City." *Political Theory* 16/2: 281–99.

Saxonhouse, Arlene W. 2006. *Free Speech and Democracy in Ancient Athens*. Cambridge: Cambridge University Press.

Seeskin, Kenneth. 1982. "Is the 'Apology of Socrates' a Parody?" *Philosophy and Literature* 6/1–2: 94–105.

Sprague, Rosamund K. 1993. "Some Platonic Recollections." In *Plato's Dialogues: New Studies and Interpretations*. Gerald A. Press ed. Lanham: Rowman and Littlefield: 249–58.

Strauss, Leo. 1966a. "Plato's 'Apology of Socrates' and 'Crito.'" The Leo Strauss Center, https://leostrausscenter.uchicago.edu/sites/default/files/Plato%27s%20Apology%20%26%20Crito%20%281966%29_0.pdf.

———. 1966b. *Socrates and Aristophanes*. New York: Basic Books.

———. 1975. *The Argument and the Action of Plato's Laws*. Chicago: University of Chicago Press.

———. 1983. "On Plato's 'Apology of Socrates' and 'Crito.'" In *Studies in Platonic Political Philosophy*. Thomas L. Pangle ed. Chicago: University of Chicago Press: 38–66.

———. 1989. "The Problem of Socrates." In *The Rebirth of Classical Rationalism*. Thomas L. Pangle ed. Chicago: University of Chicago Press: 103–83.

———. 2000. *On Tyranny*. Victor Gourevitch and Michael S. Roth eds. Chicago: University of Chicago Press.

Swift Riginos, Alice. 1976. *Platonica: The Anecdotes Concerning the Life and Writings of Plato*. Leiden: Brill.

Talero, Maria L. 2009. "Just Speaking, Just Listening: Performance and Contradiction in Socrates' 'Apology.'" In *Re-examining Socrates in the "Apology."* Patricia Fagan and John Russon eds. Evanston: Northwestern University Press: 16–31.

Taran, Leonardo. 1982. *Speusippus of Athens: A Critical Study with a Collection of the Related Texts and Commentary*. Leiden: Brill.

Tarrant, Dorothy. 1955. "Plato as Dramatist." *The Journal of Hellenic Studies* 75: 82–9.

Todd, S.C. 1993. *The Shape of Athenian Law*. Oxford: Clarendon.

Voegelin, Eric. 2000. *Order and History (Volume III): Plato and Aristotle. The Collected Works of Eric Voegelin*, Vol. 16. Dante Germino ed. Columbia: University of Missouri Press.

———. 2000. *Order and History (Volume II): The World of the Polis. The Collected Works of Eric Voegelin*, Vol. 15. Athanasios Moulakis ed. Columbia: University of Missouri Press.

———. 2000. *Order and History (Volume V): In Search of Order. The Collected Works of Eric Voegelin*, Vol. 18. Ellis Sandoz ed. Columbia: University of Missouri Press.

Walden, Kenneth. 2015. "The 'Euthyphro' Dilemma." *Philosophy and Phenomenological Research* 90/3: 612–39.

West, Thomas G. 1979. *Plato's Apology of Socrates: An Interpretation with a New Translation*. Ithaca: Cornell University Press.

West, Thomas G. and Grace Starry West, eds. and trans. 1998. *Four Texts on Socrates: Plato and Aristophanes*. Ithaca: Cornell University Press.

Zuckert, Catherine. 2009. *Plato's Philosophers: The Coherence of the Dialogues*. Chicago: University of Chicago Press.

Zuckert, Michael. 1984. "Rationalism and Political Responsibility: Just Speech and Just Deed in the 'Clouds' and the 'Apology of Socrates.'" *Polity* 17: 271–97.

3 Guiding *Eros* Toward Wisdom in *Alcibiades I*

Vanessa Jansche

The Socratic method is generally associated with a special type of questioning that aims at testing the consistency of an argument and usually forces the participant to reconsider his or her initial beliefs. But if one looks closely at the academic literature and the classroom practice, there seems to be no shared definition of the Socratic method that is broadly accepted. On the contrary, there are various views of what it actually consists of.[1]

In this chapter, I argue that the Socratic method consists of redirecting an erotic – and therefore potentially tyrannical – soul toward philosophy. The outline of my argument is as follows: based on passages in the *Symposium*, Socrates describes himself as an expert in matters of love with *eros* understood as a fundamental drive that deeply shapes human life. I complement this picture of *eros* by turning to the *Republic*, where Socrates explains how the philosopher's *eros* aims at wisdom and is stronger than any other desire within the philosopher's soul. Astonishingly, Socrates emphasizes that the tyrant, too, is driven by an enormously strong *eros*, which forces the affected person to live a tyrannical life strictly opposed to a philosophical one.

In a next step, I seek to elucidate in *Alcibiades I* how Socrates tries to turn his lover's *eros* toward philosophy. In this dialog, Socrates meets Alcibiades, an ambitious aristocrat, whose *eros* aims at political power to "rule the world." By working out the contradictions in Alcibiades' understandings of politics and justice, Socrates forces him to admit he does not have the necessary knowledge to become a good politician. The refutation of Alcibiades' mistaken ideas enables Socrates to redirect the young man's *eros*. Socrates further points out the importance of self-knowledge, an explicit reference to his own philosophical motivation derived from the Delphic maxim to "know thyself." Finally, I conclude with some remarks on how the Socratic method as presented in the *Alcibiades I* might be applicable to classroom practice in the twenty-first century.

Different Accounts of the Socratic Method

Scholars distinguish two forms of the Socratic method present in Plato's dialogs. The first type consists in refuting the interlocutor's opinion by pointing out its inconsistencies. This confutative method is most prominent in the early dialogs like *Charmides*, *Laches*, or *Republic I*.[2] Because all these dialogs end in *aporia*, some scholars conclude that Socrates was a skeptic and that the rejection of any definition given by his partners demonstrates the limits of human reason.[3] The second type of Socratic method is a way of imparting knowledge by asking specific questions. Commentators who favor this *maieutic* approach refer to *Meno* or *Theaetetus*.[4] They claim that Socrates' main intention is to help people "give birth" to their own ideas. Both approaches are consistent in themselves, but once we look for a way to combine them into one overall method, we stumble upon the so-called Socratic ignorance.

Socrates, as presented by Plato, claims that he does not know the things he is asking his interlocutors.[5] If Socrates' ignorance is seen simply as an ironic stylistic device, the Socratic method consequently appears as a way to impart knowledge or – in a negative way – to manipulate.[6]

However, this account contrasts with diverse passages within the Platonic corpus where Socrates insists on not knowing what matters most in life. He explains his epistemic position most prominently in the *Apology*. Socrates says that he never acted as a teacher, and he firmly rejects the idea that he ever had a pupil (*Apology*, 33b). Both aspects – the emphasis on his ignorance and the rejection of the idea of teaching – seem to contradict the thesis that Socrates' ignorance is simply ironic.

An alternative would be to take the Socratic ignorance literally. If Socrates really does not know what courage, justice, prudence, or piety mean, then his way of questioning his fellow citizens is a method which provides a basis for moral discussion that does not presuppose any specific knowledge. The Socratic method therefore seems to be a neutral procedure to lead a conversation such that it enables the interlocutor to "give birth" to his own ideas whereas the Socratic part does not interfere with the content.[7] Even though this interpretation seems promising and attractive, it fails to explain one crucial element of the Socratic dialog: Socrates is never satisfied with simply assisting his interlocutor to generate a claim. He always insists on testing the idea advanced by his partner (*Apology*, 29e; *Theaetetus*, 150c). If we take his ignorance literally, how can Socrates actually test an opinion? Socrates must have known something, but what exactly?

Against this background, I offer another approach to the Socratic method that does not focus on Socratic ignorance but rather on Socratic knowledge about *eros*. I understand the Socratic method in a broader sense: I define it by its overall philosophical motivation rather than by particular rhetorical techniques. I consequently shift my focus on Socrates' intention while discussing with his interlocutor, i.e., Alcibiades, in the dialog of the same name.

Socratic Expertise on *Eros*

As stated in the beginning, Socrates is famous for his ignorance. He frankly admits that he does not know the things he is asking his interlocutors (*Apology*, 23a). In this light, the rare passages where Socrates does claim to know something become even more interesting and call for further investigation. Maybe one of the most revealing dialogs about Socrates himself is the *Symposium*. As I later take a closer look at the relationship between Alcibiades and Socrates in the *Alcibiades I*, it is worth mentioning that Plato gives the most impressive characterization of his master through the mouth of Alcibiades. Apparently, Alcibiades knows Socrates better than anyone else does – except, of course, for Plato.[8]

In *Symposium*, Agathon celebrates his victory at an Athenian festival in honor of Dionysius and invites his guests to a banquet (*Symposium*, 173a).[9] Instead of raising their glasses to toast their host Agathon, the guests instead agree on delivering speeches to praise *Eros*[10] (177d). So, what does Socrates know about it?

Eros, i.e., love, is always love *of* something (199e). Love is a relation between the lover and the beloved – it is *not* the beloved itself. Love expresses a desire for something, but we only desire things we do not have yet or we already have but are afraid of losing (200d). Because *Eros* is attracted by beauty, it follows that he cannot be beautiful himself (201c). The previous speakers, Socrates holds, misunderstood this fundamental structure. Hence, all the positive attributes they ascribed to *Eros* are really the attributes of the beloved.

But if *Eros* is not beautiful, this does not mean necessarily that he is ugly, as Socrates explains reproducing a conversation he once had with the priestess Diotima (202b). He is in between, the *metaxy*; and *Eros* is neither ignorant nor wise – but philosophical (204b). This point is remarkable as it might give us an enriched idea of what philosophy actually means. Philosophy as the love for wisdom is relational – it has a center of reference, namely wisdom and truth, and it has not yet reached what it is seeking. The philosopher is neither ignorant (he *knows* that he does not know) nor wise (he knows that he *does not know*) – a clear reference to Socrates himself. Thus, philosophy represents the basic erotic condition of human life: we yearn for the things that we do not have yet but so desperately need. This link between *eros* and philosophy later becomes more evident when Alcibiades identifies Socrates as *Eros* (214b).

Love is not completion but the striving for it. It longs for the beautiful by which it hopes to attain the good and everyone wants to have the good forever (205a). Diotima describes how a true erotic lover can reach the highest good and hence satisfy his desire. First, as a young man, he loves a beautiful person and impregnates him with beautiful speeches (210a). After a while, he realizes that there are many beautiful people and his beloved is not the only one. At this point, the lover extends his love to all beautiful people. If there are many beautiful bodies, beauty cannot be identical to any specific one (210b). It is pivotal to note that the expansion on the physical level – many beautiful bodies – is the first step to overcome the mind's fixation on an empirical object. He thus has to overcome the sensual level and enter the intellectual sphere.[11] Therefore, he now loves his lover's beautiful *soul* which is of greater consistency than his body.

At this stage, the philosopher lover aims at improving the beloved soul through "beautiful speeches." He continues to recognize the beauty in the community's laws and morals (210c), until he becomes aware of the beauty of science and knowledge (210c/d). At this abstract level, he is only one step away from the end. By practicing sciences and training his intellect, the lover will be able to grasp the beauty itself which is absolute and perfect. Although the ascent to the beautiful becomes more and more abstract, it is worth going: once the philosopher perceives beauty itself, he knows the source of all beautiful things which are always imperfect in some way and therefore never as beautiful as their cause. Knowing beauty itself enables the lover to create true virtue (212a) and only then is he at the end of his journey: he gains the good by creating it.

If one stops reading at this point, all the prerequisites regarding Plato's concept of love seem to be met: it is impersonal, ignoring the individual, objective, and only interested in intellectual objects, i.e., the Forms.[12] But this is not actually the case. To prove Socrates' and hence philosophy's personal erotic engagement, Plato appeals to someone as a witness whose credibility regarding love no one in Athens would have dared to question: Alcibiades[13] who has the last saying in the *Symposium* and his description of Socrates is anything but prudish.[14]

Alcibiades enters Agathon's house accompanied by dancers and flutists. He is drunk and wants to share his inebriation with the other guests. Alcibiades refuses to praise *Eros* but instead wants to pay tribute to Socrates (214d). This scene introducing Alcibiades already gives an idea of the young Athenian's major characteristics: on the one hand, he is dictatorial and gives orders, and on the other hand, he is desperately in love with Socrates that he even associates his beloved with *Eros* itself.

How does he describe Socrates? Alcibiades compares him to the satyr Marsyas, a sort of demon, whose appearance is ugly but who bewitches humans by playing his flute. Socrates, by contrast, charms his fellows with his dialogs. Alcibiades confesses that he is so deeply moved by Socrates' words that he considers his own life not worth living on those terms (216a). And although it seems that Socrates mostly speaks about craftsmen, his words are full of wisdom and reason and "none are so divine, so rich in images of virtue" (222a).

Like *Eros*, Socrates always pursues the beautiful and is purely philosophical (216d). Driven by his love for wisdom, Socrates has achieved the highest level of Diotima's ascent by realizing virtue: he is braver than anyone else on the battlefield and he is modest, be it in times of shortage or abundance (220a/b, 221b). This is the reason why Alcibiades loves Socrates: he literally embodies the good. By following his *eros*, Socrates became what he was searching for.

Seemingly, Alcibiades is able to acknowledge the beauty of Socrates but is unable to follow him and lead a philosophical life. Alcibiades' *eros* was corrupted by his desire for power. Alcibiades represents another erotic character that is not philosophical but tyrannical. This will become more evident in the next section consulting the *Republic* and Plato's portrayal of the philosopher and the tyrant.

For present purposes, this short sketch of the *Symposium* shall be sufficient to show Socrates' expertise on love. Philosophy, as Socrates practices it, is erotic. One could even say that Socratic philosophy is the most profound expression of love. For this reason, Socrates knows that an erotic nature is highly deficient and yearns for its beloved object.

Eros as Common Ground of Philosophy and Tyranny

So far, we have met an erotic person going in one direction – the ascent to beauty and the good. Although Socrates' previous speakers have no philosophical ambitions, one cannot deny their enthusiasm. The most emotional speech is that of Alcibiades – he represents erotic passion that resembles madness. Alcibiades' appearance – escorted by girls, dancers, and musicians, crowned with ivy and considerably drunk (*Symposium*, 212e) – is reminiscent of Dionysus, the god of wine and ecstasy. Alcibiades is erotic, but surely not in a philosophical sense. He is in love with Socrates, but chooses another way of life. In the *Republic*, Plato describes the character which comes closest to the philosopher regarding his erotic passion – the tyrant.

It is therefore worth carving out the parallels of the philosopher in the *Symposium* and the *Republic*. After Socrates has stated that the philosophers are the ones who should rule the city (473c/d), he defines what a real philosopher is in order to meet potential objections (474b).[15] First, he remarks that loving something means wanting it completely and not just parts of it. Philosophers love all sorts of knowledge because they desire all wisdom (475b). Because philosophers are not the only ones who are curious, he specifies his definition: whereas lovers of spectacles are delighted by beautiful sounds and sights, the philosopher looks for the beauty itself. Here again, the philosopher is characterized as someone who goes beyond the phenomena and looks for the intellectual principle that manifests itself in material objects. The other lovers – those of spectacles, music, and so on – stay on the second level of Diotima's ascent: They are overwhelmed by the sheer amount and variety of sensual effects, but they are not capable of going one step further. They love many beautiful things without realizing *what* they love about them.

A philosopher is committed to *eros* and yearns for the good, but her or his passion is not necessarily satisfied. There are multiple dangers to a philosophical nature: First, the philosophical soul's so-called positive attributes – bravery, sobriety, and more – can pull it away from philosophy.[16] A second danger is miseducation: Socrates states that bad education harms endowed souls more than others (491e). The philosophical soul features cognitive skills that can be exploited for any purpose – be it in good or in bad faith. After all, "[. . .] a weak nature will never be the cause of anything great, either for good or evil" (491e). Philosophical natures can therefore potentially threaten their environment if they choose to use their excellence in a wrong sense.

Once the soul is corrupted, it becomes very difficult to recapture it for philosophy. Because his fellow men are also aware of his talents, they try to exploit the young person by cajoling him. In this regard, it is very unlikely that the young arrogant man will listen to someone who tells him the truth: he is in a deplorably ignorant state unless he starts to philosophize (494d). Later we will see how Socrates tries to convince Alcibiades of his ignorance in order to win him for philosophy, a task that Socrates ultimately fails.

To understand the consequences of a corrupted soul, a look at the decay of political constitutions in the *Republic* reveals that tyranny grows on the grounds of democracy.[17] Because every insufficient form of government fails by absolutizing its guiding principle, democracy's biggest problem is its love for liberty (562c). Democracy tends to arbitrariness and even anarchy, because democrats love their freedom so much that they disapprove of any sort of rule and hierarchy (563a). Whereas the oligarchic person is still able to control his ambitions to achieve an oligarch's aim, i.e., wealth, the democrat fails to overrule his desires, because his soul has never learned to obey.[18] Moreover, the democrat's moral indifference draws interest to those who promote egalitarianism and break common rules.

This toxic mixture of unbounded desires and weakness makes the democrat's soul very prone to the seduction of those whom Plato calls "dread magi and king-makers" (572e).[19] These people introduce the young democrat to a debauched lifestyle full of conviviality. He is overwhelmed by all sorts of pleasures; and the more he follows his lust, the more he destroys prudence in his soul. Finally, he is willing to devote himself completely to his desires, even the forbidden and most wicked ones,[20] and "all [his] doings [. . .] are entirely swayed by the indwelling tyrant *Eros*" (573d).

The development from a democratic to a tyrannical person is illuminating: by indulging his numerous passions, he loses control to one desire that eventually dominates all others. Plato calls this ruling passion *eros*; and the tyrant himself is subjected to the tyrant *Eros*. Some translations try to avoid the word "*eros*" in this context, although the Greek text leaves no doubt that *eros* also stands for ruthless appetite.[21] And it is indeed astonishing that the same force that earlier was described as the decisive drive toward wisdom and beauty might also deprave a man or even a whole state; or, as Scott puts it: "*eros* is to the soul of the tyrant as a tyrant is to his city."[22]

Apparently, the philosophical and the tyrannical *eros* are not similar with regard to contents, but they do share some formal characteristics: Once *eros* is unleashed, it is impossible for the obsessed to resist: the philosopher is unable to do anything else than search for truth, whereas the tyrant must indulge his unnecessary desires no matter what the cost. From an outside perspective, this radicalism may manifest itself in asocial behavior. Whereas the philosopher in his admiration for truth is unwilling to engage in the conventional struggle for power, honor, and money, the tyrant ignores social rules and anything else that might limit his *pleonexia*.[23] Philosopher and tyrant are driven by the same force to the extreme, but in opposite directions. Both share the same talent for enthusiasm, but, unfortunately, the tyrant choses the wrong object of love and is condemned to live an unjust and therefore unhappy life (576c).[24]

It is worth repeating that only a gifted person with certain capacities can achieve greatness, which also means that only an exceptional character can become a veritable tyrant. As Socrates had mentioned earlier in the *Republic*, the young talent must not be corrupted by the moral standards of the many but his love must be directed toward truth. We have seen that a democratic environment is especially dangerous because its *laissez-faire* attitude promotes desires to grow unchecked.

The Socratic Method as a Deflection of *Eros*: The Case of *Alcibiades I*

In *Alcibiades I*,[25] Socrates meets the twenty-year-old Alcibiades who plans to stake out a leading position in Athens. His political ambitions are the starting point of the following conversation. In Socrates' attempt to turn Alcibiades' *eros* toward wisdom, I argue there are three steps. First, he seduces the young man and catches his attention. Second, Socrates dismantles Alcibiades' ignorance by refuting the aristocrat's incomplete beliefs about politics and justice. Once Alcibiades accepts his deficient state, Socrates can finally redirect the young man's *eros* toward wisdom by teaching him the art of self-knowledge.

Socratic Seduction

Plato's introduction of the two characters is revealing. The initial encounter of Socrates and Alcibiades resembles the idea of *paiderastia*: the ancient Athenian institution of an elder citizen taking a teenager as his lover, who is supposed to learn virtue in return. The date of their first meeting is not accidental: Socrates' *daimonion* has forbidden him to approach Alcibiades earlier although he has stalked him for years. The reason for Socrates' patience must be linked to his educational intention: now that Alcibiades' physical attractiveness is beginning to vanish,[26] his intellectual beauty is on the rise. This is a first sign that Socrates is not interested in Alcibiades' body but rather in his soul, as he later confirms (131d). At twenty, Alcibiades stands at the threshold to adulthood which is socially marked by the participation in the assembly, the most important political institution in democratic Athens at that time. If Socrates wants to influence Alcibiades' development, he cannot wait any longer: Alcibiades is now old enough to enter the political stage.

Therefore, he is potentially endangered by the corruptive effects of power and democratic public opinion, both of which can harm a talented soul (*Republic*, 494c).[27]

Socrates' further description of Alcibiades shows that the young man is already at the brink of tyranny: Alcibiades thinks that he has "no need of any man in any matter" (104a), because he is already perfect. He is very beautiful and athletic, he comes from the noblest families of Athens, he has powerful friends – his guardian is Pericles himself – and he is very rich which, however, seems the least important to him (104b–c). Socrates has observed that Alcibiades is aware of his exceptional personality, seeing that his arrogant attitude has driven away all his lovers (103b).[28]

But why does Socrates not give up on him? The following passage is a very impressive characterization of the young Athenian and delivers insight into Socrates' love: Socrates admits that he would have resigned long ago if he had seen the young man enjoying his life. But he claims that Alcibiades is not happy at all: he would probably prefer to die if he were not to "fill, one may say, the whole world with [his] name and [his] power" (105c). The desire for absolute domination clearly implies a strong *eros*. Socrates hopes to persuade Alcibiades that only Socrates can give what Alcibiades desires (105e) – Socrates claims to be the only one who can fulfill Alcibiades' love.

Socrates' statement in this passage is quite uncommon because he usually never makes promises, especially not any of such kind.[29] But if we take his expertise on *eros* into consideration, his words make sense in two ways: he seems to acknowledge Alcibiades' strong *eros* which makes him receptive to both philosophy and tyranny.[30] Thanks to Socrates' explanation,[31] Alcibiades learns about his own secret hopes and ambitions, probably for the first time in his life, because he neither refuses nor does he confirm Socrates' claim (105c).[32]

Moreover, by promising Alcibiades what he desires, Socrates easily catches the young man's attention, who actually listens full of curiosity (106c). As Zuckert remarks, " ... Socrates used his knowledge of *ta erotika* to 'seduce' Alcibiades."[33] Of course, the power Socrates promises is not quite what Alcibiades expects: before ruling others, Alcibiades has to control himself first, a task which he does not find easy.[34]

Socratic Refutation

Once Socrates secures Alcibiades' attention by having appealed to his *eros*, he explains how Alcibiades can achieve his goal. However, Socrates cannot teach him by making a long speech, but he will prove his claim if Alcibiades answers his questions (106b). Socrates is able to give a long speech, as he later demonstrates (120e–124b), so the reason for the dialogical approach cannot be Socrates' poor oratorical skills. It is rather a first hint that the dialog as a form is central to Socrates' philosophy and his method.[35] Only by conducting a Socratic dialog can Alcibiades attain power over himself and others. It is worth noting to see how the dialog influences Alcibiades' thinking and what overall function it plays in turning Alcibiades' *eros* toward philosophy. Thus, I focus on the dialog's effects and not on its subject, i.e., justice.

The starting point is Alcibiades' political ambition. By entering the assembly and participating in public deliberations, Alcibiades asserts that he is able to consult the Athenians in political affairs (106c). Giving advice to someone implies a difference in knowledge between the advisor and the advised; hence, Alcibiades' intention means that he claims to know more than his fellow citizens (106d). Socrates, however, deconstructs the young man's presumption by showing that he does not know anything at all about politics which, he says, is based on justice (109c).

Although Socrates dismantles Alcibiades' ignorance of justice (112b), the latter is not very impressed and sees no reason why he should abandon his initial claim for political leadership. Instead, Alcibiades changes the topic by stating "that the Athenians and the rest of the Greeks rarely deliberate as to which is the more just or unjust course [. . .] and consider which course will prove more expedient in the result" (113d). This tactical move from the just to the expedient reveals

Alcibiades' inconsistency and flippancy. He thinks that by arbitrarily changing the subject, he will be able to escape Socratic refutation. But he ignores that his maneuver enlarges his claim of knowledge which has already been proven baseless. He even anticipates Socrates' argument and refuses to be proven wrong in the same way as before (113e).

After Socrates has revealed that Alcibiades neither knows what justice is nor what is expedient, Alcibiades tries one final elusion. Because Alcibiades thinks that his fellow citizens do not know anything about the just and expedient, he sees no need for himself to learn about these either: "For I am sure that my natural powers alone will give me an easy victory over them" (119c). Facing this level of hubris and convenience, Socrates highlights during a long speech that Alcibiades' true rivals are not his untalented fellows, but the kings of Persia and Sparta. These monarchs excel Alcibiades' gifts by far so that his only chance to compete against them is by "pains and skill." Therefore, Socrates recommends that Alcibiades listen to him and the Delphic motto "know thyself" (124a/b).

Some interpreters criticize that Socrates would never admire wealth and power and therefore argue that this hymn on the Persian and Spartan kings proves the dialog's inauthenticity.[36] But if one takes Socrates' educational intention into account, this speech seems to have a persuasive function and rather expresses Alcibiades' thoughts than those of Socrates.[37] By pointing at his true competitors, Socrates incites Alcibiades' *eros*, for he knows that the young man is enamored of glory "more [...] than anyone else ever was of anything" (124b). Socrates' speech is also reminiscent of the educators' attempt to persuade a talented soul of its ignorance (*Republic*, 494d). All of Socrates' efforts aim at bringing Alcibiades to terms. The young man must be made to accept his ignorance and the consequences of it; otherwise, he is lost for philosophy and will probably continue his way toward tyranny.

Socratic Teaching

The last section of the dialog keeps its dialectical structure, even though Socrates is trying to pass knowledge on to Alcibiades. After the speech about his Persian and Spartan rivals, Alcibiades appears understanding and asks that Socrates enlighten him. Before Socrates starts his lesson, he emphasizes the importance of joint consideration (124d). Both partners commit to the inquiry, Socrates as well as Alcibiades. This call for cooperation anticipates the process of mutual self-knowledge described in the allegory of the reflecting eye at the end (133d).

Socrates starts once again by asking Alcibiades how to become an Athenian gentleman whose task it is to improve the city (124e). A city is well managed when its citizens are friends. But Alcibiades cannot tell how to create friendship and once again he is helpless. In contrast to his former failures he now blames himself, admitting that "I do not even know what I mean myself, and I fear that for some time past I have lived unaware in a disgraceful condition" (127d). Here, Socrates has seemingly succeeded in qualifying Alcibiades for a certain level of self-reflection. He therefore encourages Alcibiades instead of rebuking him. Alcibiades again asks what to do and Socrates again replies that the young man has to answer his questions (127e).

Now that Alcibiades does not object anymore, Socrates directs the conversation toward the question of the self. Because Alcibiades understands that he has to care for himself, Socrates reasons that self-care presupposes self-knowledge. Therefore, he concludes, they have to understand what the self actually is, for otherwise they could not improve it (129a).[38] What, then, is the self? Socrates identifies the self with the soul (130d). This implies that Socrates is Alcibiades' true lover because he loves his soul and not his physical appearance (131a). The soul knows itself by reflecting itself in another soul.

How does this work? An eye, for example, sees itself when looking into a mirror. Now, an eye is a mirror itself if another eye looks into it and reflects itself in the other eye's pupil (133a). Therefore, Socrates concludes that a soul can know itself by looking into another soul, or more precisely into its best part; that is where we find wisdom (133b).[39] Only those who know themselves by this way will make the right decisions for themselves and their community and will be good politicians.

The allegory implies that achieving self-knowledge is a procedure which involves two parts mutually reflecting one another. Because the self is the soul and more precisely the part of the soul that houses reason, the self knows itself when it becomes aware of its intellect. This only happens through dialog. By giving account to a counterpart, one is forced to reason and to reflect upon one's own thinking.[40] In Alcibiades' case, he gets to know himself through Socrates who reflects the young man's beliefs and tests them.[41]

Socrates explains that the soul only knows itself if it looks into *another* soul, "and especially at that region of it in which occurs the virtue of a soul – wisdom" (133b). Thus, self-knowledge means to achieve wisdom, which is also the greatest desire of a philosophical *eros*. In this sense, self-knowledge and the knowledge of being, beauty, and good seem to correlate. By illustrating how to know oneself, Socrates initiates Alcibiades into the heart of philosophical inquiry. The desire of this sort of knowledge implies that it is not present yet. Yearning for something that one lacks but what one desperately needs is an unambiguous description of *eros*; hence, once one has accepted his or her ignorance concerning the self and the good, *eros* becomes the driving force to search for knowledge. The Socratic dialog therefore is the methodological link between self-knowledge and philosophical inquiry.

In *Alcibiades I* Socrates' method has two main components. First, he inspires Alcibiades' *eros* by proving his ignorance. Once Alcibiades is ready to accept his deficiency, Socrates can move on to introducing him to philosophy. This also happens through dialectical inquiry, even though the last section of *Alcibiades I* is more of a monologue. This, however, does not have to be a contradiction: just as Socrates makes a long speech to cut back Alcibiades' pride, he uses the allegory to encourage and stimulate Alcibiades' mind.

At the end of the dialog, Socrates and Alcibiades have changed their parts. Alcibiades declares that he will be Socrates' lover and will make an effort to learn about justice (135d/e). However, the now beloved Socrates is skeptical about Alcibiades' love. He concludes that the seductive power of the Athenian people might overcome both, which proves later to be true.

Conclusion: Applying Guiding *Eros* Toward Wisdom

So far, I have argued that *eros* represents the decisive power which turns a person to philosophy or seduces him or her to tyranny. The philosopher Socrates who is, due to his profession, an expert on love matters, tries to redirect Alcibiades' *eros* toward wisdom. After gaining the young man's attention, Socrates reveals that Alcibiades lacks knowledge of politics, justice, and himself. To overcome his deficiency, Alcibiades has to reflect his most wise and prudent part of himself in another soul. This theory of self-knowledge refers to the dialog itself.[42] What then are the implications for the Socratic method and how can we apply it?

My interpretation of *Alcibiades I* may offer a holistic understanding of the Socratic method. Because Socrates uses many different rhetorical and didactic approaches, it seems impossible to limit the Socratic method to one technique. Still, if one hastily denies the unity of the Socratic method, one ignores the coherence it produces throughout the dialog. Therefore, I conclude that the Socratic method is the attempt to turn the interlocutor's *eros* toward wisdom. To accomplish this feat, Socrates uses dialectical refutations, exhorting monologues, or encouraging allegories – anything that may help to make the partner accept his ignorance and motivate him to overcome his current status. Of course, it is possible to distill these techniques from Socratic philosophy. However, if they are deprived of their context, there is no need to call them "Socratic" anymore.

How can we apply this understanding of the Socratic method in the classroom? To begin with, Socrates undeniably fails to persuade his partner. Alcibiades, as described in *Symposium*, has reverted to his initial beliefs and turned away from philosophy (216a). Even though he is still in love with Socrates (222c), he is unwilling to follow the way his lover illustrated in their first conversation, i.e., *Alcibiades I*. Apparently, Alcibiades does not want to subject himself to reason but to keep his own arbitrary mind. Instead of turning his *eros* toward truth and wisdom, he prefers to stay the way he is.

In face of Socrates' failure, the difficulty of his method becomes evident. Indeed, one might wonder if it is possible to apply it at all. Still, the interpretation of *Alcibiades I* offers some practical advice. *Alcibiades I* highlights the importance of *eros* for education. Only by appealing to the student's *eros* can one gain his or her attention. As long as the student is not addressed both on an intellectual and emotional – or better at an existential – level, it is unlikely that he or she is willing to listen. At this point, it is necessary for a reminder of what *eros* stands for. *Eros* is a strong desire for something we want but do not have yet. This means that if a teacher wants to inspire his or her student for the love of wisdom, the teacher needs to reveal that the student is not wise yet. Now, we see the importance of the so-called Socratic ignorance: as long as we think that we already know something, we do not search for knowledge. And we only learn of our ignorance if our pretended knowledge is refuted. Once the student has accepted his ignorance and realizes that he needs to change, he is motivated to learn.

Appealing to the student's *eros*, however, is no guarantee for success. As we have seen in *Alcibiades I*, Socrates seduces Alcibiades but still cannot redirect the young man's *eros*. The reasons for Socrates' failure are difficult to detect and require a more detailed analysis. One starting point for further research may be to put oneself in Alcibiades' shoes in his dialog with Socrates. This approach may offer insight into Alcibiades' mind and the limits of philosophical seduction – and at best, it may lead to self-knowledge.

Notes

1. Thomas C. Brickhouse and Nicholas D. Smith, "Socratic Teaching and Socratic Method," in *The Oxford Handbook of Philosophy of Education*, Harvey Siegel, ed. (Oxford: Oxford University Press, 2009), 183.
2. For chronology of the dialogs, refer to Leonard Brandwood, "Stylometry and Chronology," in *The Cambridge Companion to Plato*, Richard Kraut, ed. (Cambridge: Cambridge University Press, 1992), 90–120; Terence H. Irwin, "The Platonic Corpus," in *The Oxford Handbook of Plato*, Gail Fine, ed. (Oxford: Oxford University Press, 2009), 63–87; Gerard R. Ledger, *Re-counting Plato: A Computer Analysis of Plato's Style* (Oxford: Clarendon Press; Oxford University Press, 1989).
3. Nicholas Denyer, *Alcibiades* (Cambridge: Cambridge University Press, 2001), 3f; Andre Archie, *Politics in Socrates' Alcibiades: A Philosophical Account of Plato's Dialogue Alcibiades Major* (Cham: Springer, 2015), 4.
4. Brickhouse and Smith, "Socratic Teaching and Socratic Method," 184.
5. Plato, *Apology*, in *Plato: In twelve volumes*, R.G. Bury, ed. (Cambridge: Loeb Classical Library and Harvard University Press, 1984), 23a. All in-text citations and translations of Plato's dialogs are taken from here.
6. Brickhouse and Smith, "Socratic Teaching and Socratic Method," 179.
7. Brickhouse and Smith, "Socratic Teaching and Socratic Method," 185.
8. See Jacqueline Romilly, *Alcibiade ou les dangers de l'ambition* (Paris: Éd. de Fallois, 1996), 28.
9. For the interwoven plots and background story, see Barbara Zehnpfennig, "Einleitung," in *Symposion: Griechisch-deutsch*, Barbara Zehnpfennig, ed. (Hamburg: Meiner, 2000), VIII.
10. Capitalized *Eros* refers to the mythological god, while lower-cased *eros* denotes the psychological phenomenon of passion and love.
11. According to Zehnpfennig, the awareness of an intellectual principle behind the forms of appearance helps the lover to transcend himself: he can no longer arbitrarily define what beauty means for him personally but has to gain an objective access. This becomes even more evident when Diotima speaks about beautiful laws and virtues which, by definition, surpass the individual. Barbara Zehnpfennig, *Platon zur Einführung* (Hamburg: Junius, 2005), 152.
12. Gregory Vlastos, *Platonic Studies* (Princeton, NJ: Princeton University Press, 1981), 31.
13. Descendant of some of the most prestigious Athenian royal houses, Alcibiades was raised by Pericles. He was said to be the most beautiful, most talented, and most infamous man of his time: he provoked numerous

scandals, won the Olympic Games, led the Athenians to several military victories, was sentenced to death by his compatriots and later brought back from exile and celebrated like a star. Peter J. Rhodes, *Alcibiades* (Barnsley: Pen & Sword Military, 2011); Walter M. Ellis, *Alcibiades* (London: Routledge, 2014).

14 Nussbaum emphasizes the personal character of the whole *Symposium* and the task of self-examination that Socrates indirectly demands by challenging the previous images of love. Nussbaum is right to take Alcibiades into consideration even though she fails to link his speech to Diotima's theory and Socrates' practice. Martha Nussbaum, "The Speech of Alcibiades: A Reading of Plato's Symposium," *Philosophy and Literature* 3/2 (1979): 133f.

15 Plato was aware that people would reject his model (*Republic*, 473e).

16 To solve this paradox, one could argue that Socrates refers to Adeimantus' concept of virtue which lacks the pivotal orientation toward the good.

17 According to Plato, all constitutions which do not provide the philosopher-kings are defective. These constitutions digress from the ideal in the following order: timocracy, oligarchy, democracy, and tyranny.

18 Plato frames the transition of the constitutions by the sequence of generations. The current constitution is represented by a father who passes some characteristics to his son who represents the future constitution, e.g., a timocratic father might create an oligarch who might raise a democratic son and so on.

19 They might correspond to those who try and distract a young talented man from philosophy to manipulate him, like Socrates described earlier (*Republic*, 494c/d).

20 Socrates classifies two sorts of desires: necessary and unnecessary ones which in turn can be either legal or illegal (*Republic*, 571b).

21 For examples, see Dominic Scott, "Eros, Philosophy and Tyranny," in *Maieusis: Essays in Ancient Philosophy in Honour of Myles Burnyeat*, Myles Burnyeat and Dominic Scott, eds. (Oxford: Oxford University Press, 2007), 154.

22 *Ibid.*, 138.

23 Scott states that the philosopher is asocial, i.e., he disregards the political in favor of the divine. *Ibid.*, 151f. This seems plausible only in parts: It is true that the philosopher has no interest in common political competition as exemplified in the ship metaphor (*Republic*, 487b–489a). But Socrates calls himself the "true statesman" (*Gorgias*, 521d) who dedicates his life to Athens' cause (*Apology*, 30e). The philosopher is not interested in political affairs in general, he just has another understanding of what politics should look like.

24 One of the leading motives in the *Republic* is that Glaucon and Adeimantus pledge Socrates to prove justice is better than injustice in every way (367e).

25 Because of Schleiermacher's harsh comment on *Alcibiades I* in the nineteenth century, the dialog's authenticity is regularly put into question. Nicholas D. Smith, "Did Plato Write the 'Alcibiades I?'" *Apeiron: A Journal for Ancient Philosophy and Science* 37/2 (2004): 93–108; Jakub Jirsa, "Authenticity of the Alcibiades I: Some Reflections," *Listy filologické/ Folia philologica* 132/3–4 (2009): 225–44. At present, scholars tend to be accepting Plato's authorship, with which I agree. Eugenio Benitez. "Authenticity, Experiment or Development: The *Alcibiades I* on Virtue and Courage," in *Alcibiades and the Socratic Lover-Educator*, Marguerite Johnson, ed. (London: Bristol Classical Press, 2012), 119–33; Francois Renaud, "Self-Knowledge in the *First Alcibiades* and the commentary of Olympiodorus," in *Inner Life and Soul: Psychē in Plato*, Maurizio Migliori, ed. (Sankt Augustin: Academia, 2011), 207; Denyer, *Alcibiades*.

26 According to the idea of *paiderastia*, the relationship, which was clearly hierarchical, usually ended when the young lover's beard started to grow. The twenty-year-old Alcibiades was too old for a conventional love affair. Carola Reinsberg, *Ehe, Hetärentum und Knabenliebe im antiken Griechenland* (München: Beck, 1993), 165.

27 For a detailed comparison between Alcibiades and the tyrant described in *Republic*, see Annie Larivée, "Eros Tyrannos: Alcibiades as the Model of the Tyrant in Book IX of the Republic," *The International Journal of the Platonic Tradition* 6/1 (2012): 1–26.

28 The historical Alcibiades allegedly mocked his numerous lovers on various occasions. Rhodes, *Alcibiades*, 25f.

29 For some interpreters, this passage proves the dialog's inauthenticity, see Smith, "Did Plato Write the 'Alcibiades I?'" 101.

30 Gordon and Kühn suggest this reading, too. Gordon adds that Socrates' way of claiming his power over Alcibiades may also impress the young man. Jill Gordon, "Eros and Philosophical Seduction in *Alcibiades I*," *Ancient Philosophy* 23/1 (2003): 27; Ulrich Kühn, "Das Liebesverhältnis zwischen Alkibiades und Sokrates: Der platonische Bericht," *Perspektiven der Philosophie: Neues Jahrbuch* 37 (2011): 96.

31 Rider adds that by this way, Socrates forces Alcibiades to reflect on his ambitions and what he wants for his life. Benjamin A. Rider, "Self-Care, Self-Knowledge, and Politics in the 'Alcibiades I,'" *Epoche: A Journal for the History of Philosophy* 15/2 (2011): 403.

32 See the twenty-fifth endnote.
33 Catherine H. Zuckert, *Plato's Philosophers: The Coherence of the Dialogues* (Chicago: University of Chicago Press, 2009), 229.
34 Brüschweiler notes that Socrates may veil the difference between his and Alcibiades' understanding of power on purpose to keep the young man's expectations high. Andreas Brüschweiler, *Sokrates' Jugend und seine ersten philosophischen Gespräche* (Würzburg: Königshausen & Neumann, 2010), 182.
35 For a dialectical interpretation of the whole dialog, see Albert Joosse, "Dialectic and Who We Are in the Alcibiades," *Phronesis* 59/1 (2014): 1–21.
36 Gregory Vlastos, *The Presocratics*. Daniel W. Graham, ed. (Princeton: Princeton University Press, 1996), 291; Friedrich Schleiermacher, *Über die Philosophie Platons: Geschichte der Philosophie. Vorlesungen über Sokrates und Platon (zwischen 1819 und 1823). Die Einleitungen zur Übersetzung des Platon (1804–1828)*, P.M. Steiner, A. Arndt, J. Jantzen with assistance (Hamburg: Felix Meiner Verlag, 2013), 321.
37 Carpenter and Polansky offer a slightly different interpretation: they distinguish two types of refutations. First, Socrates argues that Alcibiades' prejudice on his enemies has bad consequences, namely deficient self-care. Second, Socrates shows in his long speech that Alcibiades' view is likely to be false. Still, both approaches seem to intertwine. Michelle Carpenter and Ronald M. Polansky, "Variety of Socratic Elenchi," in *Does Socrates Have a Method? Rethinking the Elenchus in Plato's Dialogues and Beyond*, Gary A. Scott, ed. (University Park: Pennsylvania State University Press, 2002), 95; see Gordon, "Eros and Philosophical Seduction in *Alcibiades*," 15; Christopher L. Lauriello, "Political Science and the Irrational: Plato's Alcibiades," *Interpretation. A Journal for Political Philosophy* 37/3 (2010): 245.
38 Karl observes that the practical problem – how to become a good politician – turns into the existential question of what it means to live a good life. Jacqueline Karl, *Selbstbestimmung und Individualität bei Platon: Eine Interpretation zu frühen und mittleren Dialogen* (Freiburg: K. Alber, 2010), 90.
39 In the following, Socrates states that this is the most divine part of the soul. This means that by looking at God the soul knows itself. Because this passage is peculiar in many aspects, some scholars assume that it was inserted *ex post*. For further discussion see Joosse, "Dialectic and Who We Are in the Alcibiades," 16ff.
40 This counterpart does not necessarily have to be another person. In *Theaetetus*, Socrates explains that thinking is nothing more than dialoguing with oneself (189e).
41 According to Rider, Socrates offers Alcibiades two dimensions of self-knowledge. First, he shows the young man what he really wants in life; second, by accepting his deficiency, Alcibiades is able to look for the standard he has to achieve, i.e., he needs to look for the true self. Annas argues in a similar way, however she emphasizes that the self which Alcibiades is looking for is his personal self and no impersonal incorporation of the good or even God. In her view, self-knowledge means knowing one's social position. Rider replies that this reading fails to integrate the aspect of self-cultivation: improving one's soul only makes sense if it is not perfect yet. Moreover, Gordon criticizes Annas' interpretation of self-knowledge by pointing at the "inner dimensions of the self." For her, Socratic self-knowledge focuses on getting to know and cultivating one's *eros*. Rider, "Self-Care, Self-Knowledge, and Politics in the 'Alcibiades I,'" 405–7; Julia Annas, "Self-knowledge in Early Plato," in *Platonic investigations*, Dominic J. O'Meara, ed. (Washington, DC: Catholic University of America Press, 1985), 121; Gordon, "Eros and Philosophical Seduction in *Alcibiades I*," 21.
42 The idea that self-knowledge is only accessible through dialog also explains why Socrates emphasizes several times the importance of joint consideration and the necessity of Alcibiades answering his questions. For this interpretation see Rider, "Self-Care, Self-Knowledge, and Politics in the "Alcibiades I,'" 402–5; see Joosse, "Dialectic and Who We Are in the Alcibiades," 20.

Bibliography

Ambury, James M. 2011. "The Place of Displacement: The Elenchus in Plato's Alcibiades I." *Ancient Philosophy* 31/2: 241–60.

Annas, Julia. 1985. "Self-knowledge in Early Plato." In *Platonic Investigations*. Dominic J. O'Meara ed. Washington, DC: Catholic University of America Press: 111–38.

Archie, Andre. 2015. *Politics in Socrates' Alcibiades: A Philosophical Account of Plato's Dialogue Alcibiades Major*. Cham: Springer.

Benitez, Eugenio. 2012. "Authenticity, Experiment or Development: The *Alcibiades I* on Virtue and Courage." In *Alcibiades and the Socratic Lover-Educator*. Marguerite Johnson ed. London: Bristol Classical Press: 119–33.

Brandwood, Leonard. 1992. "Stylometry and Chronology." In *The Cambridge Companion to Plato*. Richard Kraut ed. Cambridge: Cambridge University Press: 90–120.

Brickhouse, Thomas C. and Nicholas D. Smith. 2009. "Socratic Teaching and Socratic Method." In *The Oxford Handbook of Philosophy of Education*. Harvey Siegel ed. Oxford: Oxford University Press: 177–94.

Brüschweiler, Andreas. 2010. *Sokrates' Jugend und Seine Ersten Philosophischen Gespräche*. Würzburg: Königshausen & Neumann.

Carpenter, Michelle and Ronald M. Polansky. 2002. "Variety of Socratic Elenchi." In *Does Socrates Have a Method? Rethinking the Elenchus in Plato's Dialogues and Beyond*. Gary A. Scott ed. University Park: Pennsylvania State University Press: 89–100.

Denyer, Nicholas. 2001. *Alcibiades*. Cambridge: Cambridge University Press.

Ellis, Walter M. 2014. *Alcibiades*. London: Routledge.

Gordon, Jill. 2003. "Eros and Philosophical Seduction in *Alcibiades I*." *Ancient Philosophy* 23/1: 11–30.

Irwin, Terence H. 2009. "The Platonic Corpus." In *The Oxford Handbook of Plato*. Gail Fine ed. Oxford: Oxford University Press: 63–87.

Jirsa, Jakub. 2009. "Authenticity of the Alcibiades I: Some Reflections." *Listy filologické/ Folia philologica* 132/3–4: 225–44.

Joosse, Albert. 2014. "Dialectic and Who We Are in the Alcibiades." *Phronesis* 59/1: 1–21.

Karl, Jacqueline. 2010. *Selbstbestimmung und Individualität bei Platon: Eine Interpretation zu frühen und mittleren Dialogen*. Freiburg: K. Alber.

Kühn, Ulrich. 2011. "Das Liebesverhältnis zwischen Alkibiades und Sokrates: Der platonische Bericht." *Perspektiven der Philosophie: Neues Jahrbuch* 37: 75–114.

Larivée, Annie. 2012. "Eros Tyrannos: Alcibiades as the Model of the Tyrant in Book IX of the Republic." *The International Journal of the Platonic Tradition* 6/1: 1–26.

Lauriello, Christopher L. 2010. "Political Science and the Irrational: Plato's Alcibiades." *Interpretation. A Journal for Political Philosophy* 37/3: 237–57.

Ledger, Gerard R. 1989. *Re-counting Plato: A Computer Analysis of Plato's Style*. Oxford: Clarendon Press; Oxford University Press.

Nussbaum, Martha. 1979. "The Speech of Alcibiades: A Reading of Plato's Symposium." *Philosophy and Literature* 3/2: 131–72.

Reinsberg, Carola. 1993. *Ehe, Hetärentum und Knabenliebe im antiken Griechenland*. München: Beck.

Renaud, Francois. 2011. "Self-Knowledge in the *First Alcibiades* and the Commentary of Olympiodorus." In *Inner Life and Soul: Psychē in Plato*. Maurizio Migliori ed. Sankt Augustin: Academia: 207–24.

Rhodes, Peter J. 2011. *Alcibiades*. Barnsley: Pen & Sword Military.

Rider, Benjamin A. 2011. "Self-Care, Self-Knowledge, and Politics in the 'Alcibiades I.'" *Epoche: A Journal for the History of Philosophy* 15/2: 395–413.

Romilly, Jacqueline D. 1996. *Alcibiade ou les dangers de l'ambition*. Paris: Éd. de Fallois.

Schleiermacher, Friedrich. 2013. *Über die Philosophie Platons: Geschichte der Philosophie. Vorlesungen über Sokrates und Platon (zwischen 1819 und 1823). Die Einleitungen zur Übersetzung des Platon (1804–1828)*. With the assistance of P.M. Steiner, A. Arndt and J. Jantzen. Hamburg: Felix Meiner Verlag.

Scott, Dominic. 2007. "Eros, Philosophy and Tyranny." In *Maieusis: Essays in Ancient Philosophy in Honour of Myles Burnyeat*. Myles Burnyeat and Dominic Scott eds. Oxford: Oxford University Press: 136–54.

Smith, Nicholas D. 2004. "Did Plato Write the 'Alcibiades I?'" *Apeiron: A Journal for Ancient Philosophy and Science* 37/2: 93–108.

Vlastos, Gregory. 1981. *Platonic Studies*. Princeton: Princeton University Press.

Vlastos, Gregory. 1996. *The Presocratics*. Daniel W. Graham ed. Princeton: Princeton University Press.

Zehnpfennig, Barbara ed. 2000. "Einleitung." In *Symposion: Griechisch-deutsch*. Hamburg: Meiner.

Zehnpfennig, Barbara. 2005. *Platon zur Einführung*. Hamburg: Junius.

Zuckert, Catherine H. 2009. *Plato's Philosophers: The Coherence of the Dialogues*. Chicago: University of Chicago Press.

4 Skepticism and Recollection in Socrates

Ann Ward

In *The City and Man*, Leo Strauss famously asserts that Socrates' theory of ideas "is very hard to understand; to begin with, it is utterly incredible, not to say that it appears to be fantastic," and "no one has succeeded in giving a satisfactory or clear account of this doctrine of ideas."[1] Taking Strauss's cue, I seek to provide clarity on the role of the ideas in Socratic dialectic by comparing the purpose of Socratic questioning in Plato's *Apology* to its purpose in Plato's *Meno*. In the *Apology* Socratic questioning provides knowledge of ignorance. When we turn to the first part of the *Meno*, Socratic questioning also provides knowledge of ignorance, but crucially by way of questions about the idea. Socrates refutes Meno's attempt to say what virtue is, not by critiquing the content of the definitions provided but rather their form: they are particular examples of virtue and not the universal characteristic or essential "nature" that all particular examples share. Socrates' refutation, therefore, proceeds through questions about the idea of virtue that Meno cannot answer. Moreover, the idea here is not conceived of as self-subsisting, or as existing separately from its particular manifestations, in the visible world.

The first epistemological function of the ideas, therefore, as illustrated in the *Meno* is to facilitate Socrates' refutation of his interlocutors; it is a technique or method that gives the interlocutor knowledge of their own ignorance. However, the second epistemological function of the ideas is to ground Socrates' theory of recollection which in turn appears to ground the process of human learning. After Socrates refutes his various attempts to define virtue, Meno asks: if we don't know what virtue is, how can we know when we have found it? Although learning is necessary, it appears impossible. Socrates responds that the soul knows and can recollect all things, having seen the ideas before birth.

Socrates' response, however, is problematic in two ways. First, it would seem as if the purpose of Socratic questioning in the *Apology* and that in the second part of the *Meno* are irreconcilable. In the *Apology*, Socrates first encounters persons who are ignorant but do not know this. His questioning teaches them that they don't know what they think they know, and in acquiring such knowledge of ignorance they learn that "we are non-knowers who think we know." In the second part of the *Meno* the purpose of Socratic questioning is to allow his interlocutor to recollect the universal truths or ideas that were in their soul but which they had forgotten. Socratic questioning, therefore, appears as something more than mere technique or method to bring his interlocutors to *aporia*, but rather as a pathway to discovery that the search for truth, in oneself, is possible. The second problem with Socrates' theory of recollection is that it assumes the self-subsistence of the ideas.

Jacob Klein casts doubt on how seriously the theory of recollection in the *Meno* should be taken, claiming that the account of recollection and the soul which experiences it is presented by Socrates as a myth and not an argument.[2] Yet, in arguing that the ideas are a crucial part of the *Meno*, I agree with scholars such as Gregory Vlastos, Steven S. Tigner, and R.E. Allen. Vlastos, Tigner, and Allen argue that in the *Meno* Plato is referring to the ideas or Forms as the objects of knowledge that are recollected when one looks within the self to recall what the soul has seen separated from the body.[3] Focus, therefore, is shifted by these scholars from the theory of recollection to the theory of ideas or Forms, recollection being a vehicle to arrive at the latter phenomena. Moreover, Vlastos argues that knowledge of the ideas, "is freed completely from evidential dependence on sense-experience," and Allen that, as we cannot know them through objects of sensation, "knowledge of Forms is epistemically prior to knowledge of the particulars which exemplify them, and from this Plato concludes [...] that knowledge of the Forms is temporally prior as well."[4] Thus, for Vlastos and Allen the ideas that ground the theory of recollection in the *Meno* are self-subsisting and hence exist independently of their particular manifestations in the material world.

Although building upon them I go beyond these scholars in arguing that the ideas also play a crucial role in the first part of the dialog before Socrates' discussion of recollection emerges. In the first part of the dialog, Meno cannot give Socrates a satisfactory answer to the question of what virtue is because he cannot articulate what Socrates would regard as the idea or form of virtue. Using the concept of the idea to repeatedly refute his interlocutor's attempt at a definition, Socrates brings the ideas to light as that which can give us knowledge of our own ignorance. Yet, contrary to the theory of recollection which suggests that we are all knowers who don't know we know, the ideas as central to refutation suggest that we are in fact non-knowers who think we know. Also, the ideas as part of refutation or the dialectical method do not need to be conceived of as self-subsisting or separate from their particular manifestations.

Questioning Authority

Plato's *Apology* tells the story of the quest for self-knowledge. This story begins when Socrates, on trial for his life, denies the longstanding public opinion against him reflected in Aristophanes' comedy *The Clouds* – that he is a wise man who studies things in the heavens and under the earth and makes the weaker speech the stronger – and does not believe in gods (18b–c, 19c).[5] Socrates then raises the question that one of his reasonable listeners might ask given the opportunity: if this longstanding public opinion is wrong, where did your unique reputation for wisdom come from (20c–d). In response to this hypothetical question, Socrates proceeds to give an autobiographical account of his quest for self-knowledge, beginning with the oracle given to his friend Chaerophon.

Socrates reports that Chaerophon once went to Delphi and asked the oracle whether there was anyone wiser than Socrates. The Pythia, according to Socrates, "replied that no one was wiser" (21a). Socrates' initial response to the oracle is that the god Apollo has posed a riddle making it hard to understand what the god is saying. Socrates, contrary to the oracle, believes that he is "not at all wise, either much or little" (21b). To discover the god's meaning, Socrates sets out to refute the oracle and hence prove the god wrong. Socrates' methodology in refuting the oracle involves questioning those in Athens reputed to be wise to show that they are in fact wiser than him, thus revealing the error of the god (21b–c).

The means by which Socrates proceeds with his attempted refutation – questioning the reputedly wise men of Athens to show that they are wiser than he – does not appear to be commanded by the god but is rather Socrates' own device.[6] Also, even if Socrates eventually comes to accept the correctness of the oracle, he does not do so simply on its authority as divine, but only after it passes the test of his own rational inquiry into its truth. Thus, for Socrates, revelation must be made consistent with reason if the word of the god is to be accepted as true. In addition to the god Apollo himself, Socrates proceeds to question four other authorities within the city: the politicians, the poets, the artisans, and the fathers.

Upon examination the politicians fail miserably to meet Socrates' design. Having questioned one reputed to be wise, Socrates learns that this man is not as wise as he and his followers thought him to be. Socrates then tries to show him that he is not wise. Incurring the hatred of the politician and those present during the examination, Socrates concludes:

> I am wiser than this human being. For probably neither of us knows anything noble and good, but he supposes he knows something when he does not know, while I, just as I do not know, do not even suppose that I do. I *am* likely to be a little bit wiser than he is in this very thing: that whatever I do not know, I do not even suppose I know (21d).

Socrates is thus wiser than the politicians because he has knowledge of his own ignorance, whereas they do not.

After the politicians Socrates then questions the poets, "those of tragedies [. . .] and the others, in order that there I would catch myself in the act of being more ignorant than they" (22b). The poets, however, like the politicians, fare badly under Socrates' questions. Because the poets "do not make what they make by wisdom, but by some sort of nature and while inspired, like the diviners and those who deliver oracles," they are not as wise as they think they are (22c). Guided by passion, divine or otherwise, the poets cannot give a rational explanation of what their poems and tragedies mean. Another problem with the poets for Socrates is that because they think they are wise with respect to their poetry, they believe they are wise in "other things" too, but they are not (22c). Socrates leaves the poets in the belief that he is wiser than they for the same reason he is wiser than the politicians: unlike the poets and the politicians, at least he knows what he doesn't know, or has knowledge of ignorance.

The artisans are the next authority within Athens that Socrates questions. They fare better than the politicians and the poets, proving wiser than Socrates in one respect: at least they have knowledge of their art or trade (22d). However, the artisans suffer from the same problem as the poets: because they are wise in their trade, they believe themselves wisest in the "greatest" things (22d).

Although it is not explicitly stated, Socrates also questions the fathers of Athens.[7] For instance, Socrates tells us that he questioned a father named Callias as to who had the knowledge to teach his sons the virtue of a human being and citizen. Having "paid more money to sophists than all the others," Callias responds that the sophist Evenus of Paros has such knowledge (20b). Socrates' low opinion of this answer is indicated when he insists that he lacks the knowledge Evenus is said to have. More subtly, Socrates' questioning of the fathers surfaces when he denies the longstanding slander against him reflected in Aristophanes' *Clouds*. Socrates, speaking to the jury, claims that those who spread this slander, "got hold of the many of you from childhood" (18b). Thus, refuting the slander, Socrates is refuting the fathers of the jurors sitting in judgment of his case. He thus calls into question the wisdom of the older generation. Like the young who imitate him and examine others, Socrates, considering the fathers, "discover[s] a great abundance of human beings who suppose they know something, but know little or nothing" (23c–d).

After his examination of the politicians, poets, and artisans, Socrates, having intended to prove the god wrong, concludes that the god is right. He, Socrates, is the wisest human being, because he has knowledge 1) of his own ignorance, and 2) that, "really the god is wise, and that in this oracle he is saying that human wisdom is worth little or nothing" (23a). Thus, as a result of his attempt to refute the oracle, Socrates gains knowledge not of his own ignorance, which he had prior to his investigations, but of universal human ignorance; human wisdom is worthless as only the god is wise.

Refutation

In the *Apology* Socrates illustrates that his questioning can provide knowledge that we don't in fact know what we think we know. In the *Meno* Socrates shows that such questioning can proceed by way of asking about the ideas. In the first part of the latter dialog, Socrates uses the concept of the idea to repeatedly refute Meno's attempt to say what virtue is, therewith providing his interlocutor an awareness of his own ignorance on the subject. In response to Meno's opening question, "Can you tell me, Socrates, can virtue be taught?" Socrates claims that before he can answer he must discover what virtue itself is (70a, 71a–b).[8]

Following on this Meno attempts three times to say what virtue is, or to give the definition of virtue, as it were. In his first attempt Meno characterizes virtue as multiple and diverse. According to Meno, a man's virtue consists in being able to manage public affairs and in so doing to benefit his friends and harm his enemies and to be careful that no harm comes to himself; [. . .] the virtue of a woman [. . .] [is to] manage the home well, preserve its possessions, and to be submissive to her husband; the virtue of the child [. . .] is different again, and so is that of an elderly man, [. . .] [and] that of a free man or a slave. And there are many other virtues (71e–72a).

Socrates does not accept Meno's first attempt to say what virtue is, but proceeds to refute his definition. Yet, in his refutation, Socrates does not take issue with the content of Meno's definition. For instance, Meno says that part of man's virtue is helping friends and harming enemies. In other dialogs justice has been defined or understood in similar terms. In the *Republic*, Polemarchus defines justice as helping friends and harming enemies, and in the *Crito*, Crito understands justice in a similar way. Yet, in these dialogs Socrates refutes his interlocutors by taking issue with the content of this understanding: he argues to Polemarchus that harm makes the true enemy worse but justice cannot make a person worse in the sense of more unjust, so a just man harms no one, and similarly, to Crito he argues that it is always wrong to return a harm for a harm.[9] Yet, in the *Meno*, Socrates takes issue not with the content of Meno's definition of virtue, but rather with its form or structure. Thus, Socrates asks:

> Meno, [. . .] on the image of swarms, if I were asking you what is the nature of bees, and you said that they are many and of all kinds, what would you answer if I asked you: "Do you mean that they are many and varied and different from one another insofar as they are bees? Or are they no different in that regard, but in some other respect, in their beauty, for example, or their size or in some other such way?" Tell me, what would you answer if thus questioned?
>
> (Meno): I would say that they do not differ from one another in being bees (72b).
>
> The issue that Socrates has raised with this question is the distinction between the "nature" of something and its various kinds or particular manifestations. For example, with respect to the bee, there is the "nature" or species characteristics of the bee – that quality of "beeness," as it were – and particular kinds of bees, such as bumble bees, hornets, and wasps. Socrates continues and asks Meno: If I went on to say: "Tell me what is this very thing, Meno, in which they are all the same and do not differ from one another?" Would you be able to tell me?
>
> (Meno): I would. The same is true in the case of the virtues. Even if they are many and various, all of them have one and the same form which makes them virtues, and it is right to look to this when one is asked to make clear what virtue is (72c–d).

Socrates thus clarifies to Meno that as he should tell him what the nature or "form" of bee is when he asks "What is a bee?," so Meno should tell him what the nature or form of virtue is when he asks "What is virtue?" The form or nature of a thing is that which makes the many particular examples of a thing the same rather than different; it is the universal or common characteristics that they share, and thus makes them what they are.

For instance, with respect to bee, there are bumble bees, hornets, and wasps, but the universal characteristics that these particular bees share, or that quality of "beeness" that makes them all bees – they all have wings, can buzz, and sting – is their nature or form. With respect to virtue, there may be man's virtue, woman's virtue, children's virtue, and the virtues of freemen and slaves, but what Socrates wants to know is the universal characteristic that all these particular examples of virtue share that make them virtues. This universal characteristic or quality of virtue, is its nature, or form. Thus, Socrates clarifies that when he asks "What is virtue?" he does not want Meno to give him many particular examples of it, but the universal characteristic, or characteristics that all the particular examples share. In asking for the universal characteristic that all the particular examples share,

Socrates is asking for the idea or form of virtue itself.[10] Socrates' refutation, therefore, will flow from Meno's inability to say what the idea of virtue is as opposed to its many particular examples.

Meno initially responds to Socrates' request for the idea of virtue with the claim that virtue is not like this. Although there are particular virtues, there is no common characteristic to unite them all or to cohere them into a single definition. Yet, with Socrates' encouragement, Meno attempts for the second time to say what virtue is according to the standard that Socrates has set. Meno's second definition of virtue is the ability "to rule over people" (*Meno*, 73d). Socrates' refutation of this definition again has to do not with the content of the definition, but the form or structure in which it is given. Socrates asks if the virtue of a child or a slave is to rule over the parent or the master. Meno answers in the negative, with the implication that ruling is not then the common characteristic that all the virtues share. Again, Meno has given a particular example rather than the idea.

Moreover, remaining with the concept of rule, Meno confirms in response to Socrates' question that virtuous rule requires ruling justly rather than unjustly because, according to Meno, "justice is virtue" (73d–e). Ruling as the definition of virtue, is thereby transformed into justice, and Socrates asks if justice is virtue itself, or one among many virtues. Meno answers that justice is one among many virtues, including courage, moderation, and magnificence. Socrates thus points out that Meno again has given a particular example of virtue – justice – rather than its idea (73e–74b).

Having failed in his second attempt to define virtue, Meno asks Socrates for further clarification of what he wants when he asks for the nature of virtue or the common characteristic that all the virtues share. Socrates further illustrates what he means by the nature or idea of a thing with the examples of shape and color. Although there may be many different shapes, such as circle, square, triangle, and others, the nature or idea of shape is that characteristic that is the same for all of these different shapes and allows us to call them shapes. Shape so understood, according to Socrates, "is that which alone of existing things always follows color" (75c). Socrates appears to mean that shape is what allows color to be seen or manifest itself.

For example, the color red does not manifest itself as abstract particles floating formless through the air, but rather it always manifests itself in particular shapes formed by objects such as lips, apples, roses, and others. All these objects have very different shapes, but they all allow us to see the color red. In response to Meno's question, "if someone were to say that he did not know what color is, [...] what do you think your answer would be?," Socrates gives a second definition of shape (75c). Is Socrates conceding that there is no common characteristic or single definition for shape, just as Meno had claimed about virtue? Nonetheless, Socrates' second definition of shape is "the limit of a solid" (76a). Shape is thus a boundary to matter, which appears to mean that like color, we never see abstract particles of matter floating formless through the air, but matter always manifests itself in particular shapes, such as lips, apples, and roses.

That shape is what allows color and matter to be seen is illustrated in Socrates' definition of the nature or idea of color. According to Socrates, "color is an effluvium from shapes which fits the sight and is perceived" (76d). "Effluvium" is a flowing out or an outflow in the form of a stream of particles. Color, for Socrates, is thus an outflow from shapes that is then perceived by sight. Shape, therefore, uniting Socrates' two definitions, is what allows color and matter to manifest themselves, and thus in a sense allows color and matter to be color and matter, or what they are according to the perceiver.

So understood, virtue will be like shape, or the idea of things in the material world will be matched by the idea of virtue in the non-material world, as Socrates will define it. Thus, Socrates later in the dialog will eventually hypothesize that, "virtue, being beneficial, must be a kind of wisdom" (88d). The hypothesis that virtue is wisdom results from Socrates' reasoning that particular things that we take as virtues – moderation, justice, courage, and magnificence – if not guided by wisdom in the soul can actually turn into vices (88a–d). Thus, wisdom allows particular virtues to be virtues rather than vices. As shape allows color and matter to manifest themselves and hence be what they are, so wisdom allows virtue to manifest itself or be what it is; wisdom is the necessary condition for virtue to appear and the common characteristic that all the virtues share.

After Socrates' illustration of how to properly define or articulate the idea of a thing through his discussion of shape and color, Meno attempts for the third time to say what virtue is: it is "to desire beautiful things and have the power to acquire them" (77b). Thus, we are back to Meno's second definition – virtue is power or ruling – but now power is reduced to a means to an end, the acquisition of beautiful things. Socrates' refutation proceeds by equating the beautiful with the good, and then getting Meno to agree that all persons actually desire what they believe to be good. Even if persons desire what is actually bad, they are misguided and believe that what they desire is good and will be beneficial to them and make them happy. Yet, if all persons desire what they believe to be good then to desire good things doesn't distinguish human beings and hence cannot be virtue (77b–78b). Meno, sharing Socrates' assumption that virtue is something that distinguishes or separates human beings, agrees to modifying his third definition of virtue to be "the power of securing good things" (78c). If the desire for good things does not distinguish human beings, the power to acquire them does.

Settling on this revised version of his third definition, Meno, in response to Socrates' questions, affirms that virtue requires that good things such as wealth and public office be acquired justly and piously. If acquired through injustice and impiety, such acquisition is vice. Virtue, therefore, according to the definition, is actually justice and piety, but, similar to what was agreed to before, justice and piety are particular examples of virtue among others (78c–79b). Meno, in his third attempt to say what virtue is, has again given particular examples of virtue rather than the nature or idea of virtue itself.

After three attempts to say what virtue is, Meno has not been able to provide an answer that articulates the idea of virtue or the universal characteristic that all the particular examples of virtue that he mentions share. They must, therefore, return to the question with which they started: "What is virtue?" Meno, however, is hesitant because Socrates, like a "torpedo fish," has made him "numb." According to Meno:

> Before I even met you [Socrates], I used to hear that you are always in a state of perplexity and that you bring others to the same state, and now I think you are bewitching and beguiling me, simply putting me under a spell, so that I am quite perplexed. Indeed, if a joke is in order, you seem, in appearance and in every other way, to be like the broad torpedo fish, for it too makes anyone who comes close and touches it feel numb, and you now seem to have had that kind of effect on me, for both my mind and my tongue are numb, and I have no answer to give you. Yet I have made many speeches about virtue before large audiences on a thousand occasions, very good speeches as I thought, but now I cannot even say what it is (80a–b).

Socrates' questions, Meno indicates, show you that you don't know what you thought you knew, such as what virtue is, and are like the touch of the torpedo fish that makes your mind and tongue numb so you cannot speak. Emptying his interlocutors of their false opinions, Socrates gives them knowledge of their own ignorance that leaves them not knowing what to say. Socrates' interlocutors such as Meno, therefore, are brought to the same condition in which Socrates begins the *Apology* and which he tries to give to the reputedly wise men he questions: at least having knowledge that you do not indeed know what you thought you knew (see *Apology*, 21b–d).

Recollection

Socrates assures Meno that if he, like a torpedo fish, perplexes others, he himself is perplexed and does not know what virtue is, yet still wishes to seek together with Meno for the answer. In response, Meno asks

> How will you look for it Socrates, when you do not know at all what it is? How will you aim for something you do not know at all? If you should meet with it, how will you know that this is the thing that you did not know? (80d).

Socrates responds sympathetically by claiming,

> I know what you want to say Meno [...] that a man cannot search either for what he knows or for what he does not know? He cannot search for what he knows – since he knows it, there is no need to search – nor for what he does not know, for he does not know what to look for (80e).

In the above exchange between Meno and Socrates, a number of conditions toward truth are revealed. The first condition is that of the ignorant or the non-knowers. Non-knowers are complex, however, as they can actually take two forms. The first form of the non-knower, that form which Meno takes at the beginning of the dialog and is made more thematic in Socrates' account of his interrogation of the politicians, poets, and artisans in Plato's *Apology*, are the ignorant who lack knowledge of their ignorance (*Apology*, 21d, 22c, and 22d–e). If they remain unaware of their need to learn, they will never begin the search for truth. The goal of Socratic questioning, as described in the *Apology* and displayed in the *Meno*, is to give the questioned this crucial knowledge of ignorance, a knowledge more likely to arouse hostility toward Socrates rather than love (see *Apology*, 21d, 24b. Also see *Meno*, 80b).

The second form of the non-knower, that to which Meno is brought after three failed attempts to provide the idea of virtue, are those who know they are ignorant and hence need to learn the truth, but fear that learning is impossible. For instance, if we do not know what virtue is before we begin, how will we know or have confidence that we have found it in the end. The irony brought out by this condition is that it seems you have to have knowledge of something before you can learn it. This leads us to the third condition toward truth: the wise, or those who know. Knowers will not search for truth because they already know it and learning, for them, is unnecessary.

The search for truth requires knowledge of ignorance. But even with knowledge of ignorance how can we begin the search if we do not know what we are looking for? As Meno says, "How will you aim for something you do not know at all? If you should meet with it, how will you know that this is the thing that you did not know?" Human learning which seeks to grasp the truth appears to be an impossible activity. To resolve this problem and keep the idea of the search for truth alive, Socrates draws on or develops the theory of recollection.[11] Recounting what he says he heard from (perhaps Pythagorean) priests and priestesses as well as poets such as Pindar, Socrates speculates that:

> The human soul is immortal; at times it comes to an end, which they call dying; at times it is reborn, but it is never destroyed, and one must therefore live one's life as piously as possible [...] As the soul is immortal, has been born often, and has seen all things here and in the underworld, there is nothing which it has not learned; so it is in no way surprising that it can recollect things it knew before, both about virtue, and other things. As the whole of nature is akin, and the soul has learned everything, nothing prevents a man, after recalling one thing only – a process men call learning, discovering everything else for himself, if he is brave and does not tire of the search, for searching and learning are, as a whole, recollection (*Meno*, 81b–e).

By recollection Socrates appears to mean that the learner, when questioned in the right way, remembers truths, such as the idea of virtue, they knew before but had forgotten. The questioner, such as Socrates, does not therefore impart or give knowledge, but rather reminds the learner of the knowledge in their souls that they had forgotten was there. Socratic questioning, it seems, is thus not merely a technique or method to induce *aporia*, but is transformative or is a pathway, as it were, to the discovery of truth within oneself. Moreover, learners, it appears, do have knowledge of the truth they are looking for before they "learn" it, as it were.

In drawing on the theory of recollection to resolve the problem of learning, Socrates also suggests the immortality of the soul. In the above passage, Socrates speculates that upon death the soul separates from the body and goes through an eternal cycle of birth, death, and rebirth. In its endless transmigration or cycle from life to death and death to life when it enters the body of a new person upon being born, the soul has contemplated and therefore learned all things, which it can then recollect when questioned in the right way.

Socrates' discussion of recollection in the *Meno* is thus very similar to his discussion of recollection, as a demonstration of the immortality of the soul, in the *Phaedo*. In this latter dialog Socrates argues that when we sense two equal things in this world, such as two equal sticks and stones, if we think about them in the right way we are reminded of the "Equal Itself," or the idea or form of the Equal (*Phaedo*, 74a–b).[12] This same process of recollection holds for all of the ideas or Forms; whenever we consider particular manifestations of a thing in this world, such as particular manifestations of beauty, if we contemplate them correctly we are reminded of the universal classification, such as the idea or Form beauty itself that groups the particulars into a class (*Phaedo*, 75d).[13] The knowledge in the soul, therefore, that the learner recollects, is knowledge of the universal ideas or Forms.

But, where did we get this knowledge of the ideas or Forms such that we can be reminded of them when considering their particular manifestations? Socrates concludes that the soul must have acquired knowledge of them before we were born, and then "forgot" this knowledge when entering our body upon birth.[14] This shows that the soul, thinking the universal ideas, must exist separate from the body prior to birth, and that the process of recollecting, in this case aided through the senses but in the *Meno* through Socratic questioning about the idea, entails overcoming the inhibiting factors of the body after birth (*Phaedo*, 75c–d).

If the *Phaedo* suggests that learning is the soul's recollection of the ideas that it had contemplated while separated from the body, Socrates in the *Meno* goes further saying that, "the whole of nature is akin," or related. Thus, when the soul recollects one thing it can recollect all things, as all things are the same in some way. The image here is that all things in the *cosmos*, both material and immaterial, share some universal characteristic in common that makes them the same; there is one universal being or essence, one idea, uniting all things.[15] It is, moreover, a sweeping claim for knowledge in the soul, which seems to be opposed to the purpose of the ideas in the first part of the dialog, which is to give us knowledge of our own ignorance.

Socrates' turn to the theory of recollection in the *Meno* appears to resolve the problem of learning that arises after Meno fails in his attempts to define virtue. This impasse is a result of Socrates' dialectical method of refutation that relies on asking his interlocutor to tell him what the idea or common characteristic of virtue is. Yet, although apparently resolving the impasse and allowing the conversation to continue, bringing in the theory of recollection seems problematic in two key ways.

First, in the dialectical part of the dialog, in which Meno cannot satisfy Socrates' request for the idea of virtue, the purpose of Socratic questioning, as in the *Apology* and understood as technique, is to lead Meno to knowledge of his own ignorance and an understanding of the human condition as that of non-knowers who think we know. Socrates, in other words, teaches Meno and us that we don't know what we think we know and hence that the truth is not within us. Yet when the dialog turns to recollection, it appears that the purpose of Socratic questioning, understood as a pathway to discovery, is to lead Meno to knowledge of his prior knowledge as he recollects universal truths or ideas that are already within him, and he and we come to understand the human condition as that of knowers who don't know we know. Socrates thus teaches that we all in fact have the truth within us but have forgotten that this is the case.

The purposes of Socratic refutation and Socratic recollection seem irreconcilable. However, if we consider the *Apology* and the two parts of the *Meno* together, perhaps the teaching is as follows. Socrates first encounters persons such as Meno who are ignorant but don't know this. His questioning concerning the ideas, such as the idea of virtue, teaches them that they don't know what they thought they know, and in acquiring such knowledge of their ignorance Socrates' interlocutors can discard the false opinions about truth that they hold. Yet, this discarding of false opinion would then make possible the second stage of Socratic questioning, the purpose of which is to bring about recollection.

In this second stage the purpose of Socratic questioning is to allow the interlocutor to recollect the universal truths or ideas that were in their souls but which they had forgotten and had been obscured by the false opinions which they had previously held. Having swept away our false opinions Socratic questioning can help us bring to mind the universal truths we do hold, and Socratic technique is a preparatory stage for the transformative experience or pathway to discovery that Socratic questioning can bring.

But this still leaves us with another key problem. In the first stage of Socratic questioning, the ideas sought for, such as the idea of virtue, although distinct do not necessarily exist separate or apart from their particular manifestations in this world: they are not conceived of as self-subsisting. In the second stage of Socratic questioning, however, having been contemplated by the soul when separated from the human body and its senses, the ideas are conceived of as self-subsisting as they are eternal and exist apart from their particular manifestations that come to be and pass away. How to reconcile these two ideas remains yet to be solved.

Notes

1 Leo Strauss, *The City and Man* (Chicago: University of Chicago Press, 1964), 119.
2 Jacob Klein, *A Commentary on Plato's Meno* (Chapel Hill: University of North Carolina Press, 1965), 95–96, 131.
3 Gregory Vlastos, "*Anamnesis* in the *Meno*," in *Plato's Meno in Focus*, Jane M. Day, ed. (London: Routledge, 1994), 102; Steven S. Tigner, "On 'Kinship' of 'All Nature' in Plato's *Meno*," *Phronesis* 15/1 (1970): 4; R.E. Allen, "Anamnesis in Plato's *Meno* and *Phaedo*," *The Review of Metaphysics* 13/1 (Sep. 1959): 167–70, 172.
4 Vlastos, "*Anamnesis*," 102, and Allen, "Anamnesis," 171.
5 Plato, *Apology of Socrates*, in *Five Dialogues: Euthyphro, Apology, Crito, Meno, Phaedo*, G.M.A. Grube, trans. (Indianapolis: Hackett Publishing, 2002). All subsequent citations will be taken from here.
6 David Leibowitz, *The Ironic Defense of Socrates: Plato's Apology* (Cambridge: Cambridge University Press, 2010), 64–65, 87, 101; Claudia Baracchi, "The 'Inconceivable Happiness' of 'Men and Women': Visions of Another World in Plato's *Apology of Socrates*," *Comparative Literature Studies* 43/3 (2006): 277–78; Arlene W. Saxonhouse, *Free Speech and Democracy in Ancient Athens* (Cambridge: Cambridge University Press, 2006), 106–109; Michael Zuckert, "Rationalism and Political Responsibility: Just Speech and Just Deed in the *Clouds* and the *Apology of Socrates*," *Polity* 17/2 (1984): 283–87; and Leo Strauss, "On Plato's *Apology of Socrates* and *Crito*," in *Studies in Platonic Political Philosophy* (Chicago: University of Chicago Press), 42, 44; but see Lee Ward, "The Relation between Politics and Philosophy in Plato's *Apology of Socrates*," *International Philosophical Quarterly* 49/4 (December, 2009): 504.
7 Barrachi, "Inconceivable Happiness," 278–79.
8 Plato, *Meno*, G.M.A. Grube, trans. (Indianapolis: Hackett Publishing), 2002. All subsequent citations will be taken from here.
9 Plato, *Republic*, Allan Bloom, trans. (New York: Basic Books, 1968), 335a–336d. All subsequent citations will be taken from here; also see Plato, *Crito*, G.M.A. Grube, trans. (Indianapolis: Hackett Publishing, 2002), 45b–46a, 49d–e.
10 For instance, see Plato, *Euthyphro*, G.M.A. Grube, trans. (Indianapolis: Hackett Publishing, 2002) 5d, and Plato, *Republic*, 476a–b; also see Ann Ward, "Divine Speech and the Quest for the Ideas in Plato's *Euthyphro*," in *Natural Right and Political Philosophy: Essays in Honor of Catherine Zuckert and Michael Zuckert*, Ann Ward and Lee Ward, eds. (Notre Dame: University of Notre Dame Press, 2013), 41; Mary P. Nichols, *Socrates and the Political Community: An Ancient Debate* (Albany: SUNY Press, 1988), 112; and R.E. Allen, *Plato's Euthyphro and the Earlier Theory of Forms*, (New York: Humanities Press, 1970), 28–9, 67–9. Yet, see Crombie who argues that in the *Meno*, although Socrates is asking for the idea of virtue, he is not in fact asking for the definition of virtue. I.M. Crombie, "Socratic Definition," in *Plato's Meno in Focus*, Jane M. Day, ed. (London: Routledge, 1994), 179–80, 191–92.
11 Moravscik denies that the paradox of learning for which recollection is brought in as a resolution and calls into question all forms of learning, including learning done through empirical inquiry. See Julius Moravscik, "Learning as Recollection," in *Plato's Meno in Focus*, Jane M. Day, ed. (London: Routledge, 1994), 113.

12 Plato, *Phaedo,* Eva Brann, Peter Kalkavage and Eric Salem, trans. (Newburyport, MA: Focus Classical Library), 1998. All subsequent citations will be taken from here.
13 Also see Paul Stern, *Socratic Rationalism and Political Philosophy: An Interpretation of Plato's Phaedo* (Albany: State University of New York Press, 1993), 197–98; and Ann Ward, "The Immortality of the Soul and the Origin of the Cosmos in Plato's *Phaedo*," in *Matter and Form: From Natural Science to Political Philosophy,* Ann Ward, ed. (Lanham, MD: Lexington Books, 2009), 26.
14 See Klein, who argues that despite the emphasis on recollection after the forgetting at birth, Socrates suggests that the soul is capable of and is understood to have engaged in learning in a time prior to rebirth. Klein, *Plato's Meno,* 131.
15 See Socrates' discussion of the Good or idea of the good in the *Republic*, in which he indicates that the Good is the cause of all things and that all things participate in goodness (*Republic*, 508c–509c).

Bibliography

Allen, R.E. 1959. "Anamnesis in Plato's *Meno* and *Phaedo*." *The Review of Metaphysics* 13/1: 165–74.
———. 1970. *Plato's Euthyphro and the Earlier Theory of Forms.* New York: Humanities Press.
Baracchi, Claudia. 2006. "The 'Inconceivable Happiness' of 'Men and Women': Visions of Another World in Plato's *Apology of Socrates*." *Comparative Literature Studies* 43/3: 269–84.
Crombie, I.M. 1994. "Socratic Definition." In *Plato's Meno in Focus.* Jane M. Day ed. London: Routledge: 172–207.
Klein, Jacob. 1965. *A Commentary on Plato's Meno.* Chapel Hill: University of North Carolina Press.
Leibowitz, David. 2010. *The Ironic Defense of Socrates: Plato's Apology.* Cambridge: Cambridge University Press.
Moravscik, Julius. 1994. "Learning as Recollection." In *Plato's Meno in Focus.* Jane M. Day ed. London: Routledge: 112–28.
Nichols, Mary P. 1988. *Socrates and the Political Community: An Ancient Debate.* Albany: State University of New York Press.
Plato. 1968. *Republic.* Allan Bloom trans. New York: Basic Books.
———. 1998. *Phaedo.* Eva Brann, Peter Kalkavage and Eric Salem trans. Newburyport: Focus Classical Library.
———. 2002a. *Apology of Socrates.* In *Five Dialogues: Euthyphro, Apology, Crito, Meno, Phaedo.* G.M.A. Grube trans. Indianapolis: Hackett Publishing.
———. 2002b. *Crito.* In *Five Dialogues: Euthyphro, Apology, Crito, Meno, Phaedo.* G.M.A. Grube trans. Indianapolis: Hackett Publishing.
———. 2002c. *Meno.* In *Five Dialogues: Euthyphro, Apology, Crito, Meno, Phaedo.* G.M.A. Grube trans. Indianapolis: Hackett Publishing.
Saxonhouse, Arlene W. 2006. *Free Speech and Democracy in Ancient Athens.* Cambridge: Cambridge University Press.
Stern, Paul. 1993. *Socratic Rationalism and Political Philosophy: An Interpretation of Plato's Phaedo.* Albany: State University of New York Press.
Strauss, Leo. 1964. *The City and Man.* Chicago: University of Chicago Press.
———. 1985. "On Plato's *Apology of Socrates* and *Crito*." In *Studies in Platonic Political Philosophy.* Chicago: University of Chicago Press: 38–66.
Tigner, Steven S. 1970. "On 'Kinship' of 'All Nature' in Plato's *Meno*." *Phronesis* 15/1: 1–4.
Vlastos, Gregory. 1994. *"Anamnesis* in the *Meno*." In *Plato's Meno in Focus.* Jane M. Day ed. London: Routledge: 88–111.
Ward, Ann. 2009. "The Immortality of the Soul and the Origin of the Cosmos in Plato's *Phaedo*." In *Matter and Form: From Natural Science to Political Philosophy.* Ann Ward ed. Lanham, MD: Lexington Books: 19–34.
———. 2013. "Divine Speech and the Quest for the Ideas in Plato's *Euthyphro*." In *Natural Right and Political Philosophy: Essays in Honor of Catherine Zuckert and Michael Zuckert.* Ann Ward and Lee Ward eds. Notre Dame: University of Notre Dame Press: 36–49.
Ward, Lee. 2009. "The Relation between Politics and Philosophy in Plato's *Apology of Socrates*." *International Philosophical Quarterly* 49/4: 501–19.
Zuckert, Michael. 1984. "Rationalism and Political Responsibility: Just Speech and Just Deed in the *Clouds* and the *Apology of Socrates*." *Polity* 17/2: 271–97.

Part II
The Socratic Method and Other Approaches

5 The Socratic Method in Plato and Kant

Steven F. McGuire

Liberal education is struggling to maintain its place in the contemporary university. In some ways, the challenges it faces are as old as liberal education itself. Plato's dialogs provide plenty of evidence of the difficulties that attend the attempt to find and educate pupils in philosophy. In other ways, the challenges are peculiar to, or at least exacerbated by, the character of the modern age. Think of the economic and social pressures that attend the democratization of higher education in a modern mass democracy, for instance. Is it surprising that many students, parents, voters, and politicians ask how we can justify the cost of a four-year liberal arts degree that does not immediately place a graduate into a lucrative and productive position in the economy? Other phenomena such as the ongoing trend toward vocational education and the rise of outcome-based assessment can be partly attributed to these pressures.

On a deeper level, these and other trends in modern higher education (including increasing bureaucratization, and emphases on innovation, utility, and social change) are amplifications of the modern turn toward instrumental reason. In the history of philosophy, we see this turn, for example, in the works of Hobbes, Hume, and Bentham, who argue that reason can be used to calculate means but not ends, i.e., we can rationally calculate how to achieve our ends, but those ends are given to us by our passions. The noetic function of reason that one finds in the thought of Plato and Aristotle – the mode of reason by which we discern and choose the ends we ought to pursue – appears to be absent, or even intentionally excluded.

This turn to instrumental reason manifests itself in a variety of ways in modern life. It contributes to technological progress, economic growth, political efficiency, the belief in social progress, and so forth. But the logic of instrumentality also has a tendency to overwhelm all other considerations. The danger is not necessarily instrumental reason in itself, but, rather, the displacement of noetic reason (and faith, for that matter) by instrumental reason, so that the question of whether we ought to do something is simply left behind by the process of determining how to do it.

In the educational context, the worry is that instrumentalism threatens to undermine or displace humane learning by obscuring its nature, which is ultimately problematic because it is dehumanizing. Just as maximizing profit without regard for its human cost, maximally exploiting the environment, or reducing politics to a supposedly efficient bureaucracy are dehumanizing, so is the reduction of education to outcomes or vocational training. In this context, practicing the Socratic method might be seen as essential to maintaining and promoting our humanity in the modern age. Certainly, we must count ourselves lucky if we can find the time and space (and participants) to undertake it. The Socratic method does not fit well within the rigors of time and money, and it does not meet the demand for results or outcomes.

It does, however, create a space in which persons can encounter one another as persons, in which teacher and students can explore together the perennial questions that make us human. Rather than simply conveying or even implanting some piece of knowledge in the student's mind, the teacher seeks to elicit it from the student him or herself in his or her own time. The student thus learns through a "realization," an "insight," or a moment of "recognition" – in a flash it suddenly "occurs" to the student that something is the case. And it seems correct to express the experience in the passive voice. The teacher and student are actively engaged, they are working, but the actual moment in which something is learned just unpredictably happens. We can see this in the fact that sometimes the method works and sometimes it does not: in any group of students, it is common for some to see something that others among them do not. There is an air of mystery over the whole thing.

We can discern from Plato's dialogs that the mystery is owing in part to the fact that the knowledge sought is transcendent. In Plato's account, human beings live in a "between" state: we exist in empirical reality, but we also participate in the eternal reality of reason. He refers to education as a process of recollection because he wants to indicate that we are capable of knowledge that is not reducible to the empirical world (which is the realm of instrumental reason). But Plato advances this idea through the medium of myth (rather than offering a "theory" or "doctrine," as is often attributed to him) because this kind of education is not reducible to a discursive theory by its very nature. His idea of recollection points us toward the mysterious reality of education toward transcendence as he experiences it.

In the wake of the modern philosophers mentioned above, Kant attempts to recapture a similar conception of the human being and, by extension, education. Neither Kant's personal disposition nor his philosophy exhibits much to suggest he was a friend of mystery or myth or transcendence. A partisan of the Enlightenment, he strove to test everything against the "touchstone" of reason, and he appears to want to discard everything that cannot pass the test. He often demonstrates his desire to undermine and dismiss all superstition, enthusiasm, dogmatism – thus he circumscribes religion "within the boundaries of mere reason."

Yet, even in Kant there is the occasional spark, a rhetorical flourish, or a moment of admission that exhibits the presence of the mysteries. Kant was reportedly quite taken when he read Rousseau, he marvels at the "starry heavens above me," the "moral law within,"[1] and the shining power of virtue.[2] Moreover, there are moments in his thought showing that not everything can be resolved into reason, such as his treatment of freedom, the moral law, and even grace.

Perhaps Kant's commitment to human dignity grounded in freedom and reason stands out most prominently in this regard. Kant himself is trying to stop instrumentalism from overtaking the person in modernity by emphasizing that our participation in freedom and reason transcends the mechanical nature of the empirical world, as he understands it. Thus, Kant does embrace mystery insofar as he recognizes that we cannot offer a complete account of the human being. He acknowledges this in his own language in terms of freedom, because he recognizes that freedom is not free if it can be explained. Thus, Kant does remain open to mystery in a way similar to Plato, as he also recognizes that human beings are not exhaustively contained within empirical reality. Thus, Kant, like Plato, advocates for the Socratic method as the only possible way of educating human beings in those matters that concern their participation in a reality that transcends the empirical world. The Socratic method is not merely a technique, but the necessary path by which teachers can respect the humanity of their students while leading them toward moral and intellectual transformation and growth.

Socratic Method and Recollection in Plato

The bulk of this chapter will be devoted to analyzing Kant's remarks on recollection and the Socratic method. However, to show how Kant is recovering a Socratic mode of education, it will be useful to present first a brief summary of Plato's account of the Socratic method. In Plato's dialogs, we find Socrates employing question-and-answer and other forms of exchange (including speeches, storytelling, myth-making, etc.) to lead others, usually non-philosophers, toward wisdom and virtue. He also seems to modify his approach to meet different pupils or interlocutors where they are along the path toward these ends. Thus, he is harsh with the corrupt and dangerous Callicles, circumspect but effective (practically speaking) with the unpromising Euthypro, and more deeply engaged with the more noble souls of Glaucon and Adeimantus. It is also worth noting that none of the Platonic dialogs exhibits a conversation between philosophers, which suggests that the Socratic method is appropriate to people at all stages of their education toward wisdom and virtue.

We see that Socrates relies heavily on a dialogical form of education. This form, including the exchange of question-and-answer most commonly associated with the Socratic method, could be extracted from their Platonic context and employed productively in various educational contexts (as they commonly are, for example, in law schools). In Plato's works, however, their full meaning and significance are found only in their connection to his understanding of education and philosophy as a whole. The Socratic method in Plato is meant to awaken students to their participation in eternal reason and encourage them to develop their reason both theoretically and practically as they turn toward a life devoted to wisdom and virtue. Moreover, it is necessary in this context because of the nature of both human existence and the knowledge that is sought. Plato attempts to communicate this understanding of education by referring to it as *anamnesis*: a process of remembrance or recollection.

Socrates discusses recollection most extensively in the *Meno* and the *Phaedo*, but elements of the account are present in many other dialogs as well, including the *Phaedrus* and the *Republic*. The idea of recollection is meant to communicate the experience that human beings are capable of rational knowledge that transcends empirical reality such as mathematical concepts and ethical universals. Because this knowledge is not derivable from experience (there are no empirical examples of a perfect circle or perfect justice), it seems that students already possess (if inchoately) knowledge of such things – otherwise, how could anyone acquire such knowledge? In the *Meno*, Socrates references Pindar and "others of the divine among our poets" to offer the following mythological account of the idea:

> They say that the human soul is immortal; at times it comes to an end, which they call dying, at times it is reborn, but it is never destroyed, and one must therefore live one's life as piously as possible.... As the soul is immortal, has been born often and has seen all things here and in the underworld, there is nothing which it has not learned; so it is in no way surprising that it can recollect the things it knew before, both about virtue and other things. As the whole of nature is akin, and the soul has learned everything, nothing prevents a man, after recalling one thing only – a process men call learning – discovering everything else for himself, if he is brave and does not tire of the search, for searching and learning are, as a whole, recollection.[3]

Many scholars claim that Plato has a "doctrine" or "theory" of recollection, but it is surely significant that Socrates turns to poetic authorities to encapsulate his view. Plato often uses poetry and myth in his dialogs, and it is almost certain that he uses them in a non-literal fashion to communicate insights into realities that cannot be reduced to discursive rational accounts.[4]

Thus, it is open to question whether he held to "the thesis that the immortal soul, in a disembodied state prior to its incarceration in a body, viewed these Forms, knowledge of which is then recalled by incarcerated souls through a laborious process" as one contemporary scholar defines the "doctrine of recollection."[5] It is more likely that Plato uses poetry in this case to call our attention to, and explore the parameters of, a certain kind of educational experience that he cannot simply explain dialectically because it deals with human participation in transcendent reality. The teacher is like a midwife (as Socrates sometimes calls himself), because he draws knowledge out of the student that must already be inchoately present in the mind (because it cannot be derived from empirical experience).

Socrates picks up on this idea in the *Republic* as well, where he also stresses the moral dimension of Socratic education (which is mentioned in the *Meno* passage quoted above as well). Cultivating knowledge that is already present in the mind includes the cultivation of personal character, which Socrates identifies as a kind of conversion experience, a "turning-around." As he says:

> "Then, if this is true," I said, "we must hold the following about these things: education is not what the professions of certain men assert it to be. They presumably assert that they put into the soul knowledge that isn't in it, as though they were putting sight into blind eyes."
>
> "Yes," he said, "they do indeed assert that."
>
> "But the present argument, on the other hand," I said, "indicates that this power is in the soul of each, and that the instrument with which each learns – just as an eye is not able to turn toward the light from the dark without the whole body – must be turned around from that which is coming into being together with the whole soul until it is able to endure looking at that which is and the brightest part of that which is. And we affirm that this is the good, don't we?"
>
> "Yes."
>
> "There would, therefore," I said, "be an art of this turning around, concerned with the way in which this power can most easily and efficiently be turned around, not an art of producing sight in it. Rather, this art takes as given that sight is there, but not rightly turned nor looking at what it ought to look at, and accomplishes this object."
>
> "So it seems," he said.[6]

This passage emphasizes the existential nature of education – that it involves the whole person and a "turning-around" or conversion in the student. Like the passages involving recollection in the *Meno*, it also stresses that education involves working with something that is already present in the student. Finally, it once again illustrates how Plato turns to a story or image (in this case, the cave analogy) to communicate his insights into the nature of education. Rather than offering a theory or doctrine, Plato offers stories and myths that are meant to communicate our participation in a transcendent reality that cannot be presented adequately in human thought or language.

Plato's presentations of Socratic education thus coincide with his view that human beings exist "between" being and becoming, and that we "erotically" strive toward being from within the realm of becoming.[7] Human existence is thus characterized by movement between mortality and immortality or empirical and transcendent reality. The idea of recollection, like that of "turning-around" calls attention to the need to turn the student's attention toward his or her participation in transcendent reality. The Socratic method is thus not simply one educational method among others, but the necessary way of cultivating persons to become fully what they already are by nature. Because the knowledge they seek is non-empirical, they must be encouraged to find it for themselves. As will be seen, Kant holds a similar view, even if he does not endorse Plato's idea of recollection in its entirety.

Kant on Recollection and Ideas

As will be discussed below, Kant argues that the education of reason, especially but not exclusively in its practical mode, requires the Socratic method. Based on his own account, his reasons cannot be fully Platonic ones, because he does not accept the full epistemological and metaphysical implications of Plato's idea of recollection. Kant wants to maintain a distinction between Plato's transcendent ideas, which make a claim about the nature of reality in itself, and his own "transcendental" ones, which do not. Still, he sees the Socratic method as necessary because he agrees with Plato that the person is not exhausted by empirical reality. Moreover, as will be argued in the present section, reflection on his discussions of Plato's philosophy suggest that he comes much closer to Plato, especially in the field of practical philosophy, than one might initially expect. He agrees with Plato that the person is not exhaustively contained within empirical reality, and this remains a crucial step in Kant's historical context (and our own) toward resisting the reductionist tendencies in modern thinkers such as Hume (who Kant famously regarded as an important foil and influence).

Kant acknowledges his debt to Plato in the *Critique of Pure Reason* when he acknowledges appropriating Plato's language of "ideas" to label his own conception of the "transcendental ideas." In the course of this discussion, Kant highlights what he takes to be the important difference between their respective positions as he offers his own account of the meaning of recollection in Plato:

> Plato made use of the expression "*idea*" in such a way as quite evidently to have meant by it something which not only can never be borrowed from the senses but far surpasses even the concepts of the understanding (with which Aristotle occupied himself), inasmuch as in experience nothing is ever to be met with that is coincident with it. For Plato ideas are archetypes of the things themselves, and not, in the manner of the categories, merely keys to possible experiences. In his view they have issued from highest reason, and from that source have come to be shared in by human reason, which, however, is now no longer in its original state, but is constrained laboriously to recall, by a process of reminiscence (which is named philosophy), the old ideas, now very much obscured.[8]

As the passage suggests, Kant rejects the claim that ideas correspond to a reality beyond human reason, or, more specifically, he rejects the claim that we can know that they correspond to a reality beyond human reason. For example, in Kant's account, we cannot know whether God exists, but we do know that we have an idea of God. Thus, we do not arrive at an idea of God by "remembering" a prior knowledge of God. Rather, our reason "produces" the idea of God when it applies its natural desire for the unconditioned to "the highest condition of the possibility of all that can be thought (the being of all beings)."[9] This leaves open the possibility that our ideas might or might not correspond to reality as it is in itself, a question on which Kant insists we must remain agnostic (at least from a theoretical perspective).

Despite this distinction between remembering and producing the ideas, Kant and Plato still agree that we have ideas that transcend any and all empirical examples, thus suggesting that they are not derivative of experience. Kant also seems to agree with Plato that reason has an "erotic" quality insofar as it needs or desires ideas that transcend empirical reality.[10] As Kant notes with approval:

> Plato very well realized that our faculty of knowledge feels a much higher need than merely to spell out appearances according to a synthetic unity, in order to be able to read them as experience. He knew that our reason naturally exalts itself to modes of knowledge which so far transcend the bounds of experience that no given empirical object can ever coincide with them, but which must none the less be recognized as having their own reality, and which are by no means mere fictions of the brain.[11]

Thus, for Kant, as for Plato, reason naturally strives toward transcendent knowledge. The difference between them is on the question of whether it can successfully arrive at this knowledge. Kant answers in the negative, but his own words suggest that he has difficulty resting with this answer. For, if the ideas "have[e] their own reality" and are not "mere fictions of the brain," but do not correspond to reality as it is in itself, then what is their status? It is not clear that the difference between Plato and Kant is as stark as so far presented.

This is especially the case when Kant turns to the subject of practical philosophy. Kant singles out Plato's employment of the ideas in this field:

> It is, however, in regard to the principles of morality, legislation, and religion, where the experience, in this case of the good, is itself made possible only by the ideas – incomplete as their empirical expression must always remain – that Plato's teaching exhibits its quite peculiar merits.[12]

In the realm of the practical, Kant agrees with Plato that our ideas cannot come from empirical reality because they transcend it by their very nature. For Kant, the moral law is a purely rational idea. This can be illustrated by his claim that our ability to recognize examples of morality (and immorality) in the world depends on our already-existing knowledge of the moral law. As he writes:

> ... if anyone is held up as a pattern of virtue, the true original with which we compare the alleged pattern and by which alone we judge of its value is to be found only in our minds. This original is the idea of virtue, in respect of which the possible objects of experience may serve as examples (proofs that what the concept of reason commands is in a certain degree practicable), but not as archetype. That no one of us will ever act in a way which is adequate to what is contained in the pure idea of virtue is far from proving this thought to be in any respect chimerical. For it is only by means of this idea that any judgment as to moral worth or its opposite is possible; and it therefore serves as an indispensable foundation for every approach to moral perfection.[13]

This passage is reminiscent of later ones dealing with the meaning and significance of Jesus Christ in *Religion within the Boundaries of Mere Reason*. There Kant argues, "there is no need, therefore, of any example from experience to make the idea of a human being morally pleasing to God a model to us; the idea is present as model already in our reason." He adds that if someone requires "miracles as credentials," he "confesses to his own moral unbelief, to a lack of faith in virtue." His point is that miracles do not make believers, for it is only believers who will see or understand miracles as such: "such faith alone can validate miracles, if need be, as effects coming from the good principle; it cannot borrow its validation from them." Likewise, Kant goes on to explain that believers can only recognize Jesus as the Christ because they are already prepared to know the Christ when they meet him:

> ... an experience must be possible in which the example of such a human being is given (to the extent that one can at all expect and ask for evidence of inner moral disposition from an external experience). For, according to the law, each and every human being should furnish in his own self an example of this idea. And the required prototype always resides only in reason, since outer experience yields no example adequate to the idea; as outer, it does not disclose the inwardness of the disposition but only allows inference to it, though not with strict certainty.[14]

These passages seem to suggest that the appearance of Christ in history is unnecessary or unhelpful. Counterbalancing this impression, it is interesting to note in this context that Kant admits that we do not know the genetic origin of the moral law within us:

> But, precisely because we are not its authors but the idea has rather established itself in the human being without our comprehending how human nature could have even been receptive of it, it is better to say that that prototype has come down to us from heaven, that it has taken up humanity.[15]

Similarly, in a footnote on faith and reason in the *Critique of Judgment*, Kant suggests that Christianity is a kind of midwife to reason:

> But this is not the only case where this wondrous religion has in the greatest simplicity of its statement enriched philosophy with far more determinate and pure concepts of morality than philosophy itself had until then been able to supply, but which, once they are there, reason sanctions *freely* and accepts as concepts that it surely could and should itself have hit upon and introduced.[16]

Thus, much like Plato, Kant seems to be claiming that experience can enable us to recognize ideas that are in themselves not derivable from experience, thus suggesting that our ideas have another, transcendent source.

Such a claim is at odds with Kant's theoretical epistemology. But then Kant himself admits at one point that his agreement with Plato is not confined to the practical:

> But it is not only where human reason exhibits genuine causality, and where ideas are operative causes (of actions and their objects), namely, in the moral sphere, but also in regard to nature itself, that Plato rightly discerns clear proofs of an origin from ideas. A plant, an animal, the orderly arrangement of the cosmos – presumably therefore the entire natural world – clearly show that they are possible only according to ideas, and that though no single creature in the conditions of its individual existence coincides with the idea of what is most perfect in its kind – just as little as does any human being with the idea of humanity, which he yet carries in his soul as the archetype of his actions – these ideas are none the less completely determined in the Supreme Understanding, each as an individual and each as unchangeable, and are the original causes of things. But only the totality of things, in their interconnection as constituting the universe, is completely adequate to the idea.[17]

Presumably, Kant would maintain that this idea is regulative rather than constitutive, i.e., a subjective idea by which we bring order to our experiences, rather than an objective piece of knowledge of reality in itself. But he adds immediately following the passage just quoted,

> If we set aside the exaggerations in Plato's method of expression, the philosopher's spiritual flight from the ectypal mode of reflecting upon the physical world-order to the architectonic ordering of it according to ends, that is, according to ideas, is an enterprise which calls for respect and imitation.[18]

Taking this with other statements Kant makes about interpreting Plato, it appears that Kant is hinting at the possibility of an alternate reading of Plato that would bring their positions closer together, even as he insists on the epistemological distinction between them. As he writes of Plato's use of the term "recollection":

> I shall not engage here in any literary enquiry into the meaning which this illustrious philosopher attached to the expression. I need only remark that it is by no means unusual, upon comparing the thoughts which an author has expressed in regard to his subject, whether in ordinary conversation or in writing, to find that we understand him better than he has understood himself. As he has sometimes spoken, or even thought, in opposition to his own intention.[19]

Shortly thereafter, while noting that Plato spoke of ideas in the fields of "speculative knowledge" and mathematics, Kant adds in a note,

In this I cannot follow him, any more than in his mystical deduction of these ideas, or in the extravagances whereby he, so to speak, hypostatized them – although, as must be allowed, the exalted language, which he employed in this sphere, is quite capable of a milder interpretation that accords with the nature of things.[20]

Kant thus sets up the possibility that Plato intends to articulate a position similar to his own. It is equally possible that Kant is arriving at a position closer to Plato's. At the very least, it is clear that Kant agrees with Plato that we are aware of ideas that we do not derive from experience, which is enough to require the Socratic method in education insofar as it elicits ideas from the student's own reason. It is this transcendence of the empirical world, which Kant accepts as a moral certainty, that requires employment of the Socratic method in moral education.

Kant on Socratic Method

There are two notable discussions of Socratic method in Kant's writings, and he gives it a strong endorsement in both instances. The first passage is found in his *Lectures on Pedagogy*, where he argues:

> ... in the formation of reason one must proceed Socratically. For Socrates, who called himself the midwife of his listeners' knowledge, gives in his dialogues, which Plato has preserved for us faithfully, examples, of how even in the case of old people, one can bring forth a good deal from their own reason. On many matters children do not need to exercise reason. They must not reason about everything. They do not need to know the reasons for everything which is meant to make them well-educated. But as soon as duty is concerned, then the reasons in question must be made known to them. However, in general one must see to it that one does not carry rational knowledge into them but rather extracts it from them. The Socratic method should be the rule for the catechetical method. The mechanical-catechetical method is also good for some sciences; for example, in instruction in revealed religion. However, in the case of universal religion one must use the Socratic method. For the mechanical-catechetical method particularly recommends itself for what must be learned historically.[21]

In this passage Kant clearly intends to invoke and recommend the Socratic method, as he refers to Socrates, the image of the teacher as midwife, and the idea that the teacher must "extract" knowledge from the student.

The passage also makes clear that Kant has in mind moral education in particular. Students of Kant's ethical thought will understand that he requires the Socratic method because it is the only way to preserve the autonomy of the student. Kant allows that early education might not follow this method (presumably one might teach children to memorize information they do not yet understand, although even this raises interesting questions for a Kantian), but he insists that true moral education must proceed dialogically, so that the student can become autonomous. If morality depends on duty for duty's sake, then it requires personal knowledge of one's duty, and so morality can only be taught by developing the autonomy of the student. But notice also that this is a metaphysical necessity in addition to an ethical one: because the moral law transcends experience, it would simply be impossible to educate a student to virtue if he or she did not already have access to the moral law. In Kant's language, autonomy cannot be heteronomously planted in the student. Thus, on Kant's account, it is both ethically wrong and impossible to educate someone in any other way in the field of ethics.

Further, the passage hints that the Socratic method is necessary in the field of speculative metaphysics too. While Kant focuses on ethical education, he opens the passage by referring to the education of reason as a whole, which would include the transcendental ideas. The Socratic method is required in this field as well because the only way to educate students in these matters is to offer them an opportunity to cultivate their own reason. Thus, ideas such as God and the immortality of the soul – just like the moral law – are purely rational and transcend empirical experience. As such, they are produced by each individual's reason, and, therefore, the only way to access them is through one's own reason. Just as it is impossible to plant the moral law in someone's mind, so also is it impossible with the transcendental ideas. By Kant's account, the teacher can help the students to recognize and develop their understanding of these ideas, but that is only possible because they are already present in their minds.

Finally, Kant distinguishes between rational and empirical or historical education. He juxtaposes the Socratic method to the "mechanical-catechetical" method, which he argues is an acceptable mode of education in empirical and historical matters such as revealed religion. The distinction between "universal" and "revealed" religion tracks Kant's distinction between the purely rational and the empirical or historical. Universal religion therefore can only be taught Socratically because it is purely rational like the moral law on which it hinges, whereas revealed religion can be taught empirically because it consists of a series of historical facts.

Kant's second discussion of Socratic method, which is found in the section on "Teaching Ethics" in the "Doctrine of Method" at the end of the *Metaphysics of Morals*, uses somewhat different terminology, but makes similar points to the ones noted in the previous passage. Drawing a distinction between methods involving lecturing and questioning, he focuses on the latter, which he refers to (quite Platonically) as "erotetic." He states:

> . . . .this erotetic method is, in turn, divided into the method of dialogue and that of catechism, depending on whether the teacher addresses his questions to the pupil's reason or just to his memory. For if the teacher wants to question his pupil's reason he must do this in a dialogue in which teacher and pupil question and answer each other *in turn*. The teacher, by his questions, guides his young pupil's course of thought merely by presenting him with cases in which his predisposition for certain concepts will develop (the teacher is the midwife of the pupil's thoughts). The pupil, who thus sees that he himself can think, responds with questions of his own about obscurities in the propositions admitted or about his doubts regarding them, and so provides occasions for the *teacher* himself to *learn* how to question skillfully.[22]

This passage offers a more detailed image of the Socratic method as a process of questioning and answering, and again it shows that Kant insists that reason must be educated Socratically, using once again the image of the midwife.

In the context of a discussion of recollection, it must be noted that Kant distinguishes in this passage between reason and memory. In making this distinction, Kant is very possibly alluding to his ongoing understanding of the difference between his position and Plato's, i.e., that reason "produces" rather than "remembers" (or discovers) the ideas. Certainly, he is drawing a distinction similar to the one above between revealed and universal religion, i.e., between historical-empirical and rational knowledge, and the mode of education appropriate to each.

Still, whereas Kant rejects the traditional idea of Platonic recollection because it rests on an epistemology and metaphysics he does not accept, it is striking how similar Kant's commitment to the reality of the moral law is to a Platonic claim to transcendent knowledge. By Kant's own account, the moral law necessarily transcends empirical reality, and yet he is convinced it exists and is true, even though he is unable to reconcile this view with his own theoretical epistemology. As suggested above, Kant seems to overcome his own objections to Plato's idea of recollection in practice, if not in theory. Thus, it seems that Plato and Kant are both ultimately pointing to the transcendence or mystery that lies at the center of the process of education. Put another way, both are pointing out that the person is not exhausted by empirical reality.

Conclusion

In Plato's account, human beings exist in a "between" state, participating in both being and becoming, morality and immortality, and knowledge and ignorance. Education involves turning the person toward the transcendent pole of those indices, and he introduces the idea of recollection to illuminate the process by which a teacher leads a student to recognize the transcendent ideas in which he already participates. The Socratic method is the only way to accomplish this goal because the kind of knowledge sought must be elicited from the student's mind rather than planted in it. Education in this sense is a cultivation of the person's nature, and thus maintains and promotes the student's humanity and dignity (to use a modern notion).

Kant maintains a modern distinction between the subjective and objective that is not present in Plato's thought, which leads him to insist that we do not know whether our ideas conform to reality as it is in itself. Yet, he acknowledges his debt to Plato's language of ideas, and seems to overcome the subject–object divide in his practical philosophy to reprioritize metaphysics to epistemology.[23] Even if he accomplishes this only in practice, it is enough to lead Kant to endorse the Socratic method as part of his broader attempt to defend the person and human dignity against the instrumentalization of reason in the modern age. This is one way of understanding what Kant means when he famously says in the second introduction to the first *Critique* that he had to restrict reason to "make room for faith." He sees that the source of our personhood and dignity is our participation in the realities of reason and freedom that transcend the empirical world.

Kant's project is thus to confine instrumental or theoretical reason to the realm of the empirical to open a space for freedom and moral responsibility, which is also a space for transcendence and mystery. Like Plato, he sees that students can only be awakened to their participation in such a reality through the Socratic method. Kant stands as an instance of a modern thinker recognizing and attempting to overcome the modern trend to reduce education to vocational or technical training by employing the Socratic method to cultivate the humanity of his students.

Notes

1 Immanuel Kant, *Critique of Practical Reason*, Mary Gregor, ed. (New York: Cambridge University Press, 1997), 133 [5:161].
2 Immanuel Kant, *The Metaphysics of Morals*, Mary Gregor, ed. (New York: Cambridge University Press, 1996).
3 Plato, "*Meno*," in *Plato: Complete Works*, G.M.A. Grube, trans., John M. Cooper and D.S. Hutchinson, eds. (Indianapolis: Hackett Publishing, 1997), 880 [81b–c].
4 For a reading of Plato that reads his use of myth in this way, see Eric Voegelin, *The Collected Works of Eric Voegelin, vol. 16, Order and History, vol. III, Plato and Aristotle*, Dante Germino, ed. (Columbia: University of Missouri Press, 2000).
5 Allan Silverman, "Plato's Middle Period Metaphysics and Epistemology," in *The Stanford Encyclopedia of Philosophy*, Edward N. Zalta, ed. https://plato.stanford.edu/entries/plato-metaphysics/. Accessed August 3, 2017. It is subsequently defined in the same entry as the "doctrine of recollection, i.e., the thesis that our disembodied, immortal souls have seen the Forms prior to their incarceration in the body."
6 Plato, *The Republic of Plato*, Allan Bloom, trans. (New York: Basic Books, 1968), 518b–d.
7 This characterization of human existence is present throughout Plato's works, but is especially clear in the *Symposium*.
8 Kant, *Critique of Pure Reason*, Norman Kemp Smith, trans. (New York: Basic Books, 2003), 310 [A313–14/B 370].
9 *Ibid.*, 323 [A334/B391].
10 For discussion on metaphysical *eros* in Kant, see Richard Velkley, *Being after Rousseau: Philosophy and Culture in Question* (Chicago: University of Chicago Press, 2002).
11 Kant, *Critique of Pure Reason*, 310–11 [A314/B370-371].
12 *Ibid.*, 313 [A318/B375].
13 Kant, *Critique of Pure Reason*, 311 [A315/B372].

14 Kant, *Religion within the Boundaries of Mere Reason*, Allen Wood and George di Giovanni, trans. (New York: Cambridge University Press, 1998), 81–2 [6:63].
15 *Ibid.*, 80 [6:61].
16 Kant, *Critique of Judgment*, Werner S. Pluhar, trans. (Indianapolis: Hackett Publishing, 1987), 366 [5:472].
17 Kant, *Critique of Pure Reason*, 313 [A317–18/B374–75].
18 *Ibid.*, 313 [A318/B375].
19 *Ibid.*, 310 [A313–314/B370].
20 *Ibid.*, 311 [A314/B371].
21 Kant, "Lectures on Pedagogy," in *Anthropology, History, and Education*, Günter Zöller and Robert B. Louden, eds., Robert B. Louden, trans. (New York: Cambridge University Press, 2007), 466 [9:477].
22 Kant, *The Metaphysics of Morals*, 222 [6:478].
23 For this reading of Kant, see David Walsh, *The Modern Philosophical Revolution: The Luminosity of Existence* (New York, NY: Cambridge University Press, 2008), Chap. 1.

Bibliography

Kant, Immanuel. 1987. *Critique of Judgment*. Werner S. Pluhar trans. Indianapolis: Hackett Publishing.
———. 1996. *The Metaphysics of Morals*. Mary Gregor ed. New York: Cambridge University Press.
———. 1997. *Critique of Practical Reason*. Mary Gregor ed. New York: Cambridge University Press.
———. 1998. *Religion within the Boundaries of Mere Reason*. Allen Wood and George di Giovanni trans. New York: Cambridge University Press.
———. 2003. *Critique of Pure Reason*. Norman Kemp Smith trans. New York: Basic Books.
———. 2007. "Lectures on Pedagogy." In *Anthropology, History, and Education*. Günter Zöller and Robert B. Louden eds., Robert B. Louden trans. New York: Cambridge University Press: 434–85.
Plato. 1968. *The Republic of Plato*. Allan Bloom trans. New York: Basic Books.
———. 1997. *"Meno."* In *Plato: Complete Works*. G.M.A. Grube trans. John M. Cooper and D.S. Hutchinson eds. Indianapolis: Hackett Publishing: 870–97.
Silverman, Allan. n.d. "Plato's Middle Period Metaphysics and Epistemology." In *The Stanford Encyclopedia of Philosophy*. Edward N. Zalta ed. https://plato.stanford.edu/entries/plato-metaphysics/.
Velkley, Richard. 2002. *Being after Rousseau: Philosophy and Culture in Question*. Chicago: University of Chicago Press.
Voegelin, Eric. 2000. *The Collected Works of Eric Voegelin, vol. 16, Order and History, vol. III, Plato and Aristotle*. Dante Germino ed. Columbia: University of Missouri Press.
Walsh, David. 2008. *The Modern Philosophical Revolution: The Luminosity of Existence*. New York, NY: Cambridge University Press.

6 The Americanization of the Socratic Method

Andrew Bibby

This chapter examines the troubled relationship and complex reception of the Socratic method in the early national period of American education (1776–1840). I argue that the account of Socrates' quest for self-knowledge has been largely reduced to a "technique" for encouraging creative thinking and individual self-expression. This is not necessarily a bad thing, although it does raise a number of questions about the nature of modern higher education, and more specifically, the role played by the touchstone "Socratic method" in leading students to self-knowledge. As this account suggests, the early national period was an exciting but also transformational time for the rediscovery of Socrates in America. Readers may be surprised to find out that attitudes toward Socratic teaching and learning were surprisingly negative. For the Socratic method to succeed in the United States, it would have to be stripped of its philosophical power, modernized for polite society, and transformed to suit the purposes of a virtuous citizenry.

The first part of this chapter describes in brief and general terms the historic context of Socrates' method in educational and academic theory. The second part surveys a selection of factors contributing to the transformation of the Socratic method in the United States. The third part examines Benjamin Franklin's attempt to make the Socratic style "sociable." The fourth section looks at Thomas Jefferson's critique of Socrates, with a view to further clarifying the moral and political reasons for the "Americanization" of the Socratic method.

The Problem of the Socratic Method

A number of problems plague any attempt to study the reception of Socrates' teaching in post-revolutionary America. First, there is what I would call a "speciation" problem. It is not obvious to anyone even vaguely familiar with Plato's or Xenophon's Socrates whether the modern Socratic method (as practiced in law schools, for example) is meaningfully similar to the "method" as practiced by the historical Socrates. Even today, the exact nature of the *elenchus* as practiced by Socrates is fairly open to debate: should we understand it as a positive method leading to knowledge or as a negative method used essentially to refute false claims to knowledge? There is also a disciplinary complexity. Socrates' trademark method may be applied in radically different ways, in a law school setting or in a Great Books program. Add to this the bewildering proliferation of pedagogical theories, one could see why it may no longer make any sense to speak of *the* Socratic method in any meaningful way. Finally, there is a historical problem. As the following will demonstrate, the utility or value of teaching in a Socratic manner varies across time and among various schools and political contexts.

Having noted only a few of the difficulties, let us turn to a brief summary of the reception of the Socratic method in the modern Western world. The following overview will be useful in providing a basic historical context for thinking about the reception of Socrates as a teacher in the early national period in the United States.

Socrates Underground

We can start by noting that the rediscovery of Plato and Socrates are separate historical problems. Whereas one could trace the rediscovery of Plato to the renewal of interest in the scholarship of ancient Greece in the works of Alfarabi and other eighth- and ninth-century Arabic scholars, the rediscovery of the Socratic method does not appear to follow the same timeline, at least not in any obvious way. In fact, the renewed interest in Socrates as a teacher lags – by hundreds of years – behind the renewed interest in Socrates' ideas.

The first evidence of a reawakening of the Socratic method does not appear until the sixteenth century. Interest in Socratic teaching methods appears to coincide with interest in the study of *maieutics* during this century. *Maeutica*, generally, can be defined as a pedagogical technique in which the teacher proceeds primarily with questions, in lieu of a lecture or arguments. The goal of *maeiutics* is to lead the student either to discover the answer for themselves or, to lead the student to a more profound sense or awareness of the limits of knowledge. Examples include several published works on Socratic-inspired "dialectical methods" in the works of the French scholar Pierre de la Ramée (1543–1555); and in the writings of the German humanist Johannes Sturm (1507–1589).

The first sustained discussion of a "Socratic teaching" does not appear, at least in written form, until the early eighteenth century.[1] The word *elenchus* appears in English texts in 1748. The term "Socratic method" does not appear to have been used commonly until much later still, when it was popularized in educational settings at the turn of the twentieth century. Even then, the phrase "Socratic method" does not appear to be used nearly as frequently as the more technical term *elenchus*, the preferential phrase of classicists and historians.

The earliest written reflections on the Socratic approach for modern republics are positive and complimentary. One particularly positive review appears in the works of the Scottish scholar, David Fordyce, who asserted that the "*Socratic* Doctrine ... sets [the mental] Faculty a working, and supplies it with materials to fashion."[2] English writer Isaac Watts makes similar arguments: the Socratic method provides an effective alternative to rote learning. It is, in Watts' words, a "more pleasant, and a more sprightly way of instruction." It was "more fit to excite the attention and sharpen the penetration of the learner" than traditional methods, including "silent attention to the lecturer."[3] Watts' book on education was printed in Boston in 1754. It was the first print reference focused on Socrates as teacher in the American colonies.

Not all commentaries on the Socratic method were positive. Fordyce, who described Socrates as a "quickener of wit," followed this positive comment with an observation that illustrates the problem Socrates gave later thinkers – including Franklin and Jefferson – pause. As Fordyce noted, the method was not entirely open-ended or content-neutral. It had the tendency, as Fordyce observed, to "free the mind" from "Dependence on Authority." Fordyce was only repeating what had already been well established by critics of Socrates in Europe; namely, that Socrates and Plato's teaching methods were "Enemies to dogmatizing, and rather doubting and denying than asserting anything."[4]

Jack Schneider has provided a detailed account of the ways in which the Socratic method was further altered, processed, and filtered in the United States. The emergence of public schooling in the 1830s increased pressure on paid teachers to keep their students' attention, including a few misguided attempts to combine "catechizing with Socratizing." The opening of private and religious schools to a wider American public put more pressure on traditional "lecture and rote memorization" teachers to diversify their approaches to education. After the Civil War, there was an increased demand for professionalization, and as a result, a renewed effort by administrators and educators in schools to employ the Socratic method as a "credentialing" tool (Socrates' teaching as the "inheritance of antiquity"). Compulsory schooling laws in the nineteenth century motivated teachers to find different ways to engage their students. New laws against corporal punishment further limited the "teacher's toolkit for controlling the classroom." In the twentieth century, the

Socratic method enjoyed renewed attention from three different sources. John Dewey was effective in changing the emphasis on student-centered instruction. Law schools took up Socrates' example to increase the effectiveness of legal training. A movement to restore general education and the Great Books resulted in the emergence of an updated "Socratic seminar" setting.

This history of education approach is useful for thinking about broad trends. It does not, however, provide a full account of the reasons why the Socratic method was transformed in America by leading intellectual and educational reformers. The Americanization process includes a number of cultural-historical factors, not generally accounted for in educational history, such as religion, democracy, and practical culture – factors that Hofstadter famously led to an "unpopularity of the intellect" in the United States. A brief look at these factors will help to clarify why the Socratic method could never be embraced wholeheartedly in the United States, at least not in its original unadulterated form.

Socrates and the American Character

When Tocqueville arrived in the United States, he made a few remarkable observations on the peculiar character – or problem – of American education. Religion, history, and commerce, he said, had created a social environment that was unfriendly to abstract and time-consuming styles of learning. Circumstances had conspired "to divert [the American] mind from the pursuit of science, literature and the arts ... and to fix the mind of the American upon purely practical objects." For Tocqueville, there had always been an "earthward" pull in American intellectual life. American education was grounded historically and materially in an habitual preference for the useful over the beautiful; as Tocqueville famously put it, even "the beautiful should be useful."[5]

Tocqueville's observation of the cultural setting of American education is a useful starting point for thinking about the Americanization of Socrates. American life, he observed, was characterized by constant action, and circumscribed by democratic politics. American life was also highly restless and commercial, a fact which necessarily changed the character of American education. In contrast to many European schools, American educators put a premium on practical education, or on the "rough and ready habits of mind."

The relevant part of Tocqueville's insight was his observation that American education was essentially pragmatic. The American regime favors quick thinking and decisive, often risky, action. Personal or individual success in the United States does not depend on perfection, theoretical clarity, or even doxastic coherence. According to Tocqueville, the United States never was and never would be an environment favorable to the cultivation of careful deliberation, theoretical analysis, or precision in thought.[6] To put the point simply, Tocqueville's description of American education illustrates part of the reason why Socrates' manner of teaching was difficult to reproduce on the American continent in its classical form. For it to become popular, it would have to adapt to the larger patterns and peculiarities of American culture. The American mind has always had a complicated and strained relationship with Socratic approaches to knowledge and teaching. This point is worth bearing in mind as we turn to the early national period, and to the influential analysis of Franklin.

Franklin's Socratism

Two guides were especially important in shaping how Americans came to think of the classics and the usefulness of Socratic education: Franklin and Jefferson. Turning to these thinkers now will allow us to examine the transformation of the Socratic method on a more concrete level. Both Franklin and Jefferson agreed that the Socratic method needed to be modernized. But they diverged on what this meant. Franklin's contention was that Socrates' method was insufficiently social. For Jefferson, Socrates was insufficiently democratic.

We can begin by contrasting Franklin with the early (positive) appraisals. The first print reference to the Socratic method in America can be traced to the English hymn writer, Isaac Watts, who dedicated a chapter to the "Socratic Way of Disputation" in his *The Improvement of the Mind*.[7] Watts' description of the Socratic method reads like a contemporary educational manual. The Socratic method was essentially a tool for keeping students awake. Questioning is a more "easy" and "more pleasant" and "more sprightly way of instruction." It is "more fit to excite the attention and sharpen the penetration of the learner, than solitary reading, or silent attention to a lecture."

Franklin, as we will now see, read the method against the backdrop of the historical experiment in republican government. The Socratic method certainly had its place, but not merely as a teaching tool. Franklin's views of Socrates are sketched briefly in his thoughts on the development of an educational curriculum for the Academy and College of Philadelphia (now the University of Pennsylvania). In his *Proposals Relating to the Education of Youth in Pensilvania* and in letters to friends,[8] Franklin emphasizes the importance of education in a modern republic. Education, he says, is the "surest Foundation of the Happiness both of private Families and of Commonwealths." In this sense, the American republic is no different from all previous experiments in popular government. By contrast to monarchies, all republics must make education "a principal Object of their Attention."

Franklin makes a few deviations from classical republicanism models of education, however. First, he notes that Americans do not need to be as well educated as the "first Settlers." The next generation have more pressing needs, and thus require an attention to practical education. The practical needs of the next century will be best achieved by an education that focuses less on rigorous philosophical analysis, and more on a proper understanding of liberal-republican morality. Importantly, moral education should be available to the common man, and it should not be confusing. It should focus on what we now call the bourgeois virtues, "the Advantages of Temperance, Order, Frugality, Industry, Perseverance, &c. &c."[9]

On occasion, Franklin notes, debates will arise as to the bigger ethical and philosophical questions, matters "of Right and Wrong, Justice and Injustice." In these circumstances, Franklin writes, the youth should break from the lecture mode to openly "debate" these questions both "in Conversation and in Writing." The purpose of debate, however, is pragmatic. Dialog and questioning will lead young Americans not to contradictions and moral confusion, but to enjoy the excitement of winning the argument – in Franklin's words, they will learn to "ardently desire Victory, for the Sake of the Praise attending it." This account is not strictly utilitarian. After the students have acquired a taste for victory, a few students will go further. Some will acquire a deeper love of learning and become acquainted with the pleasures of "discover[ing] Truth." What is truth? What sources should students turn to when they achieve this level of learning? Not Plato. The most advanced students should read Grotius, Puffendorff, and "other Writers of the same Kind."

Franklin's *Autobiography* provides a window onto the Founders' view of the problem of adopting the Socratic method. The Socratic technique is not insufficient because it is not useful (it was for some, including Franklin). Rather, Franklin views the Socratic method as deficient because it tends to create good scholars rather than a good – meaning sociable – citizenry.

Franklin is just a young man, sixteen years old, when he first encounters Socrates. Coincidentally, this is roughly during the same period that he describes his flirtation – and ultimate abandonment – of the philosophy of vegetarianism. Franklin's encounter with Socrates begins with a chance encounter with Xenophon. As a youth, Franklin, notes, he was interested especially in natural philosophy or science. He had devoured books on "Arithmetick, Navigation, geometry, and English grammar." He soon becomes interested in rhetoric and logic. Logic opened the doors to what he calls a "specimen of a dispute in the Socratic method."[10] Franklin writes:

> I was charm'd with it, adopted it, dropt my abrupt contradiction and positive argumentation, and put on the humble inquirer and doubter. And being then, from reading Shaftesbury and Collins, become a real doubter in many points of our religious doctrine, I found this method

safest for myself and very embarrassing to those against whom I used it; therefore I took a delight in it, practis'd it continually, and grew very artful and expert in drawing people, even of superior knowledge, into concessions, the consequences of which they did not foresee, entangling them in difficulties out of which they could not extricate themselves, and so obtaining victories that neither myself nor my cause always deserved.

The passage above illustrates the double-edged nature of the Socratic method. Franklin credits Socrates, on the one hand, for moderating his "abrupt" contradictory style of argument. Provocative intellectual combat is substituted out for the "humble inquirer and doubter." Notably, Franklin confesses that his turn to Socrates' style of questioning is politically motivated. The humble doubter is a guise; it gives him cover when disputing points of "religious doctrine."

Note, however, that Franklin is not entirely comfortable with recommending the Socratic style to others. Indeed, he warns against the adoption of the Socratic style by describing, with apparent regret, that it was particularly effective at embarrassing believers by "entangling" believers in contradictions. Interestingly, Franklin does not claim that these contradictions falsify the worldview of the believers. Taking what some call a non-constructivist approach, Franklin denies that the Socratic method always or necessarily establishes the truth or falsity of individual answers. In his words, the Socratic method often leads to victories that neither Franklin "nor [his] cause always deserved."

In the next part of the discussion, Franklin elaborates on his partial abandonment of the philosopher's peculiar teaching style. Key to understanding Franklin's departure from Socrates is his description of the virtues of the method he finds most compatible with modern times; i.e., intellectual modesty or "diffidence":

I continu'd this method some few years, but gradually left it, retaining only the habit of expressing myself in terms of modest diffidence; never using, when I advanced any thing that may possibly be disputed, the words certainly, undoubtedly, or any others that give the air of positiveness to an opinion; but rather say, I conceive or apprehend a thing to be so and so; it appears to me, or I should think it so or so, for such and such reasons; or I imagine it to be so; or it is so, if I am not mistaken.

It is now clearer how, in Franklin's hands, the Socratic method becomes sociable. The utility of the teaching method is adapted and redefined in terms of what the United States, an offshoot of commercial England, lacks most: a degree of civility and politeness.[11] The first step in the Americanization of Socrates requires a depreciation of the Socratic *elenchus*, and a corresponding elevation of the Socratic conversational style.[12] The point, as Franklin sees it, is not to trap opponents in definitional contradiction, which may either create resentment or deep confusion. The purpose of Socratic diffidence is to avoid the appearance of dogmatism, which helps one to acquire friends.

But modern republics also require attention to and the cultivation of commercial virtues. The Socratic method can be useful here too. Franklin notes that his imitation of Socrates gave him "great advantage" in business relations:

This habit, I believe, has been of great advantage to me when I have had occasion to inculcate my opinions, and persuade men into measures that I have been from time to time engag'd in promoting; and, as the chief ends of conversation are to inform or to be informed, to please or to persuade, I wish well-meaning, sensible men would not lessen their power of doing good by a positive, assuming manner, that seldom fails to disgust, tends to create opposition, and to defeat every one of those purposes for which speech was given to us, to wit, giving or receiving information or pleasure. For, if you would inform, a positive and dogmatical manner in advancing your sentiments may provoke contradiction and prevent a candid attention.

Here another aspect of the modern appreciation of the Socratic method comes to light. Franklin found that a "positive, assuming" and "dogmatical" manner is bad for business. American colonists do not like "assuming manner[s]" and "dogmatical" assertion. The Socratic style – or at least Franklin's version of it – is unpretentious, plain, and easy-going. These are essential virtues in Franklin's America for "doing good."

The extent to which Franklin renovated Socrates' image for a practical country devoted to liberty, can be further illustrated by reference to Franklin's "Project for Moral Perfection." Incidentally, it is the only other mention of Socrates in the *Autobiography*. In explaining his project, Franklin describes a "method" for instilling virtue that is – despite Franklin's earlier imitation of Socrates – almost entirely incompatible with the Socratic philosophizing.[13] Franklin starts by confiding in his reader that he finds little or nothing puzzling or complicated about morality and justice, "right and wrong." Franklin's "speculative conviction" is that it is "in our interest to be completely virtuous." The problem with virtue, in other words, has little to do with abstract philosophical analysis, let alone, rigorous logical consistency. The problem of virtue has little to do with the question of what it is or whether it is good, but rather how to succeed – establishing clubs, founding fire companies, inventing stoves – in doing good.

As is apparent from the above, Franklin's project for moral perfection is not built around the ideals of a life devoted to questioning, endless definition testing, and moral confusion. Franklin lists the virtues first, then asks questions about how to obtain them. Indeed, Franklin's famous catalog of the virtues contains a handy reference guide, for definitional precision. Franklin will annex to each a "short precept" that would leave little room for disputation.[14]

Franklin's reduction of moral perfection to a tidy list of non-ambiguous moral rules is perfectly Franklinian but also anti-Socratic. First, the list is designed to allow anyone to cultivate virtue. It is within every human being's reach to develop the qualities of temperance, silence, order, resolution, frugality, industry, sincerity, justice, moderation, cleanliness, tranquility, chastity, and humility. Moreover, these are evidently practical virtues. The goal is not to prepare the soul for a spiritual journey into the dark corners of self-knowledge. The goal is self-advancement in the world. And that world is liberal and egalitarian. Socratic humility may be imitated, in other words, but not Socrates' life, and certainly not the philosophical method in its traditional form.[15]

Whatever else can be said about Franklin's demotion of the noble virtues, Franklin's project does capture an underlying truth, important for understanding the early republic's hostility to Socratic philosophy. The viability of the new colonies would depend on the development of qualities of character that would put the colonies in a position to be economically, if not politically, self-sufficient. The virtues associated with economic self-reliance require discipline, but they do not require unnecessary self-sacrifice. And perhaps more importantly, they are not difficult to comprehend.[16]

Whereas Franklin's project for moral perfection does not capture Franklin's full views on education or his full moral teaching,[17] and while it would be fair to debate Franklin's impact on America's educational system, we can make a few general conclusions. First, Franklin articulated an ideal of self-learning or "self-education" that helped point the way to a broader educational revolution away from the traditional methods of lecture, rote memorization, and religious instruction, which dominated the European schools, medieval universities, and the Puritan worship service. The new education in the early national period did in fact shift focus to the acquisition of practical wisdom gained through self-education (one can think here of Franklin's Junto, or his founding of the first public library in America in 1731, chartered in 1742 as the Philadelphia Library).[18]

If Franklin is right, the Socratic method could be preserved in the American educational system only by abandoning the possibility that the exercise might lead to deep ignorance, and therefore, true self-knowledge. This is largely the story of American law schools. In the following section, we will continue exploring the Americanization of Socrates by turning to the other major figure of the early national period. Jefferson went further than Franklin: Socrates would be made safe for American democracy by making Socrates into a good citizen.

Jefferson and The Rural Socrates

Jefferson's thoughts were not far from Socrates in 1787. From Paris, he writes to John Trumbull, with a description of his viewing of the original *Death of Socrates*, by Jacques-Louis David. Jefferson describes it as "superb,"[19] the best item in the collection, and cites it as one of the treasures of Paris.

Not much is known, however, about Jefferson's interest in Socrates, either as a philosopher, or as a model teacher. Yet there is evidence that Jefferson was considering Socrates' legacy and thinking about ways to incorporate Socrates into the educational system in the United States. In 1801, John Vaughan sent Jefferson a copy of *The Rural Socrates* to review. The alternative title for the book hinted at the way in which Socrates could be recovered for Jefferson's America: "Philosophic Farmer." In the letter, Vaughan recommends that Jefferson read the book as an example of how Socrates was being reintegrated into the European educational system. Vaughan tells Jefferson that the book will not have seen "So full an acct. of [Socrates]."

The *Rural Socrates* belongs to a specialized literature on agriculture, from the nineteenth century.[20] Johnstone argues that the book, while largely neglected by intellectual historians, is significant in American history because it contains the assumptions and "moral attitudes" of the modern "back-to-nature" ideas in America. Vaughan had recommended it to Jefferson because it captured nicely the modern enthusiasm for rural life, and agriculture, in modern times. It contained all the "basic tenets of the agrarian tradition." The agrarian life is good not because it promotes leisure for the sake of seeking wisdom, but because it promotes a simple, wholesome, natural, and even "divinely ordained" way of life.

It is worth dwelling on the image of Socrates that Jefferson encountered in the book. Socrates is transformed from an urban philosopher to a rural hero. He is anti-court, anti-city, anti-commercial, and he lives in accord with a divine purpose. Vaughan recommends this version of Socrates to Jefferson because he represents a new possibility. Here is a figure who can stand astride two great unbridgeable worlds, between the urban intellectual elite and the virtuous farmers of the new republic.

What could Jefferson have seen or learned from such a possibility? As Johnstone has argued, this rendition of Socrates intrigued thinkers in the agrarian school for three reasons. First, the enthusiastic and experimental curiosity of Socrates was easily (if crudely) adaptable to the modern farmer, who needed to embrace technology and science to discover new agricultural techniques. In this context, one needs only to think of the Aristophanic Socrates to see the connection. Second, and more importantly, Socrates gave the American "gentry," as it were, a dignified and dignifying model for combining agricultural life with intellectual virtue. By taking Socrates out of the city, as it were, the book made a case for a "philosophic farmer." The intellectually curious farmer, with Socrates as a role model, could not be decried by urban snobs as merely gardening for the wealthy. Third, the "Rural Socrates" was an example of near perfect self-sufficiency. The combination of philosophy and agriculture was both intellectually rewarding and economically viable. Unlike the real philosopher, an Americanized Socrates could make a living out of philosophizing.

The Rural Socrates ideal was not new, of course. The idea was traceable to the Socrates of Xenophon. Xenophon's Socrates is quoted at length at the beginning of the book. Socrates is the originator of the idea that agricultural is the mother of all arts, and therefore, worthy of study by gentlemen. Agriculture produces good citizens and brave soldiers, people that love justice, revere the gods, and appreciate simplicity. Jefferson, in short, did not have to reinvent or transform the Platonic Socrates for a virtuous republic. The citizen-Socrates model was there, preexisting in the works of Xenophon. John Vaughan's copy of *The Rural Socrates* was a reminder for Jefferson of the compatibility of philosophy with the agrarian ideal. And using the "Rural Socrates" as an ideal, Jefferson could help set an example for others. He could study farming himself, without the ghost of a Platonic Socrates nagging him that the study of natural man was in reality a study of the souls of the lowly. The Socratic method could be extracted, in other words, to dignify the agrarian social creed. In 1819, Jefferson wrote to William Short with an argument to this point; namely, that "of Socrates, we have nothing genuine but in the *Memorabilia* of Xenophon."[21]

The significance of Socratic method, for Jefferson, is relevant, not because it provided a technique for self-realization, but because it provided an example of a deep commitment to a questioning way of life.[22] While it is arguable whether Jefferson's view of Socrates – through Xenophon – was influential in changing attitudes toward the Socratic method, what is clear is that there has always been an uneasy relationship between the ideal of Socrates and the ideals of the American character, whether they are best represented by the urbane Franklin or Jefferson's virtuous farmer.

Clearly there were elements of the Socratic method that were compatible with either vision of the American character. The Socratic method displaces or makes redundant divine explanations in favor of natural or rational accounts of things.[23] Second, the Socratic method seeks logical consistency as a touchstone for the truth, even if it means questioning the moral consistency with respect to the gods. Third, the Socratic method assumes a fundamental equality among human beings with respect to the possibility of self-knowledge.[24]

These elements were not incompatible with American liberal democracy. In regard to favoring natural explanation over divine ones, Jefferson frequently makes note of his consternation with Plato and his "misrepresentations" of Socrates. Jefferson said that Plato's dialogs were "in truth" "libels on Socrates,"[25] meaning that Plato had attributed to Socrates a transcendent meaning to his investigations that were at the least misleading. Jefferson saw the philosopher in hindsight as a proponent of secular rationalism: the Socratic method was not merely an aid to philosophical wisdom; the method itself was primary. Woodruff has explained that primacy as "Socrates accepted a belief-system that is defined under the *elenchus*."[26] The truth is what is left behind after the method: Socrates accepts only "what is left of traditional beliefs after *elenchus*."[27]

The Socratic emphasis on the equal human capacity for self-knowledge is also clearly compatible with both Jefferson and Franklin's democratic educational vision. In the *Gorgias* (508d–509a), for example, Socrates takes the position that each individual has the intellectual capacity to make a good judgment on basic human questions. Most individuals are capable of self-knowledge, and therefore, good judgment, if the process by which they arrive at knowledge is sound. Practical wisdom is the result not of rote learning, but conversation, dialectic, and with the guidance or under the pressure of a Socratic questioner.

Yet it is easy to overlook the profound difficulties of a true recovery of Socrates' method of disputation in democratic America. As applied to moral questions, the method encourages doubt, if not skepticism or incredulity. In the context of republican government, the method can produce distrust in tradition, such as Socrates' critique of the goodness of democracy (*Apology*, 29d; *Protagoras*, 319d) or the greatness of political or military heroes (*Gorgias*, 514a). Considering justice, Socrates' relentless probing leads to confusion or suspicion. In relation to the gods, the method aims at hypothesis elimination – but with no promise or guarantee that any better hypothesis will be found.

The problem of the Socratic method, in other words, is not limited only to pedagogical means and aims; it touches on the greatest questions of politics and of being. It is this recognition that is the basis of the worst accusations of Socrates – that he was good only at confounding his enemies, or that he would say anything to win an argument, or that he was guilty of introducing new gods or corrupting the youth. The trial of Socrates is an example of the stakes involved, a point often lost on modern educators. That is, Socrates viewed his method as inseparable from a life of philosophy, and that life he considered to be worthy of great sacrifice, even death. The city's laws, in short, have no real claim over his inquiring way of life. Socrates will "obey the god" rather than the city. There will be no end to his criticism, even of the best men of Athens. Socrates will accost the worthiest citizens, even those who do not want to talk to him. The Socratic method, in other words, has no city. He will examine, test, and "rebuke," both the young and old, citizen and stranger, whoever he happens to meet (30a–c). In its purest form, the Socratic method does no service to the city, except insofar as it is a service to the truth. Socrates will die for this way of living, even if he is to "die for it many times over" (30c).

Conclusion

This chapter has argued that the Socratic method underwent subtle transformations during the early national period of American education (1776–1840). The above summary is not meant to demonstrate causation or influence. It is meant only to raise a few questions about the role played by the touchstone Socratic method in leading students to self-knowledge in the colleges and universities today. Franklin found the Socratic method to be valuable, but with two important qualifications: that it be tempered by politeness and sociability, especially in the context of theological or religious debate. Second, that the goal or aim of questioning not interfere with the larger commercial or economic self-sufficiency of the developing colonies. Democratic republicans like Jefferson went further and suggested a deeper transformation. Socrates, in Jefferson's view, had been ruined by Plato. The true Socrates was closer to the "Rural Socrates," whose way of life was better understood through a careful reading of Xenophon. Through Xenophon, Socrates' strange manner of teaching could be made safe for democracy by making Socrates into a good citizen.

The examples of Franklin and Jefferson are illustrative, insofar as they underline or deepen the problem of using Socrates' method in the classroom. In the long view, Franklin's and Jefferson's attempts at revising the legacy of Socrates' teaching method can be considered relatively minor. But these early attempts at alteration prefigure a more profound change to the Socratic method in the twentieth century. Today, pedagogic debate regarding the value of the Socratic method for the classroom tends to focus less on the problem of sociability (Franklin) or democratic virtue (Jefferson). Increasingly, the discussion centers on the compatibility of the Socratic method with personal comfort and classroom engagement. Perhaps this is not a bad thing. But it is worth talking about what is lost when the original Socratic quest for self-knowledge is replaced with a classroom "technique" for encouraging creative thinking and individual self-expression.

Notes

1 According to Schneider, these discussions were often of a superficial and casual nature. See Jack Schneider, "Remembrance of Things Past: A History of the Socratic Method in the United States," *Curriculum Inquiry* 43/5 (2013): 616.
2 In Schneider, "Remembrance," 616.
3 *Ibid.*
4 *Ibid.*
5 He added that the average American intellectual was (unlike the European intellectual elite) not philosophically minded. Or more accurately, she was not indoctrinated in to any one particular philosophical school. Americans, Tocqueville noted, "have no philosophical school of their own, and they worry very little about all those that divide Europe; they hardly know their names." Alexis de Tocqueville, *Democracy in America*, Harvey C. Mansfield and Delba Winthrop, trans. (Chicago: University of Chicago Press, 2000): II 1.3, 403.
6 Tocqueville, *Democracy in America*, II, 525–6.
7 Quoted in Schneider, "Remembrance," 616.
8 See Ralph Ketchum, ed. *The Political Thought of Benjamin Franklin* (Indianapolis: Hackett Publishing, 2003), 54–57.
9 History, likewise, should not focus on the utility and beauty of "Virtue of all Kinds." It should encourage oratory, political leadership, and it should instill in Americans an appreciation for the "Necessity of a *Publick Religion*" and the "Excellency of the Christian Religion above all other ancient or modern."
10 This led to a study of Xenophon's *Memorable Thoughts of Socrates*.

11 For interest, see Steven C. Bullock, "What Ben Franklin Could Teach Us about Civility and Politics," *The Wall Street Journal,* November 7, 2016. www.wsj.com/articles/what-ben-franklin-could-teach-us-about-civility-and-politics-1478564982.
12 To put this more sharply, the utility of the Socratic method in America, one could say, is in its preserving sociability and politeness while having difficult conversations about religion. The ideal form of Socratic style is one of ironic modesty, the kind used by Socrates in *Euthydemus*.
13 For a comparison, see Lorraine Smith Pangle, "Ben Franklin and Socrates," in *Benjamin Franklin's Intellectual World*, Paul E. Kerry and Matthew S. Holland, eds. (Madison: Fairleigh Dickinson University Press, 2014).
14 Temperance, for example, would not require debate or dialectical scrutiny. Its ambiguity would be defined away by the philosopher Franklin in advance. Temperance is: "Eat not to dullness; drink not to elevation." It does not mean, and does not need to include, the moderating of "every other pleasure, appetite, inclination, or passion."
15 Which Socrates had argued was the source of his humility.
16 Temperance, for example, notoriously hard to define in Plato's *Charmides*, means "Eat not to Dulness. Drink not to Elevation." Justice, the central theme of Plato's second longest dialogic masterpiece, requires memorizing a fairly simple rule of thumb: "Wrong none, by doing Injuries or omitting the Benefits that are your Duty." How does one know if one is virtuous? Franklin recommends everyone to ask two questions every day. In the morning: What good shall I do this day? In the evening: What good have I done today?
17 Jerry Weinberger, *Benjamin Franklin Unmasked: On the Unity of his Moral, Religious and Political Thought* (Lawrence, KS: University Press of Kansas, 2008), 16–42.
18 This is not to say that Franklin did not value formal education (e.g., Franklin's plan for an English-language grammar school).
19 "From Thomas Jefferson to John Trumbull, 30 August 1787," *Founders Online*, National Archives, last modified June 29, 2017, http://founders.archives.gov/documents/Jefferson/01-12-02-0076. [Original source: Julian P. Boyd, ed. *The Papers of Thomas Jefferson, vol. 12, 7 August 1787–31 March 1788*, (Princeton: Princeton University Press, 1955), 69.]
20 Paul Johnstone, "The Rural Socrates," *Journal of the History of Ideas*, 5/2 (April 1944): 151–175.
21 In Thomas Jefferson, *Writings*, Merrill D. Peterson, ed. (New York: Library of America, 2011), 1431.
22 The scholarly opinion of Jefferson in relation to education is summarized by Merrill D. Peterson, who noted that public education was "the backbone of Jefferson's republic." The importance of public education to Jefferson's vision is clear: from the transfer of the College of Geneva, to the Constitutional amendment for public education funding, to Jefferson's work to establish a library, and a national curriculum, to his accomplishment as "father of the University of Virginia." Darren Staloff, "The Politics of Pedagogy: Thomas Jefferson and the Education of a Democratic Citizenry," in *The Cambridge Companion to Thomas Jefferson*, Frank Shuffleton, ed. (Cambridge: Cambridge University Press, 2009), 127.
23 See Paul Woodruff, "Socrates and the New Learning" in *The Cambridge Companion to Socrates,* Donald R. Morrison, ed. (Cambridge: Cambridge University Press, 2011), 95.
24 Woodruff, "Socrates," 96.
25 To John Adams, in Jefferson, *Writings*, 1342.
26 Woodruff, "Socrates," 103.
27 What this means is that Socrates could only believe a subset of what is commonly believed to be true about the gods given a particular view of the gods, specifically, the gods "as moral exemplars." A "Socratic method" approach to religious truth is entirely consistent with Jefferson's thoughts on education. Indeed, this is the program outlined in the above letter to John Vaughan, where Jefferson describes his project for a fundamental rewriting of the Christian Bible.

Bibliography

Bullock, Steven C. November 7, 2016. "What Ben Franklin Could Teach Us about Civility and Politics." *The Wall Street Journal*. www.wsj.com/articles/what-ben-franklin-could-teach-us-about-civility-and-politics-1478564982.
Jefferson, Thomas. 1787. "From Thomas Jefferson to John Trumbull, 30 August 1787." *Founders Online*, National Archives, last modified June 29, 2017, http://founders.archives.gov/documents/Jefferson/01-12-02-0076. [Original source: Boyd, Julian P. ed. 1955. *The Papers of Thomas Jefferson, vol. 12, 7 August 1787–31 March 1788*. Princeton: Princeton University Press].
Jefferson, Thomas. 2011. *Writings*. Merrill D. Peterson ed. New York: Library of America.
Johnstone, Paul. 1944. "The Rural Socrates." *Journal of the History of Ideas* 5/2: 151–75.

Ketchum, Ralph ed. 2003. *The Political Thought of Benjamin Franklin*. Indianapolis: Hackett Publishing.

Pangle, Lorraine S. 2014. "Ben Franklin and Socrates." In *Benjamin Franklin's Intellectual World*. Paul E. Kerry and Matthew S. Holland eds. Madison, NJ: Fairleigh Dickinson University Press: 137–52.

Schneider, Jack. 2013. "Remembrance of Things Past: A History of the Socratic Method in the United States." *Curriculum Inquiry* 43/5: 613–40.

Staloff, Darren. 2009. "The Politics of Pedagogy: Thomas Jefferson and the Education of a Democratic Citizenry." In *The Cambridge Companion to Thomas Jefferson*. Frank Shuffleton ed. Cambridge: Cambridge University Press: 127–142.

Tocqueville, Alexis de. 2000. *Democracy in America*, Harvey C. Mansfield and Delba Winthrop trans. Chicago: University of Chicago Press.

Weinberger, Jerry. 2008. *Benjamin Franklin Unmasked: On the Unity of his Moral, Religious and Political Thought*. Lawrence: University Press of Kansas.

Woodruff, Paul. 2011. "Socrates and the New Learning." In *The Cambridge Companion to Socrates*. Donald R. Morrison ed. Cambridge: Cambridge University Press: 91–110.

7 The Socratic Method and John Dewey

David W. Livingstone

In the wake of Ernest Boyer's work in the 1990s on scholarship in the academy, the scholarship of teaching and learning has grown from a small cottage industry of interested faculty members into a thriving industry embedded in the administrative structure of higher education.[1] Centers for teaching and learning have sprouted on many campuses, offering teaching support, mentoring, and workshops to professors, especially for new faculties. They frequently draw upon scholars and scholarship trends that originate in faculties of education. This appears to be reasonable enough: who better to turn to for teaching advice than to curriculum and pedagogy experts who teach our public school teachers and sometimes serve as education policy advisors to governments?

Yet, the infusion into universities of education theories popular in the K-12 world should raise questions, particularly for the discipline of political science.[2] Faculties of education have weathered criticism in the past for their overreliance upon education theories that can be traced to the influential work of John Dewey.[3] In Canada, these criticisms along with the battle over progressive reforms in public schools go back at least to the early 1950s. Critics lament the effect these theories will have on political culture, tying the discussion of instructional method to worries about potential regime changes. Indeed, there is some basis for this concern. Dewey was clear that his educational reforms were intended to advance a particular model of democracy: egalitarian, historicist, pragmatist, and progressive. The intention now, at least as far as some influential reformers are concerned, is to push the changes that have swept through the public school systems into universities and colleges.[4] And while Dewey's theories, which university faculties are being encouraged to adopt, are sometimes presented in a glossier package called twenty-first-century education, their intellectual parentage is still evident.

Political science can trace its origins to another educational pioneer, Socrates, who employed a method of learning with only superficial similarities to twenty-first-century education phrases like inquiry-based learning or even student directed learning (SDL). The Socratic method, at least as exemplified in Plato's *Republic*, differs from Dewey's prescriptions in terms of what it tells us about knowledge, political life, and democracy. If the assumption of university centers of teaching and learning – and the university administrators who support them – is that teaching methods have little bearing on what is being taught to students, this would be inconsistent with how both John Dewey and Socrates regarded the matter. Both were clear: pedagogy presumes prior epistemological and metaphysical commitments, and the character of those commitments entail radically different consequences for both individuals and society. Therefore, political scientists ought to guard against surrendering its authority with respect to teaching and learning, and not be too quick to outsource this "expertise" to those who are not deeply familiar with the Socratic method or abandon the Socratic method for something that merely resembles it. The Socratic method is not simply a technique that can be abstracted from its original context and applied anywhere we would like. Political scientists above all should be cautious about jumping on the SoTL (scholarship of teaching and learning) bandwagon insofar as it entails having to embrace twenty-first-century education pedagogy.

First, it is worth clarifying what is meant by the phrase "twenty-first-century education." A report issued in 2009 by the Education Directorate of the OECD states:

> Developments in society and economy require that educational systems equip young people with new skills and competencies, which allow them to benefit from the emerging new forms of socialization and to contribute actively to economic development under a system where the main asset is knowledge. These skills and competencies are often referred to as 21st century skills and competencies, to indicate that they are more related to the needs of the emerging models of economic and social development than with those of the past century, which were suited to an industrial mode of production.[5]

Learning conditions have so significantly changed in the twenty-first century, the argument goes, that the education systems built in the twentieth century are no longer adequate to meet the contemporary learner's needs. Noticeably the learners and their natural needs – needs and potentials that may remain fairly consistent across generations – should not guide educational policy and pedagogy. Rather, the OECD report assumes that when external conditions change, so too must the entire project of education, including its ends and goals.

The OECD report also implies that one of the most relevant changes in this century is the widespread acknowledgment among educational theorists that knowledge is constructed. According to Krahenbuhl:

> The philosophy of constructivist pedagogy has dominated the fields of teaching and learning for nearly the entire twenty-first century.... Constructivism ... is an epistemological view of knowledge that argues knowledge is derived in a meaning-making process through which learners construct individual interpretations of their experiences and thus, construct meaning in their minds. This is considered opposed to objectivism which suggests that truth exists independently of the learner and is transferred when encountered in a meaningful way.[6]

Several Canadian provincial governments, such as those in Alberta and British Columbia (BC), have adopted the language of twenty-first-century education at the policy level and are implementing the new curricula to bring their school systems into line with the OECD report. BC's Ministry of Education website, for example, alerts parents that schools will now begin to place less emphasis on learning facts and greater emphasis on high order conceptual learning. It will encourage students to pursue their passions by developing personal learning initiatives: "The deep understanding and application of knowledge is at the center of the new model, as opposed to the memory and recall of facts that previously shaped education around the globe for many decades."[7] Alberta's "transformative" education plan was introduced in 2010.[8] These twenty-first-century approaches to education have several names: "discovery-learning" or "independent inquiry" or even "experiential learning," though they often seem to be interchangeable, or at minimum, they flow from the same perspective about knowledge as a "meaning-making" rather than truth-discovering endeavor.[9]

Along with the claim that knowledge is widely regarded as a sociocultural creation, at least as far as educational thought leaders are concerned, it is sometimes added that the sheer pace of economic and technical change demands this new approach to education. Whereas schools are reportedly still adhering to a model of education the foundations for which were laid at the end of the nineteenth century, businesses today are demanding skills and competencies that will prepare students to enter into the new knowledge economy: "The task is not to do better now what we set out to do then: it is to rethink the purposes, methods and scale of education in our new circumstances."[10] According to its advocates, the new education is similar to the old education in one important respect, however: both are, or ought to be, preoccupied with training students to become productive participants in the economy. As the material modes of economic production change, one might say, so too must society's superstructure in light of those historical shifts. Education reformer, Michael Fullan, suggests "It is no exaggeration to say that the new pedagogies have the potential to support a fundamental transformation in human evolution. The result is that action, reflection, learning and living can now become one and the same."[11] The emphasis is on novelty and change. Much less attention, however, is paid to skills or competencies the earlier form of education may have encouraged, and whether some of those are worth preserving, or whether the new form of education places any of those prior goals – however they may be categorized – in jeopardy.

There seems to be little regard in the OECD report, for example, for the pursuit of wisdom or learning for its own sake. Occasionally the twenty-first-century education model promises to foster "deeper learning," facilitated by deprioritizing the memorization of mere facts and by pulling away from "passive reading."[12] To that end, teaching strategies based on constructivist ideas usually promote students' active engagement in learning and in the construction of knowledge. John Dewey, the pioneer and first serious advocate of discovery-learning in public schools, asserts that "The [ideal] teacher operates not as a magistrate set on high and marked by arbitrary authority."[13] Modern reformers pick up where Dewey left off. Carao, Lenkeit, and Kyriakides conclude in 2012 that "Student-oriented instruction for example promotes activating and cooperative learning environments through discussions between students and the teacher, as well as among students themselves."[14] The teacher's role is therefore to support the processes that are necessary for the student to construct knowledge.

By emphasizing the socio-constructivist idea of education, however, one devalues the role of teacher as expert knower and changes the students' self-perception as learners. Classroom hierarchies are flattened, which promotes greater equality between the students and teacher, a consequence consistent with Dewey's insistence that pedagogies promote egalitarian democratic citizens. In fact, Dewey intended to bring about this egalitarianism by undermining what he felt was an aristocratic elitism based on "book learning."[15] "Sharing in actual pursuit, whether directly or vicariously in play, is at least personal and vital.... Formal instruction, on the contrary, easily becomes remote and dead – abstract and bookish, to use the ordinary words of depreciation." Steel notes that a teacher competent in their discipline is regarded as outmoded these days. Ironically, the refrain that we are living in the knowledge-based society renders the teacher's knowledge superfluous.[16] Teachers, we are told, must focus more on developing learning competencies than on imparting knowledge. Thus the assumption that teaching methods are one thing and subject expertise – that university centers for teaching and learning are merely helping departments convey their content more effectively – begins to collapse under social constructivism's assumptions concerning truth, because the method now replaces the content.

Malcolmson, Myers, and O'Connell note the curious fact that this argument concerning the flattening of classroom hierarchies affects professors in the humanities and social sciences more than those in the so-called STEM fields (science, technology, engineering, math): "it is interesting that people never argue that it is unacceptably elitist for a professor of mathematics or engineering to have a preeminent role in math or engineering class."[17] The superior knowledge and technical expertise of STEM instructors is not in doubt: "Obviously, the assumption is that Ph.D.s in arts cannot make the same claim to expertise that Ph.D.s in mathematics can. In other words, the call for a non-hierarchical arts classroom is based on the premises of value relativism."

Former Dean of the Yale Law School, Anthony Kronman, points to further repercussions of the constructivist assumptions for university students: they learn, either directly or indirectly, that nothing has an independent "essence" or "nature," and thus there is no human nature *per se*. Who and what we are is simply a product of social construction. "Constructivism," Kronman notes, "further insists that this activity of meaning-making receives its motive and direction from a desire to assert power and control over someone or something (oneself, others, or the world)." And the purpose of education is "to expose these motives." Moreover, "it also asserts that there can be no criteria for ranking the relative worth of the meanings that human beings make or the desires that drive them to do so" because each meaning is equally an outgrowth of the same basic element: power.[18]

This idea may be motivated by a sincere desire for advancing equality and by a genuine concern for society's unfairly marginalized groups, yet it has the unintended consequence of making rational debate and compromise meaningless. If students are convinced they are merely "representatives" of a marginalized group, and opinions – including the instructor's – are merely covert assertions of power, then there is little reason for students to be moderate when advancing their own opinions or the interests of whichever group or sub-group with which they identify. Students will no longer come to class as individuals thirsty for new and foreign insights into the meaning of life, they will come as delegates.

> The more a classroom resembles a gathering of delegates speaking on behalf of the groups they represent, the less congenial a place it becomes in which to explore questions of a personally meaningful kind including, above all, the question of what ultimately matters in life and why. In such classrooms, students encounter each other not as individuals but as spokespersons instead.[19]

Kronman's analysis may help explain why students on some North American campuses have become increasingly less tolerant of academic freedom and free speech, more willing to shout down rather than listen respectfully to invited speakers with whom they disagree, and why a proportion of them are becoming *less* fit for life in a democratic republic or parliamentary democracy.[20]

In addition, there is evidence that the new strategies modeled on twenty-first-century education theory are less effective than are traditional strategies when it comes to developing deep learning. Psychologists Kirschner, Sweller, and Clark's analysis of discovery-learning concludes that,

> although unguided or minimally guided instructional approaches are very popular and intuitively appealing, the point is made that these approaches ignore both our cognitive architecture and evidence from empirical studies over the past half-century that consistently indicate that minimally guided instruction is less effective and less efficient than instructional approaches that place a strong emphasis on guidance of the student learning process.[21]

Minimal guidance learning overloads the student's short-term cognitive functions and frustrates the development of conceptual skills and deep learning. "Everything we see, hear, and think about is critically dependent on and influenced by our long-term memory."[22] It does the learner little good if the information they need to build upon is stored on Google servers rather than in their own memory. They cannot merely "look" up the facts that form the schema into which the new facts they are learning must be fitted. "Minimally guided instruction," these authors conclude, "appears to proceed with no reference to the characteristics of working memory, long-term memory, or the intricate relations between them."[23]

And work done over the last thirty years by E.D. Hirsch and the Core Knowledge initiative supports these findings:

> The central insight of Core Knowledge is the scientific finding that language comprehension requires a mountain of unseen shared knowledge that is not spoken – a kind of dark energy that governs verbal comprehension. The schools' neglect of this hidden knowledge has depressed language competence and perpetuated inequality.[24]

A sizable portion of the knowledge a student requires in order to develop deep learning must already be available in the form of stored information – facts and dates, for example – in long-term memory rather than information that is stored in an external source, like an internet database.

Perhaps more concerning is the fact that, as Kirschner *et al.* point out, the empirical data demonstrating that discovery-learning is ineffective appears to have little persuasive power over educational experts and policy advisors who continue to promote these strategies.

> In each decade since the mid-1950s, when empirical studies provided solid evidence that the then popular unguided approach did not work, a similar approach popped up under a different name with the cycle then repeating itself. Each new set of advocates for unguided approaches seemed either unaware of *or uninterested* in previous evidence that unguided approaches had not been validated.[25]

Stokke illustrates this phenomenon: when education officials in the province of Alberta recently faced criticism over the discovery-learning method they introduced into the math programs, they simply changed the name but maintained the same methodologies: "education officials argued that Alberta Education was actually promoting inquiry-based learning" not "discovery-learning."[26] Christodoulou reports she "was shocked to stumble across an entire field of educational and scientific research which completely disproved so many of the theories I had been taught when training and teaching. I was not just shocked; I was angry."

Neatby detected the same tendencies toward group-think among education policymakers in the 1950s. She complained that the career educator can become "a specialist in 'education' without ever having been subjected to a liberal education."[27] In Canada, at least, the educational experts essentially have a monopoly on education training and curriculum development. So every prospective teacher in Canada and a great many in the United States will wander "for some time in the Dewey maze," and it is only by a stroke of good luck that they will ever hear a serious critique of progressivism or be compelled to think through any alternative teaching philosophies.[28] Yet these are frequently the same sources for the pedagogies promoted by teaching and learning centers on university campuses.

So what about the Socratic method? How does it compare to discovery-learning and inquiry-based learning? Insofar as what is meant by this method is that an instructor conducts their teaching through questioning and answering, i.e., dialog, with the students in small seminar settings, does this method not derive much of its strength from the sorts of theories that underlie the progressive methodologies? By eliciting responses from the students rather than lecturing to them, the method's practitioners seem to share the view that memorizing "mere facts" is not the point of education. In the *Republic,* Socrates famously advises Glaucon that no forced learning abides in the soul.[29] And contemporary scholar Martha Nussbaum states that "Undoubtedly the most influential and theoretically distinguished American *practitioner of Socratic education*, John Dewey (1869–1952), changed the way virtually all American schools understand their task" (emphasis added).[30]

Yet Malcolmson, Myers, and O'Connell maintain that the identification of Dewey-esque discovery-learning or inquiry-learning with the Socratic method is misleading. The Socratic method often promoted or even used in the contemporary university has only superficial similarities to the genuine article. Socrates referred to his educational activity as dialectic through which Socrates would "lead people to the discovery of their own ignorance, that they did not know what they thought they knew."[31] And whereas Socrates often refused to state exactly what he thought the right answer to any particular question was, he "always had a very clear idea of what his students needed to give more thought to."[32] Because Socrates had already given more thought to the question than they had he was in a superior position to lead the discussions. He had at least determined more adequately than they what the genuinely important questions are. This in itself is not discountable knowledge. Indeed, it may even be an example of trans-historical knowledge that in its timelessness undermines the historicist claims that lie at the root of much of the progressive and constructivist pedagogies.[33]

Moreover, whereas the emphasis is rightly placed on dialog, Socrates did not eschew book reading. In fact, in a lovely and oft quoted passage from Xenophon's *Memorabilia*, Socrates points out that a favorite and profitable activity for him and his friends is to comb through books and discuss them together, divining their meaning and taking from them what grains of truth and wisdom they might have to offer.[34] The shared text, particularly if it is a profound one, can provide the necessary starting point for the discussion between teacher and student, provided it is read with care and attention. Yet, according to Dewey,

> every advance in the influence of the experimental method is sure to aid in *outlawing the literary, dialectic*, and authoritative methods of forming beliefs which have governed the schools of the past, and to transfer their prestige to methods which will procure an active concern with things and persons, directed by aims of increasing temporal reach and deploying greater range of things in space.[35]

And

> adherence to the culture of the past ... generates a reminiscent social spirit, for this makes an individual feel more at home in the life of other days than in his own. A professedly cultural education is peculiarly exposed to this danger.

Dewey's approach, by contrast, is intended to embed the student thoroughly in the current, changing social world in which they happen to find themselves, not to put them in a position where pesky authors and books from the past might raise uncomfortable questions in the reader's mind about the wisdom (or lack of wisdom) of the emergent and the present. Dewey's goal is to socialize the learner so they can conform to the present. The point is to produce not a thinker in the Socratic mode but "a character which not only does the particular deed socially necessary but one which is interested in that continuous readjustment which is essential to [continuous] growth."[36]

As far as Neatby is concerned, this will not develop the attributes long understood as essential in the souls of a self-governing and free citizen. "Book learning reminds [Dewey] of the 'aristocrat' who did not work with their hands; and instruction directly imparted from teacher to pupil is, it seems, a denial of democratic equalitarianism." The result, Neatby argues, is that Dewey and his disciples who advocate "discovery-learning" in public school curricula are positively anti-intellectual.

> They are spreading "education for democracy" at the expense of the best liberal traditions of education. In their desire to "teach" democracy and social morality they have quite forgotten that both must be founded on a true liberation of the mind.[37]

Dewey's method – far from being either neutral or innocuous – is antithetical to the development of the characteristics and knowledge required by citizens of a free society. And to repeat, Dewey's methods are generally acknowledged to be largely at the heart of both the K-12 and the higher education reforms that go by the name of twenty-first-century education.

Of course the single biggest difference between the Socratic method and progressive reforms is how they divide on the question of the status of truth and being. "Knowledge," Socrates claims in the *Republic*, "is presumably dependent on what is, to know of what is, that it is and how it is." Whereas "Opinion is a different power and must rest on something different." Opinion cannot rest on non-being, not entirely at any rate, for, as Socrates observes, the one who opines opines *something*. Opinion is situated between knowledge (resting on stable being) and ignorance (resting on non-being). Opinion is dependent upon what is between these two: the realm of becoming (*Republic*, 477c–478d). The pragmatists, insofar as they insist that students must be engaged with real-world problems, and who assume that there is no stable knowledge – only ever-changing socially constructed knowledge – would confine the learner's attention to the realm of opinion.

Socrates also argues that political society "in its education and want of education" can aptly be compared to a cave in which prisoners are shown shadows that are believed by the cave's denizens to represent the truth of things. In fact, these changing, flickering shadows are merely the basis of opinions (*doxa*). But because this is all the cave prisoners have ever experienced, and because everyone else in the cave repeats the same things in conversation, they are prevented from realizing the limitations of their "knowledge." Those who are most adept at describing and predicting which images will follow are hailed by their peers as expert knowers. From the Socratic perspective, the pragmatist – by privileging practical learning, assigning readings that mirror back only current opinions, by cutting off access to great authors from the past, and denying Being (replacing it with endless historical change) – simply condemns the student to live within the environs of the cave and to accept *uncritically* the dogma broadcast on the cave walls. The immersion into the actual, into the realm of flux and becoming, is merely the consequence of denying the significance of universal norms.[38] This is why Neatby called Dewey's approach to education "totalitarian" and called attention to the fact that it is incompatible with responsible self-government properly understood.

Dewey's understanding of the future of democracy, and the education he proposes as the suitable pathway to its realization, is much closer to the democracy criticized by Socrates in Book Eight of *Republic*. Democratic man, and the soul after whom the democratic regime is patterned, denies that there are stable truths, particularly about moral questions. Such a man living in democracy, explains Socrates,

> doesn't admit true speech or let it pass into the guardhouse, if someone says that there are some pleasures belonging to fine and good desires and some belonging to bad desires, and that the ones must be practiced and honored and the others checked and enslaved. Rather, he shakes his head at all this and says that all are alike and must be honored on an equal basis. (*Republic*, 561c)

From the Socratic perspective, Dewey simply fastens on to one of the most predictable, self-destructive, and least attractive features of untutored democracy and makes this the goal of his educational endeavors. Moreover, as we have seen, there is nothing particularly "new" or twenty-first century about this approach: it was already pointed to by Socrates some 2,500 years ago as the typical and not particularly well thought out response that a sophist in a democracy is likely to give to the question of how to educate its citizens. For the genuine health of the citizens and their souls, Socrates always found it best to try to resist this approach that Dewey hails. Yet Socrates also knew that the citizens of a democracy are always more inclined to hear the siren song of "progress" and "egalitarianism" and be less likely to see that these can ultimately be fatal to deeper principles that underlie the way of life and the freedom they enjoy.

For Dewey, however, the Socratic emphasis on Being over becoming is a non-starter. The new situation we find ourselves in is the result of Charles Darwin's insights, which, he believes, compel us to alter our definition of knowledge:

> The development of biology clinches this lesson, with its discovery of evolution. For the philosophic significance of the doctrine of evolution lies precisely in its emphasis upon continuity of simpler and more complex organic forms until we reach man. The development of organic forms begins with structures where the adjustment of environment and organism is obvious, and where anything which can be called mind is at a minimum.[39]

As a result, Dewey places his hopes in scientific positivism:

> The development of the experimental method as the method of getting knowledge and of making sure it is knowledge, and not mere opinion – the method of both discovery and proof – is the remaining great force in bringing about a transformation in the theory of knowledge. The experimental method has two sides. (i) On one hand, it means that we have no right to call anything knowledge except where our activity has actually produced certain physical changes in things, which agree with and confirm the conception entertained.[40]

But from this it seems Dewey would need to conclude that there is no stable knowledge available: everything is in flux. This, in turn, would seem to bring Dewey's thought in line with postmodernism, which is skeptical about the value of truth and knowledge. Yet in a review of Dewey's education and its impact on democracy, Fott concludes instead that Dewey has been misappropriated by later postmodern pragmatists, such as Rorty, for whom, following Nietzsche, truth is little more than a "mobile army of metaphors." By contrast, Fott points out that Dewey, unlike Rorty, still speaks about the value of knowledge – scientific and experimental knowledge.[41] Dewey's error, Fott concludes, was only in that he did not attempt to ground his assertions about the reliability of experimental science as a source of knowledge.

Despite Fott's attempt to separate Dewey's conclusions from the destructive consequences of postmodernist philosophy, Dewey's perspective eventually undermines the foundation for truth. Dewey's perspective eventually unravels knowledge and renders it a social construction which, from a Socratic perspective, means it is not knowledge at all. Dewey maintains that knowledge is merely the result of successfully changing one's environment. In the spirit of the later pragmatists, knowledge is reducible to what works. It is a temporary product of the will and the imagination working within some minimal, given restraints, such as the basic laws of physics. Because the path to a transcendent realm of permanent ideas about good and bad is cut off, it stands to reason that moral standards must also arise out of our interactions with the world here and now.

But which interactions, which drives we choose to indulge or deploy here and now, are largely up to us to decide without reference to some permanent standard by which to assess their goodness. They can be judged only by the real-world standard of their effectiveness to change the present material and social conditions – a standard dangerously seductive for any democracy, because democracy always tends to prefer utility to truth (*Republic*, 527d–e).

> The effect upon the theory of knowing is to displace the notion that it is the activity of a mere onlooker or spectator of the world, the notion which goes with the idea of knowing as something complete in itself.[42]

Dewey's doctrine of organic development means that

> the living creature is a part of the world, sharing its vicissitudes and fortunes, and making itself secure in its precarious dependence only as it intellectually identifies itself with the things about it, and, forecasting the future consequences of what is going on, shapes its own activities accordingly.[43]

We can see here why modern education theories, following Dewey, cling to the view that knowledge is socially constructed. And because nature, according to this view, is at bottom flux and not stable Dewey recommends immersing the student in the flux of becoming; he cuts off any pretended ascent to the transcendent realm of Being that Socrates thought was essential. This explains why Dewey and modern progressive reformers insist students be immersed in the practical realties of everyday life and learn to manipulate these realities to bring about greater effects. This imperative gets translated in today's educational policies as an insistence that students be engaged foremost in "real-world" problems and in activities that resemble the work-world as closely as possible. If instead students are encouraged to read great literature that stimulates thoughts about the "good as such" or "the beautiful," they are, by implication, not engaged in anything having to do with the real world.

Yet this also entails that what human beings choose to make of the raw elements of nature, including their own nature, is guided by will, not knowledge of permanent ends of goals. Dewey's thought is a form of historicist thinking about which it has been said that "No objective criterion henceforth allowed the distinction between good and bad choices. Historicism culminated in nihilism." After all, why the will should have as its goal the emancipation of slaves as opposed to the enslavement of free peoples cannot be given an answer by historicism because it has dispensed with any rationally apprehensible idea of the good. And so, Strauss concludes, "The attempt to make man absolutely at home in this world ended in man's becoming absolutely homeless."[44]

Pragmatism like Dewey's is premised on a rather truncated view of human beings and the education best suited for them. This is what worried earlier critics like Neatby, as she argues,

> In practice, however, the [progressive] teacher and the curriculum are instruments in the hands of the administrator for conditioning children in an approved manner according to the listed "value" of "democracy" or occasionally of "social living" or of "effective living". Progressive education in Canada is not liberation; it is indoctrination both intellectual and moral.[45]

Dewey's over-emphasis upon social integration and practical problem-solving to the neglect of individual appreciation of knowledge for its own sake has the perverse but entirely predictable consequence of rendering students less fit for self-government.

Brann, reviewing Nussbaum's book *Not for Profit,* notes that Nussbaum appreciatively quotes from Dewey: Nussbaum "quotes him [Dewey] as saying that 'ideas . . . devolve for the sake of the better control of action.' This is a pragmatist's view," Brann observes,

> which is surely the opposite of Socrates', for whom dialectic first leads out of the world to a transcendent realm of ideas. And although knowledge of these ideas then leads back to good human action, it is, in the first instance, for the soul's health that we engage in inquiry; right action is the indirect, one might almost say, the unintended, consequence of thinking things through. Indeed, the old understanding of liberal education is that its very liberality consists in its being pursued for its own sake, free from practical purposes – and that this way also happens, blessedly, to make for the most prudent practicality.[46]

By removing objective truth from the equation, as progressive and constructivist or twenty-first-century education apparently asks us to do, we fall back on that from which Socrates sought always to distance his own activity: the *eristical* discussions and the rhetorical techniques of the sophists. *Eristical* discussion seeks only to win an argument, to carry the day. It is an assertion of will for the sake of scoring a victory rather than a shared pursuit of knowledge. As Steel reminds us about the Socratic tradition:

> Both Schall and Thomas help us to see that there is a necessary spiritual structure to teaching and learning. This means that education, contrary to what is most often said today among reformers, cannot properly be "student-," "child-," or "learner-centered"; it must be truth-centered. Consequently, its center must lie somewhere between the teacher and the learner. . . . There can be no genuine dialog between teacher and student where the center is not somewhere *between* the discussants – if *truth* rather than either of the participants is not the central concern of both parties.[47]

When the truth drops out of the relation, sophistry emerges, and a speaker or a student has no concern for the truth of what is said.

I do not believe that the Socratic approach necessarily commits those who would adopt it to a particular set of detailed metaphysical or cosmological claims. By questioning Dewey's methodologies from a Socratic perspective, we do not have to feel compelled to adopt something about which we, and Socrates, are not entirely certain.[48] Rejecting relativism does not compel us to become dogmatists. But it is clear that Socrates consistently strove to discern the truth, and so he acted in accordance with the expectation that it existed independently of our making and could be known rather than socially constructed. We recognize that we think about the things that are in the world. And as Socrates points out, some of those things we think about are not sensible objects, rather they are perceivable only by the mind. But the thinking of these objects did not bring those objects into being, and the availability of these objects for thought, while it may have stimulated our thinking right now, did not bring our capacity to think into being. Or as Schall pithily remarks, "We find intelligibility in the universe; we do not put it there."[49] There was, so Socrates maintained, sufficient evidence of such self-existing truth and being for the thoughtful and reflective person to take this perspective as a guiding principle of their life.

Between these alternative "methods" – Dewey's and Socrates' – the decision to try as best we can to embrace Socrates' "erotic skepticism," as it has sometimes been called, is more productive and more compatible with our responsibilities as political science professors entrusted with the dual purposes of liberally educating our pupils and educating them for their regime, recognizing our situation for what it is (and what it must be for every teacher): that we inhabit a less than ideal regime, though the one which, if it is decent and permits freedom of inquiry and the rule of law, deserves our principled support more than it need us to dissolve its roots using eristic sophistry or to replace it with misplaced hopes for a socially constructed utopia.

Notes

1. Ernest L. Boyer, "Scholarship Reconsidered: Priorities of the Professoriate," *Special Report for the Carnegie Foundation for the Advancement of Teaching* (Jossey-Bass, 1997).
2. Faculty teaching and learning centers (TLCs) often offer a variety of classroom teaching supports for faculties, including curriculum design and classroom organization strategies. Some of these are basic, practical, and useful, such as reminders to be clear with students about classroom expectations and grading scales. A consistent refrain of TLCs is the promotion of "active learning," or "experiential learning" – pedagogies associated with John Dewey's theories – and the downplaying of traditional teaching methods. For example, the LEAP Institute at the University of Wisconsin promotes "philosophies that are hallmarks of learner-centered instruction" (https://teachingacademy.wisc.edu/i-leap-2/); The University of South Florida's Academy for Teaching and Learning Excellence encourages "problem-based learning, project-based learning, team-based learning, and inquiry methods of instruction." These " . . . can be thought of as mirror images of traditional instruction." (www.usf.edu/atle/teaching/teaching-methods.aspx). Among the principles listed by Carleton University which ought to guide faculty teaching are the following: education should be "learner-centered," "experiential, active and collaborative," and "innovative." The University of North Carolina, Charlotte has an Active Learning Academy associated with its Center for Teaching and Learning. The Academy's goals are to promote "active learning" which "can be understood as instructional activities involving students 'doing' and 'thinking' about what they are doing." These are just a few examples which could be easily multiplied. The point being that university TLCs by and large promote Dewey's key concepts of "experiential learning," "active learning," or "discovery-learning," and these same phrases have migrated to campuses from K-12 curriculum development, where they have been deployed since at least the early 1950s.
3. Steven Olusegun Bada, "Constructivism Learning Theory: A Paradigm for Teaching and Learning," *IOSR Journal of Research & Method in Education* 5/6 (2015): 66. The "constructivist view of learning considers the learner as an active agent in the process of knowledge acquisition. Constructivist conceptions of learning have their historical roots in the work of Dewey (1929), Bruner (1961), Vygotsky (1962), and Piaget (1980)."
4. In a talk entitled "On Schools in Need of Re-Education," (TV Ontario, June 21, 2013), education consultant Michael Fullan claims that kids in school need to be "engaged" and "they won't stand to be bored any longer." Fullan also expressed his hope that "impatient" students will pressure faculties to change their teaching methods. He likens his approach to Machiavelli's introduction of "new modes and orders." Hence one of the stated objectives of progressive, public education reform is to change the university. Fullan's website indicates he is currently helping the state of California change its education system "across the entire system and at all of its levels" (http://michaelfullan.ca/).
5. K. Ananiadou and M. Claro, "21st Century Skills and Competences for New Millennium Learners in OECD Countries," *OECD Education Working Papers*, No. 41, OECD Publishing (2009), 5. The majority of the 17 countries surveyed by the OECD responded positively when asked if they have

implemented twenty-first-century education strategies in their public school system through government policies (12).
6. Kevin S. Krahenbuhl, "Student-Centered Education and Constructivism: Challenges, Concerns, and Clarity for Teachers," *The Clearing House: A Journal of Educational Strategies, Issues and Ideas* 89/3 (2016): 31.
7. Government of British Columbia, "BC's New Curriculum," https://curriculum.gov.bc.ca/curriculum-info, accessed January 17, 2017.
8. For a critical analysis of the Alberta plan, see Sean Steel, "Transformative Education? A Philosophic-Augustinian Response to the 2010 Albertan Reform Initiatives in 'Inspiring Education'," *Interchange* 43 (2012): 43–55.
9. Paul Kirschner, John Sweller and Richard E. Clark, "Why Minimal Guidance During Instruction Does Not Work: An Analysis of the Failure of Constructivist, Discovery, Problem-Based, Experiential, and Inquiry-based Teaching," *Educational Psychologist* 42/2 (2006): 75. See Anna Stokke, "What to do About Canada's Declining Math Scores," *Commentary no. 427*, (May 2015), C.D. Howe Institute, (4), and Daisy Christodoulou, *Seven Myths About Education* (London: The Curriculum Centre, 2013) where in Chapter Three Krahenbuhl points out that "Jamin Carson (2005) outlined the metaphysical and epistemological assumptions one must adhere to if accepting constructivist pedagogy," including the claim that "reality is dependent on the perceiver, and thus constructed." But, as Krahenbuhl observes, "*these assumptions are typically unstated and less often even considered* (emphasis added)" (3).
10. Ken Robinson, "All Our Futures: Creativity, Culture and Education," National Advisory Committee on Creative and Cultural Education [England], (1999), 14, quoted in Christodoulou, *Seven Myths About Education*, 48–9.
11. Michael Fullan and Geoff Scott, "New Pedagogies for Deep Learning Whitepaper," Seattle: Collaborative Impact SPC, July 2014, 3. "For the first time in history the mark of an educated person is that of a doer (a doer-thinker; a thinker-doer) – they learn to do, and do to learn. They are impatient with lack of action" 3.
12. Richard E. Mayer, "Should there be a Three Strikes Rule Against Pure Discovery Learning? The Case for Guided Methods of Instruction," *American Psychologist* 59/1 (2004): 14. "According to this interpretation, passive venues involving books, lectures, and online presentations are classified as non-constructivist teaching whereas active venues such as group discussions, hands-on activities, and interactive games are classified as constructivist teaching."
13. John Dewey, *Democracy and Education* (Paradigm Publishing, 2014 [Macmillan, 1916]). Kindle edition, 10.
14. Daniel H. Carao, Jenny Lenkeit and Leonidas Kyriakides, "Teaching Strategies and Differential Effectiveness Across Learning Contexts: Evidence from PISA 2012," *Studies in Educational Evaluation* 49 (2016): 31.
15. Dewey, *Democracy and Education*, 13. "When the acquiring of information and of technical intellectual skill do not influence the formation of a social disposition, ordinary vital experience fails to gain in meaning, while schooling, in so far, creates only 'sharps' in learning – that is, egoistic specialists."
16. Christodoulou, *Seven Myths*, 38.
17. Patrick Malcolmson, Richard Myers and Colin O'Connell, *Liberal Education and Value Relativism: A Guide to Today's BA* (Lanham: University Press of America, 1996), 56.
18. Anthony T. Kronman, *Educations' End: Why Our Colleges and Universities Have Given Up on the Meaning of Life* (New Haven: Yale University Press, 2007), 180–83.
19. *Ibid.*, 151.
20. Leon Craig argues, "the acceptance of this view undermines all confidence in the principles that have guided Western life for almost three millennia, while it precludes our discovering any that are better (denying as it does any rational basis for judging better or worse). The fact-value distinction represents nothing less than the rejection of reason as adequate for disclosing how one ought to live." Leon Craig, *The War Lover: A Study of Plato's Republic* (Toronto: University of Toronto Press, 1994), note 19: 329.
21. Paul Kirschner *et al.*, "Why Minimal Guidance," 75.
22. *Ibid.*, 76.
23. *Ibid.*, 76.
24. E.D. Hirsch Jr., "Sustaining the American Experiment," in *Knowledge at the Core: Don Hirsch. Core Knowledge, and the Future of the Common Core*, Chester E. Finn and Michael J. Petrilli, eds. (New York: Thomas Fordham Institute, 2014), 7.
25. Paul Kirschner *et al.*, "Why Minimal Guidance," 79. Emphasis added.
26. Anna Stokke, "What to Do About Canada's Declining Math Scores," *Commentary No.427*, (CD Howe Institute, May 2015), 4.
27. Hilda Neatby, *So Little for the Mind* (Toronto: Clarke Irwin and Company, 1953), 95.
28. *Ibid.*, 90.
29. Plato, *The Republic of Plato*, Allan Bloom, trans. (New York: Basic Books, 1968), 536e. All subsequent citations are in-text.

30 Martha C. Nussbaum, *Not for Profit: Why Democracy Needs the Humanities* (Princeton: Princeton University Press, 2010), 64.
31 Eva T.H. Brann criticizes Martha Nussbaum for not noticing a crucial difference between Dewey and Socrates: "The 'Socratic method' [as Nussbaum presents it]... incites students not so much to question-asking as to 'questioning'; thus it has in its very conception a subversive tone: ... [yet] Socrates inquired into people's notions so as to ground, not to subvert them, and he refuted more the thoughtlessness with which individuals hold their opinions than the beliefs by which communities live." "Liberalism and Liberal Education," a review of *Not for Profit: Why Democracy Needs the Humanities* by Martha Nussbaum (Imaginativeconservative.org); accessed September 14, 2016.
32 Malcolmson, Myers, and O'Connell, *Liberal Education and Value Relativism*, 55.
33 Leo Strauss, *Natural Right and History* (Chicago: University of Chicago Press, 1953): "If the fundamental problems persist in all historical change, human thought is capable of transcending its historical limitation or of grasping something trans-historical.... No more is needed to legitimize philosophy in its original, Socratic sense" (23–4, 32).
34 "Others have a fancy for a good horse or dog or bird: my fancy, stronger even than theirs, is for good friends. And I teach them all the good I can, and recommend them to others from whom I think they will get some moral benefit. And the treasures that the wise men of old have left us in their writings I open and explore with my friends. If we come on any good thing, we extract it, and we set much store on being useful to one another." Xenophon, *Xenophon in Seven Volumes*, E.C. Marchant, ed. (Cambridge: Loeb Classical Library and Harvard University Press, 1923). Accessed from www.perseus.tufts.edu, March 21, 2017.
35 Dewey, *Democracy and Education*, 366.
36 *Ibid.*, 388.
37 Neatby, *So Little for the Mind*, 24–5, 235.
38 Strauss, *Natural Right and History*, 15.
39 Dewey, *Democracy and Education*, 364–65.
40 *Ibid.*
41 David Fott, "John Dewey and the Mutual Influence of Democracy and Education," *The Review of Politics* 71 (2009): 7–19. "But his [Dewey's] failure to think more rigorously – more philosophically – about the relation between philosophy and science allowed Richard Rorty, his most famous recent spokesman, more plausibly to claim Dewey's thought for his own, postmodern ends than would otherwise have been possible" (19).
42 Dewey, *Democracy and Education*, 364.
43 *Ibid.*
44 Strauss, *Natural Right and History*, 18.
45 Neatby, *So Little for the Mind*, 41.
46 Brann, "Liberalism and Liberal Education."
47 Sean Steel, *The Pursuit of Wisdom and Happiness in Education: Historical Sources and Contemplative Practices* (Albany: SUNY Press, 2014), 136.
48 "To understand man in the light of the whole means for modern natural science to understand man in the light of the sub-human. But in that light man as man is wholly unintelligible. Classical political philosophy viewed man in a different light. It was originated by Socrates, and Socrates was so far from being committed to a specific cosmology that his knowledge was knowledge of ignorance." Leo Strauss, "What is Political Philosophy?" in *An Introduction to Political Philosophy: Ten Essays by Leo Strauss*, Hilail Gildin, ed. (Detroit: Wayne State University Press, 1989), 37–8.
49 James V. Schall, "The Universe We Know In," *Crisis Magazine*, September 21, 2012 (crisismagazine.com), accessed January 22, 2017.

Bibliography

Ananiadou, K. and M. Claro. 2009. "21st Century Skills and Competences for New Millennium Learners in OECD Countries." *OECD Education Working Papers*, No. 41. OECD Publishing.

Bada, Steven Olusegun. 2015. "Constructivism Learning Theory: A Paradigm for Teaching and Learning." *IOSR Journal of Research & Method in Education* 5/6: 66–70.

Boyer, Ernest L. 1997. "Scholarship Reconsidered: Priorities of the Professoriate." *Special Report for the Carnegie Foundation for the Advancement of Teaching*. Jossey-Bass.

Brann, Eva T.H. "Liberalism and Liberal Education." A review of *Not for Profit: Why Democracy Needs the Humanities* by Martha Nussbaum. Imaginativeconservative.org: accessed September 14, 2016.

Carao, Daniel H., Jenny Lenkeit and Leonidas Kyriakides. 2016. "Teaching Strategies and Differential Effectiveness Across Learning Contexts: Evidence from PISA 2012." *Studies in Educational Evaluation* 49: 30–41.

Christodoulou, Daisy. 2013. *Seven Myths About Education*. London: The Curriculum Centre.

Craig, Leon. 1994. *The War Lover: A Study of Plato's Republic*. Toronto: University of Toronto Press.

Dewey, John. 1916. *Democracy and Education*. New York: Macmillan Company. Reprint. Kindle edition. Paradigm Publishing, 2014.

Fott, David. 2009. "John Dewey and the Mutual Influence of Democracy and Education." *The Review of Politics* 71: 7–19.

Fullan, Michael and Geoff Scott. "On Schools in Need of Re-Education." TV Ontario, Pod Cast. June 21, 2013.

———. 2014. "New Pedagogies for Deep Learning Whitepaper." Seattle: Collaborative Impact SPC.

Government of British Columbia, "BC's New Curriculum": http://curriculum.gov.bc.ca/curriculum-info, accessed January 17, 2017.

Hirsch Jr., E.D. 2014 "Romancing the Child: Curing American Education of its Enduring Belief that Learning is Natural." In *Knowledge at the Core: Don Hirsch. Core Knowledge, and the Future of the Common Core*. Chester E. Finn and Michael J. Petrilli eds. New York: Thomas Fordham Institute: 15–21.

———. 2014. "Sustaining the American Experiment." In *Knowledge at the Core: Don Hirsch. Core Knowledge, and the Future of the Common Core*. Chester E. Finn and Michael J. Petrilli eds. New York: Thomas Fordham Institute: 7–14.

Kirschner, Paul, John Sweller and Richard E. Clark. 2006. "Why Minimal Guidance During Instruction Does Not Work: An Analysis of the Failure of Constructivist, Discovery, Problem-Based, Experiential, and Inquiry-Based Teaching." *Educational Psychologist* 42/2: 75–86.

Krahenbuhl, Kevin S. 2016. "Student-Centered Education and Constructivism: Challenges, Concerns, and Clarity for Teachers." *The Clearing House: A Journal of Educational Strategies, Issues and Ideas* 89: 97–105.

Kronman, Anthony T. 2007. *Educations' End: Why Our Colleges and Universities Have Given Up on the Meaning of Life*. New Haven: Yale University Press.

Malcolmson, Patrick, Richard Myers and Colin O'Connell. 1996. *Liberal Education and Value Relativism: A Guide to Today's BA*. Lanham: University Press of America.

Mayer, Richard E. 2004. "Should there be a Three Strikes Rule Against Pure Discovery Learning? The Case for Guided Methods of Instruction." *American Psychologist* 59: 14–19.

Neatby, Hilda. 1953. *So Little for the Mind* (2nd edition). Toronto: Clarke Irwin and Company.

Nussbaum, Martha C. 2010. *Not for Profit: Why Democracy Needs the Humanities*. Princeton: Princeton University Press.

Plato, *The Republic of Plato*. 1968. Allan Bloom trans. New York: Basic Books.

Schall, James V.S.J. 2012. "The Universe We Know In." *Crisis Magazine*. www.crisismagazine.com.

Steel, Sean. 2012. "Transformative Education? A Philosophic-Augustinian Response to the 2010 Albertan Reform Initiatives in 'Inspiring Education.'" *Interchange* 43: 43–55.

———. 2014. *The Pursuit of Wisdom and Happiness in Education: Historical Sources and Contemplative Practices*. Albany: SUNY Press.

Stokke, Anna. 2015. "What to do About Canada's Declining Math Scores." *Commentary no. 427*, C.D. Howe Institute.

Strauss, Leo. 1953. *Natural Right and History*. Chicago: University of Chicago Press.

———. 1989. "What is Political Philosophy?" In *An Introduction to Political Philosophy: Ten Essays by Leo Strauss*. Hilail Gildin ed. Detroit: Wayne State University Press: 3–58.

Xenophon. 1923. *Xenophon in Seven Volumes*. E.C. Marchant ed. Cambridge: Loeb Classical Library and Harvard University Press. Accessed March 21, 2017. www.perseus.tufts.edu.

8 The Courage of the Socratic Method

Jordon B. Barkalow[1]

The ongoing debate over what should be taught or emphasized in American higher education obfuscates a concern that is intimately connected to the question of what we should teach: how should we teach? We neglect this question at our peril as doing so undermines efforts to educate the entire person. If we fail to address it, we fail to satisfy the requirements of a liberal education and the consequences of this failure threaten the great experiment that is democratic government.

In its original sense, liberal education refers to practicing the virtue of liberality.[2] If ancient philosophers are to be believed, the object of a liberal education is the cultivation of a virtuous person who is capable of living freely.[3] The preoccupation with virtue and living a free and noble life should not be interpreted to mean that liberal education ignores skills. In fact, an educated person requires many of the skills emphasized in higher education today (reading, writing, counting, and reckoning). The difference between the contemporary emphasis on skills and liberal education's concern with virtue is that the former views skills as ends whereas the latter sees skills serving the higher purpose of cultivating persons capable of self-government.

This vision of liberal education stands in marked contrast to a dominant method of teaching in higher education today – student-centered learning. Defined as a broad teaching approach that encompasses replacing lectures with active learning, integrating self-paced learning programs and/or cooperative group situations, student-centered learning focuses on student needs, satisfaction, or skill development. This view is in need of revision as it incorrectly identifies skill development as the proper end of education. In its place, we should employ an understanding of Socratic student-centered learning. Like contemporary theories of student-centered learning, Socratic student-centered learning focuses on the individual and encourages students to be responsible for their own learning. Whereas contemporary theories give primacy to project development and completion, Socratic student-centered learning's emphasis on asking the right question, listening, and contradiction requires learners to reflect on one's own life through critical reflection. Thus, unlike contemporary theories, the Socratic version of student-centered learning focuses on developing good persons and citizens.

This argument is developed by first providing a critical review of contemporary theories of student-centered learning. This is followed by an overview of the three tenets of the Socratic method: 1) The emphasis on virtue in Socratic philosophy; 2) The method of Socratic education as refutation (*elenchus*); and 3) The form of Socratic philosophy as dialog. The third and fourth sections analyze these tenets through an analysis of Plato's *Laches* to demonstrate what Socratic student-centered learning looks like. The final section identifies a pedagogical practice (discussion boards) that instructors may use to facilitate the face-to-face interaction in class required by the Socratic method.

Contemporary Theories of Student-Centered Learning

On their surface, contemporary theories of student-centered learning appear to share a great deal with the Socratic method as both views reject the lecture as an appropriate mode of education.

Whereas lectures seek to transfer knowledge from teacher to student passively, student-centered learning employs interactive activities that allow learners to address their own learning interests and needs.[4] According to these theories, student needs consist of developing the "twenty-first century skills" desired by future employers.[5] The key to developing these skills is to require students to focus on projects having real-world implications.[6] As shown in the next section, differences regarding the question of what constitutes student needs distinguishes Socratic from contemporary student-centered learning.

To provide students with these skills, the classroom must be transformed into a dynamic learning environment where students can clearly see the connection(s) between what they learn and their personal experiences. The keys to transforming the classroom can be identified by looking at the four core values of student-centered learning.[7] First, learners define their own meaning. Unlike the traditional classroom where meaning is externally defined, the first value of student-centered learning places the responsibility for constructing meaning on the student.[8] Working with the instructor to set goals and objectives, learners ultimately determine how to proceed on a project that focuses on a single topic based on an assessment of their individual needs and questions.

Second, the focus on a single, iterative project requires scaffolding: the process of managing inquiry through structures and guidance that are embedded in the learning environment.[9] Student-centered learning's reliance on working on a single, open-ended question requires the learning environment to bridge the gap between learners who are newcomers to a topic and the expertise of the practitioner. Scaffolding connects learning to the kinds of problems and practices that many learners will encounter in the real world.[10] Failure to connect learning with the experiences of learners is thought to undermine the learning process more generally.[11]

Third, because personal experiences serve as the conceptual references by which new knowledge is organized and assimilated, there must be a clear connection between what one learns and one's personal experiences. It is necessary to situate new information in these environments if learners are to know how to apply concepts and why they are useful.

Finally, having access to multiple perspectives, resources, and representations enhances learning. Exposing learners to varied methods and perspectives is critical to developing deeper, divergent, and more flexible thinking processes. Together, these core values provide an understanding of the educated individual produced by student-centered learning. The educated individual is a self-guided learner who has the ability to see a project through from conception to completion. This person is able to apply her knowledge to real-world contexts by drawing on personal experience, and is a flexible thinker capable of viewing things from a variety of perspectives. Cumulatively, this person possesses the skills most sought after in the real world.

The Socratic Method as Student-Centered Learning

The Socratic method contains three constituent parts. First, the subject matter of Socratic philosophy is virtue: Socrates and his interlocutors are in agreement that virtue is the proper object of education and inquiry.[12] Second, the Socratic method proceeds *via* the process of *elenchus*, which can be understood as meaning to examine, refute, or put to shame.[13] In having one's understanding examined and possibly refuted, *elentic* questioning facilitates discovery: "the soul must free itself of the anger, arrogance, and laziness present in so many of Socrates' companions."[14] The refutation of Socratic inquiry is central not only to philosophical inquiry into virtue, but to the respondent's own life. Finally, Socratic texts are written in the dialog form. This emphasizes the dialectic quality of the Socratic method which transforms the reader from a passive into an active participant. Each of these aspects is dealt with in greater detail below.

Socratic Subject Matter is Virtue

Unlike the emphasis on skill development that constitutes the goal of contemporary student-centered learning, the relationship between the individual and virtue sits at the heart of Socratic student-centered learning. In placing the individual at the center, Socrates proves to be an innovator whose pedagogical greatness "is based on another innovation: he made his pupils do their own thinking and introduced the interchange of ideas as a safeguard against self-deception."[15] Given the concern with the virtue of the individual, one can conclude that the worst form of self-deception consists of thinking oneself virtuous when, in actuality, one is not. This explains why virtue in the Socratic sense requires one to "do the right thing" and be able to "say why it is right."[16] Ultimately, Socrates seeks to understand virtue as a "phenomenon" that applies beyond the moral tests that arise in a temple, on a battlefield, or at a feast.[17] To see and to understand why something is right, "one must face the test on inquiry."[18]

Socratic Method as Refutation

Plato never discusses the *elenchus* in any sustained way. The closest he comes to doing so is in the *Meno* (86c–87c), the *Phaedo* (99d–101e), and the *Republic* (532b–d).[19] One must look elsewhere for a model of *elentic* questioning and such a model is provided by watching Socrates in action.

The starting point of the *elentic* questioning is the opinion of the respondent. Seeskin writes:

> In Socratic conversation, true and primary principles are the outcome of the intellectual process, never the starting point. Truth is something the participants in the discussion seek out. The starting point is the body of opinion the respondent brings to the discussion. But these opinions are not starting points in the sense that their truth is taken for granted; they are not premises. Rather they are things to be examined and, if needed, overturned.[20]

By starting *elenchus* with individual opinion, Socrates takes a fundamentally practical position. The purpose of Socratic inquiry has more to do with showing the respondent the pathway (*hodos*) "to a philosophical stance rather than a way of certifying the truth of various propositions."[21] It is a method for getting individuals to examine their own lives and, in turn, to lead better, more virtuous lives. This is only possible, however, when one understands why "they [one's original propositions] are false" and to recognize that one is in a better position to seek the truth as a consequence of being refuted or shamed.[22] It is not the job of *elentic* questioning to replace false propositions with true propositions.

The student-centered quality of *elentic* questioning is obvious in its aim as persuasion is "not aimed at a general audience but at the individual respondent: its purpose is to get him to change his mind."[23] Socrates' focus on the respondent is so strong that he rejects Polus's appeals to popular opinion as "worthless, as far as truth is concerned, for it might happen sometimes that an individual is brought down by the false testimony of many reputable people" (*Gorgias*, 472a).[24] Ultimately, the purpose of refutation is to help the respondent to "remove the obstacles which prevent him from being perfectly satisfied with his own response. Unless these responses are subject to criticism, he will never know whether they express his real convictions."[25] This is something the respondent must discover on her own. If one were to come to this conclusion in any other way, it would "be tantamount to putting sight into blind eyes" (*Republic*, 518b).

The implications of this for how one understands the concept of teaching are profound. Socrates famously denies being anyone's teacher in the *Apology* (33a) because the respondent is truly her own teacher.[26] For Socrates, the respondent is not actually ignorant as she already possesses knowledge. The problem is that she is having difficulty accessing this information. Thus, one needs to be aware when one takes an inconsistent position and one becomes aware of this as a result of *elentic* examination.[27] The same reason that Socrates cannot be seen as a teacher informs the conclusion that Plato is not the teacher of the reader of a dialog. Plato, like Socrates, employs a series of devices to make the reader aware of her own ignorance. This does not mean that *elenchus* is destructive.

As shown in the *Sophist* (230b–d), the purpose of refutation is not to destroy the respondent or the positions taken by the respondent. While the respondent needs to be made aware that she does not, in fact, possess knowledge, this serves as a springboard toward knowledge. After feeling shame and getting mad at one's self, the respondent begins to undergo a transformation. Having lost the inflated and rigid beliefs that previously prevented the respondent from seeking the truth, Socrates argues that this person is not only more pleasant, but that she will enjoy the more lasting effect of being capable of learning. In this context, the purpose of refutation and the responsibility of Socrates and Plato is to enable the respondent/reader to say what she was trying to say all along.

By allowing the respondent to "certify the truth of what is said, *elentic* education assumes the respondent's opinions have some value. They are the views of a person who has a partial grasp of the truth but is having trouble seeing it clearly."[28] This, in turn, explains why Socrates is described as a midwife of the intellect, which turns out to be an appropriate comparison given the understanding of *elenchus* provided here: 1) the respondent/reader gives birth to the idea; 2) Socrates/Plato only facilitate delivery of knowledge; and 3) the respondent/reader is given every possible motive to inquire.[29]

Socratic Form is Dialog

Plato writes in the dialog format for two reasons. First, *elenchus* is a method that lends itself to the dialog because it requires that at least two voices are heard. The two-voice requirement is important as "it is not enough to have a thesis, antithesis, and explanation: there must be people willing to defend them."[30] Second, a distinction between a dialog and a sermon or treatise can be drawn. Whereas the latter are essentially prolonged speeches, a dialog is a directed conversation. As such, dialog opens the possibility of connecting form and content and engaging the reader in the same way a piece of literature does. In contrast, a sermon or treatise approaches the topic of virtue "in the same way we traditionally understand how a student approaches a teacher – with the latter imparting wisdom to the former."[31] Thus, where the dialog identifies the student as its primary concern and employs the best means possible to engage the student, the sermon or treatise focuses on the transfer of knowledge that is accepted not because of its truth, but because of the authority of the one providing the information.

The Platonic dialog itself is a form of art where written conversation is transformed into real conversation. As a pedagogical form, the dialog "must sound like actual talk; otherwise, it does not fulfill its task of being model and guide."[32] As real conversation, readers of a Platonic dialog should employ the same tools and information used daily to distill the meaning of actual conversations. Readers are required to "grasp the character, wishes, opinions, and prospects" of the figures in the dialog and to "attend to the flow of the conversation, to moments of anger, befuddlement, and silence, to changes from one interlocutor to another, and to Socrates' comments when he is narrating a dialog."[33]

Additionally, readers should be aware of Plato's use of literary devices such as irony, flattery, satire, parody, myth, and mockery. These devices are not simply employed for their literary value, but serve the purpose of fostering the conceptual breakthrough which Socrates wants the respondent to achieve and Plato wants the reader to achieve.[34] Like the respondent, the reader is shown the effect an argument has on the person to whom it is addressed. It is the intention of Socrates as an interlocutor and Plato as the author to force the respondent/reader to confess their ignorance. In doing so, the roots of one's dogmatism are cut and one leaves behind one's prejudices and opens up to the world of knowledge. On the relationship between *elenchus* and the dialog format, Nelson writes,

> Only persistent pressure to speak one's mind, to meet every counter question, and to state the reasons for every assertion transforms the power of that allure into an irresistible compulsion. This art of *forcing* minds to *freedom* constitutes the first secret of the Socratic method.[35]

Summary

Three aspects of the Socratic method have been identified here: 1) the subject matter of Socratic philosophy is virtue; 2) the method proceeds *via elentic* questioning; and 3) it is presented in dialog format. The student-centered quality of the Socratic method is evident not only in its starting position, i.e., the opinions held by the respondent, but in the subject matter of Socratic philosophy. Socratic philosophy is not fundamentally concerned with arriving at abstract understandings of virtue and the specific virtues. The fundamental concern is more practical: the moral development of the interlocutors. Socrates seeks to free their souls from those qualities (e.g., anger, arrogance) that undermine or threaten philosophic inquiry and prevent the respondent from examining her own life. This reorientation of the soul, of its "release and healing from bonds and folly," is a consequence of *elentic* questioning (*Republic*, 515c). Here, Socrates serves as a guide that reveals to the respondent her own ignorance. It is only after recognizing this fact that it truly becomes possible to pursue the truth. In the same way, Plato's use of the dialog format engages the reader and draws her into the conversation. Now an interlocutor of Socrates, the reader is invited to hold her position up to critical examination.

Plato's *Laches* Part I: The Socratic Method as Student-Centered Learning

The next two sections provide an analysis of Plato's *Laches* and demonstrate how Socratic student-centered learning operates in practice. They also show how this understanding provides the reader with a deeper, more nuanced understanding of the *Laches* itself. The question pursued here is as follows: what does the *Laches* reveal about the nature of the Socratic method and Socratic learning? In pursuit of this question, it is possible to treat Socrates' examinations of Laches and Nicias in the second half of the text as two examples of the Socratic method in practice that reveal insights into the nature of Socratic student-centered learning. Before turning to this, however, it is necessary to address the question: what is one to do with the first half of the *Laches*?

Socrates does not enter the dialog until 184d and it is not until the end of the first half of the dialog that Socrates assumes his standard place at the center of the conversation; and it is only after Socrates assumes this position that courage, the virtue of interest in the *Laches*, is introduced (189c, 190c).[36] The first half of the *Laches* establishes a correct understanding of the Socratic method that should be employed when analyzing the exchanges between Socrates, Laches, and Nicias that occur in the second half of the dialog. Approaching the *Laches* through the lens of the Socratic method provides readers with valuable information that helps them to overcome the obstacles preventing them from pursuing philosophy and thus avoiding the aporetic ending of the dialog itself (199e).

The Purpose of Lysimachus and Melesias

At the outset, the reader is introduced to Lysimachus and Melesias who, despite having very accomplished fathers (Aristeides and Thucydides), have amounted to little. Unable to tell their sons of any meaningful deeds of their own, Lysimachus and Melesias seek the advice of Laches and Nicias with regard to how they should educate their own sons. Interestingly, their own lack of distinction is seen as a consequence of their fathers' neglect of their own education. Whereas Lysimachus and Melesias feel shame in front of their sons, they do not take any responsibility for this and instead "blame our fathers for allowing us to take things easy when we were growing up, while they were busy with other people's affairs" (179c–d). In making this argument Lysimachus and Melesias unwittingly introduce a central concern of the *Laches* as a whole: the rift between public service and the proper cultivation of one's own, or philosophy.[37]

The question one needs to consider here is how one should interpret the introduction of this topic and the figure of Lysimachus who is almost exclusively responsible for its introduction. Lysimachus is aware of this tension (it is his formulation) and a remedy for the rift is sought in the advice of two prominent generals (179e). Sprague suggests that in recognizing the problem and seeking expert advice for a solution, that Lysimachus and Melesias embody the correct view of Socratic ignorance (not thinking that they know things they do not know).[38] If correct, then it is possible to view the contribution of Lysimachus and Melesias to the first half of the *Laches* as situating the question of courage within a larger context of questions about education and virtue.[39] For this argument to hold, it must necessarily be the case that Lysimachus and Melesias act and speak from a position of conviction. Is this the case, or does Plato employ the two for a different purpose?

The dialog format requires the reader to be mindful of the possibility that Plato employs literary devices for larger, philosophic ends. Plato is especially fond of irony and this raises the possibility that his presentation of Lysimachus and Melesias as being philosophically predisposed is done ironically.[40] If so, this would have the effect of introducing a comic element into how one should interpret the function of these characters. Tessitore makes the case for a comic reading of the *Laches* and of Lysimachus and Melesias in particular.[41] According to this reading, the promising philosophic start detailed above is undercut by what Plato reveals about these characters.

Lysimachus is shown to be unqualified for philosophic inquiry. Over the course of his interaction with Socrates, Plato reveals that Lysimachus is unable to recognize the presence of the very expert he seeks for his son as it is Socrates who "is always spending his time in places where young men engage in any study of noble pursuit of the sort [he is] looking for" (180c). This failure – combined with his inability to recognize Socrates' expertise (180d–e) and his asking Socrates to take his place in the conversation (189c–d) – leads Tessitore to conclude that Lysimachus is "an unlikely candidate for philosophic inquiry."[42] This conclusion serves as the source of the ironically comic ending of the dialog where it is only Lysimachus who invites Socrates to continue the dialog the next day (201b–c). By assigning the correct response to the experience of *aporia* to the figure least qualified to undertake and sustain philosophic inquiry, Plato provides a comic treatment of philosophy that frames the rest of the dialog.

If the comic reading is correct, one must consider the question of why Plato would choose to undermine the image of philosophy found in the exoteric reading? As suggested by Tessitore, the comic frame of philosophy in the wrong hands shifts the attention of both the interlocutors and the reader to philosophy in the right hands. As the discussion of *elenchus* in the previous section reminds us, the *elentic* quality of the Socratic method is only observable in the figure of Socrates. Thus, one must come to terms with the role of Socrates to grasp the understanding of philosophy in the right hands.

The Role of Socrates in the First Half of the Laches

When Socrates first enters the conversation, the interlocutors are in the midst of discussing who an appropriate instructor would be for the sons of Lysimachus and Melesias. Whereas Lysimachus and Melesias have grounds for consulting the two generals, their faith is quickly called into question when Laches says that he is "astonished" that he and Nicias were asked when Socrates is present (180c). Far from being recognition of Socrates as the most qualified person to ask given the subject matter, Laches' recommendation of Socrates represents an effort on his part to escape the conversation.[43] This is suggested by the fact that Socrates repeatedly has to keep Laches in the conversation (186e, 191d, 194a, and 196c) and his limited value of discussion (185e, 188c–189a).

Only after Nicias and Laches vouch for Socrates do the interlocutors arrive at a point where they can consider the question of whether fighting in armor is a worthwhile area of study for their sons? Usually, this would mark the moment where Socrates would direct the conversation, but this does not happen here. Instead, Socrates defers to the age and experience of the two generals and indicates that he will only speak up if he feels that he has something to add to the conversation and will use this as an opportunity to teach and persuade (181d). An answer to the question of why Socrates does this becomes apparent only after Nicias and Laches are unable to reach an agreement about fighting in armor (182a–184c). The lack of agreement provides Socrates with the opportunity to introduce the proper understanding of philosophy into the conversation as an alternative to the comic understanding of philosophy provided by Lysimachus and Melesias.

In response to the failure of Nicias and Laches to reach an agreement, Lysimachus asks Socrates to settle the matter by "casting the deciding vote" (184d). Socrates, in turn, asks Lysimachus whether he really intends to settle the matter by majority vote (184d). Lysimachus is unable to identify another option, so Socrates turns his attention to Melesias and asks him whether the greater number can persuade or whether one is persuaded by an expert – one with actual knowledge (184e). Melesias answers that it is an expert who can persuade which allows Socrates to conclude that "it is by knowledge that one ought to make decisions, if one is to make them well, and not by majority rule" (184e). From here Socrates can call into question the expertise of politics while simultaneously making the case for philosophic expertise by providing his interlocutors and the reader with an understanding of Socratic inquiry and knowledge.

Socrates starts down this path by first refining the question of expertise. While the interlocutors must determine "whether any one of us is an expert in the subject we are debating," they must first establish the criteria by which they will make this determination (185a). This is not simply a matter of agreeing on what constitutes an expert. They must also settle the question of this person's area of expertise. While the interlocutors can agree that an expert is one "who has studied and practiced the art and who had good teachers in that particular subject," they are unable to establish "what in the world they are consulting about and investigating..." (185b). Failure to reach agreement on this topic allows Socrates to suggest an answer by shifting the conversation from educational means to education ends and from bodily training to care for the soul (185e). Without saying it, Socrates identifies virtue as the subject matter of their common inquiry and once the subject matter is agreed on, he can lay out, albeit provisionally, what constitutes his philosophic mode of inquiry.

Socrates does this by drawing a distinction between Socratic inquiry and the methods of the sophists. According to Socrates, it is the sophists who "professed to be able to make a cultivated man of me" (186c). The problem with the sophists is that they cannot deliver on the promises they make, suggesting that the best alternative to their model of education is the Socratic model. This reasoning has political implications as Socrates connects politics with sophistry, as he "would be surprised" if Laches and Nicias did not possess this knowledge as they are not only older than him, but, more importantly, they had the means to study with the sophists (186c). Like the politicians encountered in the *Apology*, Laches and Nicias give their opinions "fearlessly on the subject of pursuits which are beneficial and harmful for the young" (186d; see also *Apology*, 21c–d). The problem, which will be exposed more completely in the second half of the dialog, is that both lack knowledge of what benefits and harms the young. Socrates drives this point home with his response to the concern that Laches and Nicias will abandon the conversation and return to the affairs of the city, persuading men "either by means of gifts or favors or both" (187a).

In making this argument, Socrates does not just establish the centrality of philosophy for the acquisition of knowledge. He also demonstrates the proper means by which one should go about acquiring knowledge when he employs *elentic* questioning. Socrates leads his interlocutors to consider the right question rather than simply tell them what they should know as would a sophist.

By transforming the interlocutors from passive into active learners, Socrates highlights the student-centered quality of the Socratic method.

However, the identification of virtue as the topic of consideration differentiates Socratic student-centered learning from contemporary emphasis on skills. In establishing virtue as the proper subject matter and the Socratic method as the proper means of pursuing knowledge, the first half of the *Laches* shows that Socrates addresses two, interrelated tensions instead of a single tension. In addition to the tension between politics and philosophy, it is shown here that Socrates also addresses the tension between himself and the sophists regarding rival accounts of what constitutes philosophy and knowledge.

This reading of the first half of the *Laches* is similar to those of Sprague and Nicholls as the question of courage is situated within a larger context of questions about education and virtue. My reading differs from their respective readings in that this understanding is provided by Socrates and not Lysimachus. The above interpretation follows the lead of Arieti and Tessitore in viewing Melesias and Lysimachus as comic figures who represent an incorrect view of philosophy and knowledge. Thus, the second half of the dialog, where Socrates examines Laches and Nicias, is both an examination of the tension between politics and philosophy as well as the tension between rival accounts of philosophy, knowledge, and virtue.

Laches Part II: Socratic Student-Centered Learning in Practice

Socrates and Laches

Having established that virtue consists of the harmony between one's words and actions (188d), Socrates proceeds to investigate Laches and Nicias. In Socratic fashion, Laches is asked to define courage, but he instead defines the courageous person (190e). Rather than admonishing Laches, Socrates employs *elentic* questioning in an effort to get Laches to see for himself that he has not defined courage. In response to Laches' definition of the courageous person as one who "is willing to remain at his post and to defend himself against the enemy without running away," Socrates asks Laches about the man who retreats (190e, 191a). Unable to recognize courage in retreating, Laches is shown two examples of courage by Socrates (Homer and the Scythians) that suggest otherwise (191a). While Laches is willing to agree with Homer, he qualifies the example of the Scythians, saying that his definition of courage applies to their horsemen and cavalry, but not their hoplites (191b). In making this argument Laches points to a problem with his understanding of courage: you cannot have different definitions of courage for each of these. Getting Laches to recognize this problem constitutes the next step in his education.

Laches' poor answer allows Socrates to expand the scope of their inquiry. Summarizing this expansion, Socrates tells Laches that "all these men are brave, but some possess courage in pleasures, some in pains, some in desires, and some in fears. And others, I think, show cowardice in the same respects" (191e). Not only does Socrates want Laches to recognize that courage is present in things as diverse as warfare and pleasure/pain/desire, but that the particular virtues are related to one another in light of the fact that they are virtues. Unfortunately, Laches is never able to recognize this and, despite the best efforts of Socrates, Laches must admit that he does not have a clear understanding of what Socrates is asking him (191d). The source of Laches' difficulty lies in the fact that he views courage as a fine thing, but that he does not understand what makes something fine (192c). Ultimately, Socrates shows Laches that fine things are regulated by wisdom and that things accompanied by folly become harmful and dangerous (192c–d). In recognition of this, Laches modifies his definition of courage from endurance of the soul to wise endurance (192d). If the latter makes it through examination, it would harmonize deed and action thus satisfying the requirements of virtue. To the extent that it does not, the reader is presented with a sense of the obstacles that stand in the way of acquiring knowledge and leading a life of virtue.

Socrates tests Laches' understanding of courage as wise endurance by presenting him with a choice. On the one hand, courage can be understood as choosing to fight "based on a wise calculation" when one's position is stronger and "fighting men who are fewer than those on his side, and inferior to them..." (193a). On the other hand, courage could be displayed by one "who is willing to remain and hold out" (193a). In selecting the second option, Laches reveals his lack of harmony and its source in his lack of understanding. Previously, they had agreed that foolish daring and endurance were disgraceful and harmful (see 192c–d, 193d). Now, Laches argues the contrary. Fortunately, Laches recognizes that they are not making sense because "their deeds are not harmonized with their words" (193e). What he does not recognize is the source of this disharmony.

The reader, however, is aware that the source lies in Laches' resistance to knowledge or philosophy. It was previously shown that Laches would willingly forego philosophic discussion in favor of attending to the affairs of the city. That Laches is never able to reconcile politics and philosophy is suggested by the qualification he adds to his definition of courage as endurance of the soul: "if it is necessary to say what its nature is in all cases" (192b). Socrates must once again keep Laches in the conversation if they are going to answer the question. He does this by encouraging Laches to act in accordance with his definition of courage as wise endurance and wants both of them to hold their "ground in the search and let us endure, so that courage itself won't make fun of us for searching for it courageously..." (194a). Whereas Laches decides to remain in the conversation, he does so for political reasons. What ultimately matters for Laches is the "absolute desire for victory" of the politician and not the steadfast endurance, or courage, of the philosopher in the face of *aporia* (194a).

Socrates and Nicias

Unlike Laches, Nicias is open to knowledge as suggested by his attempt to correct for Socrates' inability to arrive at a definition of courage with Laches. According to Nicias, Socrates is not "defining courage in the right way" because he is ignoring his own opinion on the subject matter (194c). In particular, Nicias adopts the position of Socrates that "everyone one of us is good with respect to that which he is wise and bad in respect to that which he is ignorant" (194d). Here, Nicias reasons like a sophist by providing a short, high-minded answer from another that speaks to Nicias' cleverness rather than his own understanding of courage. Arguing this way differentiates Nicias from Laches. Whereas Laches is willing to begin with his own opinion, Nicias is not. Nicias' reliance on the opinion of another reinforces the conclusion that politics is not the sole obstacle to knowledge dealt with in the dialog. As suggested in the reading of the first half of the *Laches* provided above and reiterated below, Socrates must also address the tension between rival conceptions of philosophy. It is necessary for him to do so as an improper view of education prevents one from pursuing the proper object of inquiry in the right way.

Nicias initially defines courage in this way: "if a courageous man is really good, it is clear that he is wise" (194d). What is important here is not the actual definition, but the fact that Nicias will be shown to have no idea what he is talking about. His definition has the appearance of knowledge, but only the appearance, and it is up to Socrates to reveal this to Nicias. He begins to do this by asking Nicias to clarify what type of knowledge courage consists of (194e). Nicias responds that courage consists of knowledge of what is fearful and hopeful in war and in every other station, but closer examination reveals that Nicias really understands courage to consist of knowledge of future goods and evils (195a).

Laches is the first to recognize this when he connects Nicias' definition of courage to knowledge of for whom it is better to live or die (195e). In recognition of this, Laches claims that Nicias equates seers with the knowledge of courage which allows him to identify a series of problems with Nicias' view of knowledge. First, only a god could possess such knowledge (196a). Second, and more importantly, Nicias twists his argument to avoid contradicting himself (196b). Laches concludes that Nicias' argument is not appropriate in a "gathering like this" and his concern for what is appropriate and inappropriate differentiates Laches from Nicias (196b). Nicias' problematic view of knowledge is not simply a consequence of his concern with politics. Nicias' inability to recognize what is and what is not appropriate suggests that his own understanding is informed by an incorrect understanding of knowledge. Thus, in exposing Nicias' lack of harmony Socrates must argue for an alternative understanding of knowledge and this argument is made on three levels.

On the first level, connecting Nicias with seers reminds the reader of Nicias' reputation for being superstitious.[44] Calling on the reader to make this connection raises questions regarding the appropriateness of Nicias' knowledge for the good of the city. The text clarifies this concern by connecting Nicias with the sophists which serves as the second level of argument. Whereas Socrates had previously suggested a connection between the sophists and both Laches and Nicias, it is Laches who develops this argument further when he charges Nicias of refusing to admit, as a gentleman would, that he is "talking nonsense" (186a–b, 196a). Instead, Nicias "twists this way and that in an attempt to cover up this difficulty" and, hopefully, achieve victory and avoid embarrassing himself (196b). Socrates ultimately endorses this charge when he identifies the source of Nicias' wisdom as the sophist Prodicus (197d). Whereas Laches will claim that the knowledge of the sophists is not fit for "a man the city thinks worthy to be its leader," it remains for Socrates to explain why this is the case (197d).

This argument is provided on the third level. Nicias comes to define courage as knowledge of future anticipated evils (198c). While his exclusive concern with future evils reinforces his connection to seers, the larger point Socrates makes concerns the nature of knowledge itself. Socrates tells Nicias that "there is not one kind of knowledge by which we know things that have happened in the past, and another by which we know how things are happening in the present, and still another by which we know what has not yet happened might best come to be in the future, but that the knowledge is the same in each case" (198d). Nicias' exclusive concern with future events and his superstition prevent him from recognizing the true nature of knowledge. Nicias is only able to identify about one-third of courage because he fails to understand that courage "understands not simply future goods and evils, but those of the present and past and all times, just as with other kinds of knowledge" (199b–c). This, in turn, explains Nicias' dubious decision in Sicily not to take advantage of the lunar eclipse and escape under the cloak of darkness.[45] In recognition of this, Socrates tells Nicias that one who possesses knowledge does not consider it necessary

> to be ruled by the art of the seer, but to rule it, as being better acquainted with both present and future in the affairs of war. In fact, the law decrees, not that the seer should command the general, but that the general should command the seer (199a).

Thus, Nicias' lack of knowledge not only prevents him from defining courage, it causes him to undermine the laws of the city and, consequently, the city itself.

Why this is the case is revealed when one compares the responses of Laches and Nicias upon learning of their lack of harmony. Recall that Laches recognizes his own lack of harmony and that he is willing to continue the investigation into the nature of courage (193e). Whereas he does so for political reasons (victory) and out of anger, he continues to hold himself and his opinions up for examination (194a). In contrast, Nicias does not feel any shame. Whereas Laches feels anger toward himself due to his inability to "express what I think in this fashion," Nicias lashes out at his fellow interlocutor which effectively brings the conversation to a close (194b, 200a–b). Whereas both Laches and Nicias decide to abandon the conversation and both recommend that Socrates continue to consult with Lysimachus and Melesias on the education of their sons, where they go is important (200c–d). Given his previous attempts to leave the conversation, Laches presumably returns to attending to the affairs of the city. Nicias, in contrast, will first consult with Damon and "once secure on these points," will be able to "instruct you [Laches] too and won't begrudge the effort – because you seem to me to be sadly in need of learning" (200b–c).

Nicias' response is telling for several reasons. First, he seems unaware of what Socrates' examination of him reveals. Besides revealing that Nicias lacks virtue, the examination reveals that the education he receives at the hands of the sophists provides only one-third of knowledge. Unmoved by these revelations, Nicias continues to seek out the "knowledge" of the sophists. Second, in returning to the sophists for continued instruction, Nicias continues to demonstrate a lack of courage. He will take the knowledge given to him by Damon and pass this knowledge on to Laches. He remains unwilling to start with his own opinion. While Laches remains in disharmony, at least he is courageous enough to undergo the *elentic* questioning of Socrates. Nicias' cowardice and his dependence on others renders him unfit to lead Athens and suggests an explanation for why the dialog is named after Laches and not his better-known interlocutor.

Plato's *Laches* in the Classroom

The previous section demonstrates how reading the *Laches* through the lens of the Socratic method both illuminates the nature and purpose of the Socratic method and facilitates a deeper understanding of the dialog itself. In particular, the argument and analysis show how *elentic* questioning is used to assist interlocutors in identifying the proper object of inquiry (virtue) and how it reveals one's lack of understanding. Throughout, the analysis highlights how Socrates employs certain literary devices characteristic of the dialog format to deepen one's understanding of the dialog and its subject matter. The purpose of this section is to show how the use of discussion boards (DBs) on mediums like Blackboard provides students with a clearer understanding of the procedures and rules of the Socratic method that can be applied to arriving at a better understanding of the *Laches* and any other text.

Discussion Boards

In my political theory courses students are provided with a set of discussion questions for every reading. Inspection of the discussion questions developed for the *Laches* shows that the text has been broken down into distinct parts with each part constituting the focus for a specific number of class sessions (see Appendix A). I am able to divide students into four groups of five as my theory courses are capped at 20 students. Part of the course requirements are for students to participate in DBs for each section of the text. In addition to their own post which answers a particular discussion question, each student must comment on two other posts. The comments should raise interpretive concerns and/or agreements in addition to identifying questions raised by the initial post.

Using the DBs does three things. First, they allow me to address relatively straightforward questions and issues by posting on the DB myself. I do so with an eye to clarification so that the discussion can progress. When this is not possible, second, I can identify specific passages and concepts with which the students are struggling, and begin the next class period by addressing these. Finally, the DBs are used to identify questions raised by the students that allow the class to pursue the larger issues and concerns raised by the text itself. It is ultimately these questions that serve as the foundation of class discussion. When successful, the DBs facilitate the translation of the dialog into real conversation where 20 students and an instructor become 21 interlocutors engaged in a common intellectual enterprise.

Some examples of this from my fall 2016 Western Political Thought course attest to the value of using DBs. The fifth question, for example, led to an extended conversation about what distinguishes politics from philosophy. We not only addressed the question of what differentiates a political from a philosophic understanding of courage, but spent class time discussing the requirements of justice as well. Thus, our face-to-face interaction allowed us to consider questions not addressed by Socrates and his interlocutors: the relationship between courage and the whole of virtue as well as the relationship between the particular virtues.

This conversation naturally fed into our discussion of the sixth question and how one thinks about knowledge. In particular, we addressed the distinction between knowledge and opinion and how this distinction informs the distinction between politics and philosophy. It also allowed us to revisit the second question and the topic of expertise where a good portion of our time was spent answering the questions of: 1) In what sense are philosophers and politicians experts?; and 2) What are they experts in?

The seventh question allowed us to consider how Socrates employs *elentic* questioning in his examination of Laches and for what purpose. Finally, the ninth question anticipated much of the conversation surrounding the tenth question. We thus spent two days on the distinction between Socrates and the sophists and were able to explore the question of why the former is connected with philosophy and the latter with politics. Students were asked to explain why one was preferable and whether their answer to this question depended on the type of regime one was considering.

The opportunity and ability to consider these larger questions is possible because of the DBs and the fact that students gain a better understanding of the procedures and rules associated with the Socratic method. Saran and Neisser identify four procedures and eight rules for interlocutors that characterize the Socratic method and Socratic student-centered learning.[46] Consideration of these in light of the understanding of how DBs are used in my own courses illustrates how DBs facilitate Socratic student-centered learning.

Procedures of the Socratic Method

The first procedure of the Socratic method is that a well-formulated general question or a statement is set by the facilitator before the discussion commences. The questions posted ahead of time for each of the assigned readings are designed to familiarize students with the content and action of the dialog. They are also designed to reveal areas of uncertainty or confusion that can either be addressed in the DBs or at the beginning of class. Through the process of answering these questions and commenting on the posts of others, common themes or questions arise that become the focus of face-to-face interaction. Sometimes this process is easy and you can simply borrow an observation or question found in the DBs. Other times you will need to review the discussion thread carefully with an eye to identifying these common elements. In either case, the facilitator is responsible for making these available to students ahead of time.

The second procedure provides that the facilitator is to collect examples experienced by participants which are relevant to the given topic and the third rule requires the group to choose one example. The first step in pursuit of the second level discussion questions generated by the first procedure requires students to provide examples of appropriate topics introduced in the text and/or the DBs. For example, in working through the definition of courage as wise endurance, students were asked to identify examples both supporting and calling into question this understanding. Class began with examples in support and these were listed on the board in class. From here, a single example was selected and investigated with an eye to determining the manner and extent to which the example supports the understanding of courage as wise endurance. After this was done, counterexamples were asked for, listed on the board, and the same procedure was followed.

Finally, the fourth procedure provides that significant statements made by the participants are written down so that all can have an overview of the discourse. This occurs on two levels. First, requiring students to submit a post of their own and to comment on posts of two others creates a great deal of information to assess, scrutinize, and respond to. While each group only has access to their own thread, I am able to bring these threads together in the classroom. When presenting this information in class, I make sure to identify the student(s) who raised the issue or topic addressed in class. Second, as mentioned above, I also make use of the white board in class. Here, I not only provide the list of examples provided by the class, but also break down arguments, define key terms, etc. As a general rule, I want students engaged in the conversation and not taking notes on the conversation. Doing this is nothing more than reporting, and reporting what is said is inconsistent with the requirements of active learning.

Rules for Interlocutors

The first rule for interlocutors provides that each participant's contribution is based upon what she has experienced, not upon what she has read or heard. In terms of student posts and comments on the DBs, I want them to focus on the text. As already mentioned, these questions serve the purpose of putting students into a better position from which they will be able to arrive at their own understanding of the meaning and significance of the text. Thus, their posts must be textually focused. This requirement is loosened when we consider the text in class. In the example of Laches' definition of courage as wise endurance, where students are asked to identify examples and counter-examples of their own, I specifically instruct them to select examples not provided in the text. Examining these examples in class provides students with a better understanding of the text while sharpening their own understanding of courage as well as their critical thinking skills.

The second rule is that thinking and questioning must be honest. This means that only genuine doubts about what has been said should be expressed. This rule is important for narrowing the examples down to a single example. After listing the examples on the board, I ask the class if any of the examples should be removed and to explain why they should be removed. Here, I want students to be mindful of the following criteria: 1) the example must be derived from one's particular experience; 2) it should not be overly complicated; 3) the example must be relevant for the topic of the dialog; 4) the example should deal with an experience that has already come to an end; and 5) the person providing the example must be willing to present it fully and provide all relevant factual information.[47] After the argument is presented, the individual who suggested the example is given the opportunity to respond. She can agree to its removal or she may continue efforts to persuade others that the example should be included.

The third rule makes it the responsibility of all participants to express their thoughts clearly and concisely as possible so that everyone is able to build on the ideas contributed by others. Obviously, the DB posts and comments need to be written clearly. One of the things I do, and encourage students to do as well, is request that specific aspects of a post be clarified. Blackboard allows students to quote from another post so students are able to identify the specific part of the post/response requiring clarification. I also ask students to clarify what they say in the classroom and encourage other students to do the same. Moreover, they are instructed to ask me to clarify what I say as well. As a matter of course, I regularly ask the entire class if there are any questions or if there is anything that needs clarification before moving on to the next aspect of our discussion.

The fourth rule requires everyone to listen carefully to all contributions. This also means active participation so that everyone's ideas are woven into the process of cooperative thinking. I do my best to distribute the burden of class discussion. One thing I have found that helps to alleviate some of the student concern with speaking in class is that the starting position for class discussion is already available in the DBs. By identifying the student or students that are the source of the question(s) for class discussion, they are given ownership. However, when I have to start class by correcting something I do not assign the need to do this to any student. Instead, I follow Socrates and take responsibility for this.[48] Thus, students are never connected to an error or a mistake. The goal here is to develop an environment where even the most introverted student feels comfortable participating in the common discussion.

The fifth and sixth rules reinforce the idea that we are engaged in common inquiry. The fifth rule maintains that participants should not concentrate exclusively on their own thought. They should make every effort to understand those of other participants and if necessary seek clarification. The requirement of commenting on two posts speaks directly to this. If a student is in agreement with another student, she needs to clearly explain why this is the case and be able to support her reasoning with evidence. If they are in disagreement, before moving on to explanation and evidence, she must first demonstrate that she understands the position of the other student. The DBs thus facilitate consideration of a particular topic from a variety of perspectives. The sixth rule places responsibility for progress in the conversation on the shoulders of all participants as anyone who has lost sight of the question or of the thread of discussion should seek the help of others to clarify where the group stands. It is rarely the case that I have to remind students of this as, generally speaking, they do this themselves.

The seventh rule requires that abstract statements be grounded in concrete experience in order to illuminate such statements. Like Socrates, I want to avoid the high-minded response of the sophists. This is why students are required to support the claims they make about a text in the DBs with textual evidence and why, during class discussion, students may be asked to connect what they say to a specific passage in the text, or to another text read over the course of the semester, or provide a real-world example.

Finally, inquiry into relevant questions continues as long as participants hold conflicting views or if they have not achieved clarity. Given the limits of time, it is not always possible to satisfy this rule. As much as I might like to continue a particular conversation, there are other parts of the dialog and other texts to consider over the course of a semester. Fortunately, as the examples of classroom discussion provided above show, we are able to identify and focus on recurring themes which allows us to return to previously unanswered questions and to do so from a better-informed position. Even if the questions remain unsettled, this is far from being a problem. Our inability to provide an answer illustrates an important reality about human inquiry – answers are never complete or locked in stone. Thus, whereas Socrates and his interlocutors may not have succeeded in arriving at an understanding of courage, an understanding of the Socratic method allows Plato's reader to consider the possibility that the *Laches* does, in fact, answer the question of what constitutes courage. An understanding of the Socratic method, moreover, suggests to the reader where she should look (the example of Socrates) in pursuit of this question. All of this places the reader in a position where she can consider her own understanding of courage in light of the argument and understanding provided in the *Laches*.

Conclusion

Contemporary theories of student-centered learning only educate half of the person. With their emphasis on skill development, these theories focus on preparing students to compete in the increasingly competitive twenty-first-century marketplace. While higher education must prepare students for these realities, to focus exclusively on skill development through project-based learning fails to remember that humans aspire to more than a vocation. By effectively removing anything higher from the idea of higher education, contemporary theories of student-centered learning fail to prepare students to be good citizens and persons. From a political perspective, contemporary theories pose a threat to democratic government as they ignore the fact that democracies are the regime type that "stands and falls by virtue."[49]

To return the higher to higher education and assist students in their pursuit of the noble, an alternative account of student-centered learning is necessary. As argued here, such an account is provided by the Socratic method. Like contemporary theories, the Socratic view of student-centered learning focuses on individual learners, rejects the lecture and passive student-learning model, requires students to consider topics from multiple perspectives, and encourages students to be responsible for their own education. Unlike the contemporary theories, Socratic student-centered learning recognizes that students have needs beyond the acquisition of skills and identifies the subject matter and means of pursuing these needs.

This is evident in the analysis of Plato's *Laches* provided here. Through his depiction of Socrates' engagement with Laches and Nicias, Plato provides the reader with a powerful argument for the centrality of virtue to human life and the Socratic method as the proper means of pursuing this topic. Perhaps more importantly, the *Laches* is honest with regard to the obstacles lying in wait for those who pursue higher questions and ideas. While the dialog ends without resolving the questions of what constitutes courage or the question of the relationship between courage and the whole of virtue, the action of the dialog provides both its interlocutors and its reader with explanations for why this is the case (see *Laches*, 199e, 190c–d). Whereas politics serves as an obstacle for both Laches and Nicias, the improper education Nicias receives at the feet of the sophists identifies another, perhaps more difficult, obstacle to overcome. For the reader, it is recognition of these limitations that opens up the possibility of pursuing the higher questions of the human condition.

This understanding of the nature and purpose of education relies on the face-to-face interaction between interlocutors engaged in common intellectual activity. Modern technology, especially the use of DBs, facilitates pursuit of these higher questions and issues in the classroom. The DBs allow the moderator to address questions, clarify things, and identify the question or topic of conversation for a particular reading ahead of time. Whereas the DBs focus on questions provided by the instructor, the face-to-face interaction begins where Socratic inquiry begins: the opinions of the interlocutors. With extra time at our disposal, class time can focus on putting the Socratic method into practice. Becoming aware of the obstacles found along this pathway, steps are taken toward a life of inquiry devoted to seeking the truth.

Notes

1 The Center for Democratic Governance and Leadership and the Office of Teaching and Learning (OTL) at Bridgewater State University provided generous financial support for this project. The views expressed here are solely those of the author and do not represent the views of the Center for Democratic Governance and Leadership or the OTL.
2 Leo Strauss, *Liberalism Ancient and Modern* (Chicago: University of Chicago Press, 1968), ix.
3 *Ibid.*, 10.
4 Robert E. Clausen and William E. Bowman, "Toward a Student-Centered Learning Focus Inventory for Junior High and Middle School Teachers," *Journal of Educational Research* 68/1 (1974): 9–11.
5 Stephanie Bell, "Project-Based Learning for the 21st Century: Skills for the Future," *The Clearing House* 83/2 (2010): 40.
6 See Richard M. Felder and Rebecca Brent, "Navigating the Bumpy Road to Student-Centered Instruction," *College Teaching* 44/2 (1996): 43–7; Kimberly Overby, "Student-Centered Learning," *ESSAI* 9/1 (2011): 109–12; and Allison Zmuda, "Leap of Faith: Take the Plunge Into a 21st Century Conception of Learning," *School Library Monthly* 26/3 (2009): 16–18.
7 See Susan M. Land, Kevin Olliver, and Michael J. Hannifan, "Student-Centered Learning Environments: Foundations, Assumptions, and Design," in *Theoretical Foundations of Learning Environments*, David H. Jonassen and Susan M. Land, eds. (New York: Routledge, 2012), 8–13.
8 According to analyses of the traditional classroom, learners are often denied opportunities to develop the decision-making, self-monitoring, and attention-checking skills deemed necessary for optimizing the learning experience. Consequently, learners become increasingly compliant in their learning, viewing the task as one of matching their meanings to those expected by external agents. On the traditional classroom see R. Keith Sawyer, "Introduction: The New Science of Learning," in *The Cambridge Handbook to the Learning Sciences*, R.K. Sawyer, ed. (Cambridge: Cambridge University Press, 2006), 1–18. For the consequences see Mary McCaslin and Thomas Good, "Compliant Cognition: The Misalliance of Management and Instructional Goals in Current School Reform," *Educational Researcher* 21/3 (1992): 4–17.
9 Chris Quintana *et al.* "A Scaffolding Design Framework for Software to Support Science Inquiry," *Journal of Learning Sciences* 13/3 (2004): 337–86.
10 See Quintana *et al.* "Scaffolding Design," 337–86; John S. Brown, Allan Collins, and Paul Duguid, "Situated Cognition and the Culture of Learning," *Educational Researcher* 18/1 (1989): 32–41; and Sasha A. Barab and Thomas Duffy, "From Practice Fields to Communities of Practice," in *Theoretical Foundations of Learning Environments*, David Jonassen and Susan Land, eds. (Mahwah: Lawrence Erlbaum Associates, 2003), 29–66.

11 See Philip Bell *et al. Learning Science in Informal Environments: People, Places, and Pursuits* (Washington: National Academic Press, 2009), 1–18.
12 Mark Blitz, *Plato's Political Philosophy* (Baltimore: The Johns Hopkins University Press, 2010), 34.
13 Kenneth Seeskin, *Dialogue and Discovery: A Study in Socratic Method* (Albany: State University of New York Press, 1987), 1.
14 *Ibid.*, 3.
15 Leonard Nelson, *Socratic Method and Critical Philosophy* (New Haven: Yale University Press, 1949), 17.
16 Seeskin, *Dialogue and Discovery*, 135.
17 Blitz, *Plato's Political Philosophy*, 35.
18 Seeskin, *Dialogue and Discovery*, 135.
19 Plato, *Meno*, trans. George Anastapolo and Lawrence Burns (Newburyport: Focus Publishing, 2007); Plato, *Phaedo*, trans. Eva Brann, Peter Kalkavage, and Eric Salem (Newburyport: Focus Publishing, 1998); and Plato, *Republic*, trans. Allan Bloom (New York: Basic Books, 1991). Throughout, I follow the standard practice of citing Platonic texts by Stephanus number(s). All subsequent citations will be taken from here.
20 Seeskin, *Dialogue and Discovery*, 24.
21 *Ibid.*, 42–3.
22 *Ibid.*, 99.
23 *Ibid.*, 24–5.
24 Plato, *Gorgias*, trans. James A. Arrieti and Roger M. Burius (Newburyport: Focus Publishing, 2007). All subsequent citations will be taken from here.
25 Seeskin, *Dialogue and Discovery*, 33.
26 Plato, *Apology*, trans. Thomas G. West and Grace Starry West (Ithaca: Cornell University Press, 1998). All subsequent citations will be taken from here.
27 A key aspect of *elenchus* is shame and this reliance serves as one of the most common criticisms of the Socratic method. Critics argue that a reliance on shame actually has the effect of dissuading the respondent from continued inquiry. That shame should spur one on to continued inquiry and philosophy see *Apology*, 29d–e; *Symposium*, 216b; and *Sophist*, 230c–d. Plato, *Symposium*, trans. Seth Benardete (Chicago: University of Chicago Press, 2001) and Plato, *Sophist*, trans. Seth Benardete (Chicago: University of Chicago Press, 1986). All subsequent citations will be taken from here.
28 Seeskin, *Dialogue and Discovery*, 102.
29 On Socrates as midwife see Plato's *Theatetus* (150b–c) and Seeskin, *Dialogue and Discovery*, 13. Plato, *Theatetus*, trans. M.J. Levette and Rev. Myles Burnyeat (Indianapolis: Hackett Publishing, 1997). All subsequent citations will be taken from here.
30 Seeskin, *Dialogue and Discovery*, 23.
31 *Ibid.*, 10.
32 Nelson, *Socratic Method*, 13–14.
33 Blitz, *Plato's Political Philosophy*, 4.
34 Seeskin, *Dialogue and Discovery*, 7. See also James Arieti, *Interpreting Plato: The Dialogues as Drama* (Savage: Rowman and Littlefield, 1991), 1–17.
35 Nelson, *Socratic Method*, 15. Here, one will want to point out that there is a fundamental difference between the respondent and the reader: the latter is not exposed to *elentic* questioning in the same way the respondent is. On this topic, I am inclined to side with Seeskin who argues that the act of thinking or reflecting constitutes a form of dialog. See Seeskin, *Dialogue and Discovery*, 23. Support for this interpretation is provided in Plato's *Theatetus* (189e) where Socrates defines thinking as "A talk which the soul has with itself about the objects under its consideration" and the *Sophist* (263e) where Socrates engages Theatetus again and defines thought as "speech that occurs without the voice, inside the soul in conversation with itself."
36 Plato, *Laches*, trans. Rosamund Kent Sprague (Indianapolis: Hackett Publishing, 1992). All subsequent citations are taken from here.
37 Darrell Dobbs, "For Lack of Wisdom: Courage and Inquiry in Plato's 'Laches,'" *Journal of Politics* 48/4 (1986): 830.
38 Rosamund Kent Sprague, "Introduction," in *Laches and Charmides* (Indianapolis: Hackett Publishing, 1994), 4.
39 See also James H. Nichols, Jr., "Introduction to the *Laches*," in *The Roots of Political Philosophy: Ten Forgotten Platonic Dialogues*, Thomas L. Pangle, ed. (Ithaca: Cornell University Press, 1987), 269.
40 On the centrality of irony see Charles L. Griswold, Jr., "Irony in the Platonic Dialogues," *Philosophy and Literature* 26/1 (2002): 84–106.
41 Aristide Tessitore, "Courage and Comedy in Plato's Laches," *Journal of Politics* 56/1 (1994): 115–33.
42 *Ibid.*, 124.

43 See also Katherine H. Zuckert, *Plato's Philosophers: The Coherence of the Dialogues* (Chicago: University of Chicago Press, 2009), 254.
44 See Dobbs, "Lack of Wisdom," 832, 840–41.
45 See Robert A. Strassler, *The Landmark Thucydides* (New York: Simon and Schuster, 1996), 456–59, 463–78.
46 Rene Saran and Barbara Neisser, *Enquiring Minds: Socratic Dialogue in Education* (London: Institute of Education, 2004), 171–72.
47 *Ibid.*, 173.
48 On the differences between Socrates and the sophists see Zuckert, *Plato's Philosphers*, 499–503.
49 Strauss, *Liberalism*, 4.

Bibliography

Arieti, James. 1991. *Interpreting Plato: The Dialogues as Drama*. Savage, MD: Rowman & Littlefield.
Barab, Sasha A. and Thomas Duffy. 2003. "From Practice Fields to Communities of Practice." In *Theoretical Foundations of Learning Environments*. David Jonassen and Susan Land eds. Mahwah: Lawrence Erlbaum Associates: 25–56.
Bell, Philip, Bruce Lewestein, Andrew Shouse and Michael A. Feder. 2009. *Learning Science in Informal Environments: People, Places, and Pursuits*. Washington, DC: National Academic Press.
Bell, Stephanie. 2010. "Project-Based Learning for the 21st Century: Skills for the Future." *The Clearing House* 83/2: 39–43.
Blitz, Mark. 2010. *Plato's Political Philosophy*. Baltimore: Johns Hopkins University Press.
Bransford, John D., Ann L. Brown and Rodney R. Cocking. 2000. *How People Learn: Brain, Mind, Experience, and School*. Washington, DC: National Academy Press.
Brown, John S., Allan Collins and Paul Duguid. 1989. "Situated Cognition and the Culture of Learning." *Educational Researcher* 18/1: 32–41.
Clausen, Robert E. and William E. Bowman. 1974. "Toward a Student-Centered Learning Focus Inventory for Junior High and Middle School Teachers." *Journal of Educational Research* 68/1: 9–11.
Dobbs, Darrell. 1986. "For Lack of Wisdom: Courage and Inquiry in Plato's 'Laches.'" *Journal of Politics* 48/4: 825–49.
Felder, Richard M. and Rebecca Brent. 1996. "Navigating the Bumpy Road to Student-Centered Instruction." *College Teaching* 44/2: 43–7.
Griswold, Charles L., Jr. 2002. "Irony in the Platonic Dialogues." *Philosophy and Literature* 26/1: 84–106.
Land, Susan M., Kevin Olliver and Michael J. Hannifan. 2012. "Student-Centered Learning Environments: Foundations, Assumptions, and Design." In *Theoretical Foundations of Learning Environments*. David H. Jonassen and Susan M. Land eds. New York: Routledge: 1–24.
McCaslin, Mary and Thomas Good. 1992. "Compliant Cognition: The Misalliance of Management and Instructional Goals in Current School Reform." *Educational Researcher* 21/3: 4–17.
Nelson, Leonard. 1949. *Socratic Method and Critical Philosophy*. New Haven: Yale University Press.
Nichols, James H., Jr. 1987. "Introduction to the *Laches*." In *The Roots of Political Philosophy: Ten Forgotten Socratic Dialogues*. Thomas L. Pangle ed. Ithaca: Cornell University Press: 269–80.
Overby, Kimberly. 2011. "Student-Centered Learning." *ESSAI* 9/1: 109–12.
Plato. 1986. *Sophist*. Seth Benardete trans. Chicago: University of Chicago Press.
———. 1991. *Republic*. Allan Bloom trans. New York: Basic Books.
———. 1992. *Laches*. Rosamund Kent Sprague trans. Indianapolis: Hackett Publishing.
———. 1997. *Theatetus*. In *Plato: Complete Works*. M.J. Levette and Rev. Myles Burnyeat trans. Indianapolis: Hackett Publishing: 157–234.
———. 1998. *Apology*. In *Four Texts on Socrates*. Thomas G. West and Grace Starry West trans. Ithaca: Cornell University Press.
———. 1998. *Phaedo*. Eva Brann, Peter Kalkavage and Eric Salem trans. Newburyport: Focus Publishing.
———. 2001. *Symposium*. Seth Benardete trans. Chicago: University of Chicago Press.
———. 2004. *Meno*. George Anastapolo and Lawrence Burns trans. Newburyport: Focus Publishing.
———. 2007. *Gorgias*. James A. Arrieti and Roger M. Burius trans. Newburyport: Focus Publishing.
Quintana, Chris, Brian Reiser, Elizabeth Davis, Joseph Krajcik, Eric Fretz, Ravit Duncan, Elen Kyza, Daniel Edelson and Elliot Soloway. 2004. "A Scaffolding Design Framework for Software to Support Science Inquiry." *Journal of Learning Sciences* 13/3: 337–86.

Saran, Rene and Barbara Neisser. 2004. *Enquiring Minds: Socratic Dialogue in Education*. London: Institute of Education Press.
Sawyer, R. Keith. 2006. "Introduction: The New Science of Learning." In *The Cambridge Handbook to the Learning Sciences*. R.K. Sawyer ed. Cambridge: Cambridge University Press: 1–18.
Seeskin, Kenneth. 1987. *Dialogue and Discovery: A Study in Socratic Method*. Albany: State University of New York Press.
Sprague, Rosamund K. 1994. "Introduction." In *Laches and Charmides*. Rosamund Kent Sprague ed. Indianapolis: Hackett Publishing: 3–8.
Strauss, Leo. 1968. *Liberalism Ancient and Modern*. Chicago: University of Chicago Press.
Tessitore, Aristide. 1994. "Courage and Comedy in Plato's Laches." *Journal of Politics* 56/1: 115–33.
Thucydides. 1996. *The Landmark Thucydides*. Robert A. Strassler ed. New York: Simon and Schuster.
Zmuda, Allison. 2009. "Leap of Faith: Take the Plunge Into a 21st Century Conception of Learning." *School Library Monthly* 26/3: 16–18.
Zuckert, Katherine H. 2009. *Plato's Philosophers: The Coherence of the Dialogues*. Chicago: University of Chicago Press.

Part III
The Socratic Method in the Classroom

9 "No Guru, No Method, No Teacher"

Sean Steel

Getting Back to Socrates[1]

Genuine philosophy is not pretty. In fact, its public countenance is as ugly as Socrates' face. It is most certainly unattractive to those who are pragmatically minded, seeking "solutions": checklists, methods, and toolboxes that might apply to a teacher's classroom. Many students enrolled in university harbor much pretense to know what philosophy is, and it is very hard to open their eyes about such things. Moreover, even when one does manage to help them recognize their ignorance (*agnoia*) in this regard, only a small few will be delighted, thankful, or excited by the experience of perplexity (*aporia*) that gives rise to wonder (*thauma*) and a renewed, elevated desire to know. And having been led into an awareness of such things, a far greater number will rather grow resentful and angry with you as their teacher, impatient with this thing you have been attempting to help them see: they will hear your words, perhaps; maybe they will do the assigned readings and go through the motions of the exercises but never in the genuine spirit of philosophy.

It is the underlying contention of this chapter that genuine philosophizing – that is to say, "loving wisdom" – ought to be at the core of what we do as teachers. To philosophize with our students, I suggest that we return to Socrates and his example. However, the problem is that "Socrates' example" isn't well understood. What does it mean to be like Socrates in our philosophizing as teachers? What does it mean to philosophize? Riffing on a single line from a popular Van Morrison song and album title, *No Guru, No Method, No Teacher*, and using this phrase as an organizational rubric, what follows is an attempt to begin clearing up some of our misconceptions by investigating what philosophy is *not*.[2]

Philosophy is *Not* a Method, Socratic or Otherwise

One misunderstanding about teaching philosophy is that it is to train students in methods of argumentation and forms of logical reasoning – a type of transferable "critical thinking" skill. In her book, *Children as Philosophers*, Haynes offers a valuable warning against conceiving of philosophy as a methodology for "critical thinking." She contends that, "If we are concerned to develop our thinking, we need to move beyond an overly structured, narrow and rigid tradition of logical thinking and argument." Her desire to conceive of philosophy as a "way of life" arises from her recognition that the *ratio* – the power of the mind through which we know by means of discursive reasoning and logic – when cultivated in separation from the *intellectus*, which knows not by moving through chains of reasoning but rather intuitively or all at once, breeds "a disconnection between thinker and the world."

Indeed, the commonly accepted notion among educators that philosophy inculcates a set of "critical thinking" skills that "can be taught and applied to content reflects a fundamental view of our relationship with the world." Without cultivating our awareness of the theoretic activity of *intellectus*, wherein we come to know the deep unity between seer and seen, we see the world only through *ratio*. In its cognitive capacity to work upon the objects of thought and to master those objects with critical-analytic precision, *ratio* becomes "instrumentalist in its desire to make the environment, including the world of meanings, a resource."[3] Haynes sees that this "instrumentalist view"[4] underlies conceptions of philosophy as critical thinking, and she remarks that "Philosophy probably wants to question the whole notion of thinking skills."[5]

Philosophers have always been reviled for their methods, for the use they make of these methods, and for the perceived negative effects of them. Diogenes Laertius records that Anaxagoras was banished from Athens on a charge of impiety on the grounds his manner of argument served to undermine belief in the gods.[6] Socrates was especially reviled, along with the practice of philosophy, as being indistinguishable from the sophists. Although writers like Haroutunian-Gordon have stressed the importance of philosophic conversation in teaching, and Adler has advocated for the adoption of "Socratic" discussions in the modern classroom,[7] both Socrates and the "Socratic method" of philosophic conversation continue to be scorned. Carmichael remarks that "the Socratic method" of "question-and-answer" is not well-suited to the modern classroom of thirty-five students.[8] Rud likewise views the "Socratic method" of using "withering questions" to undermine student pretensions to knowledge as "sadistic"; he deems it humiliating for students, and he cites experiences with the method as it is often used to teach law classes: "The consensus among students is that the method is not 'educational' in any traditional sense."[9]

Moreover, Rud does not agree that the use of such a "method" guarantees that self-knowledge – the purported and principle benefit of Socratic philosophic practice – will even occur. One need only look as far as the Platonic dialogs themselves to confirm Rud's skepticism here. Socrates has a rather poor track record of ever having "improved" anyone through his "methods" of disputation.[10] Both Critias and Alcibiades were among Socrates' frequent interlocutors; yet Critias became one of the Thirty Tyrants, and Alcibiades' actions during the Sicilian campaign led to the destruction of Athens.

Others who are less skeptical of Socrates and "Socratic method" as a destructive, corruptive, and pedagogically suspect manner of teaching nonetheless harbor doubts about the utility of "an easy mimicry" of Socrates in the classroom.[11] Haroutunian-Gordon has thoughtfully observed that Socrates does not actually conform to a prescribed "method." She rightly points out that in teaching dialogically, one cannot follow a method or a predetermined dialectical blueprint, because discussions are organic and unpredictable: they are what she refers to as "ill-structured teaching situations."[12]

Finally, others have questioned the legitimacy of even speaking about a "Socratic method" as though it were the peculiar technique of philosophic investigation proffered by Socrates. Mitchell, for example, has written that "the Socratic method" is not properly attributed to Socrates at all, but is rather the invention of the German philosopher Leonard Nelson.[13] Carmichael sees not one, but three methods being used by Socrates[14]; Calhoun provides an analysis of the Platonic dialogs in which he identifies seven different methods at work as well as two "pedagogical modes."[15] And Hand writes that philosophy is plainly about more than "raising philosophical questions"; and, to be "competent as a form of inquiry," philosophy must be "a matter of answering questions of a particular kind *by means of appropriate methods of investigation.*"[16]

Whether philosophers use a specific "method" to engage in their various inquiries, I wish to emphasize that there is no particular method that can specifically be termed either "Socratic" or "philosophic," as though adherence to it might distinguish one who philosophizes from one who does not. Indeed, the sophist and the philosopher use the same "methods" of inquiry and discourse. Both the philosopher and the sophist make use of stories[17]; both use long speeches as well as short ones, and both engage in question-and-answer discussions; both at various times speak to large crowds as well as to individuals. Clearly, both are familiar with the art of rhetoric and are not strangers to its methods.

It has long been recognized that Socrates' own defense speech in the *Apology* is remarkably similar (if not, in many respects, identical) in form to the sophistic speech of Gorgias in his *Defense of Palamedes*.[18] Additionally, one might observe that in the *Euthydemus*, Socrates squares off against two sophists in the use of *elenchos*, or the methods of cross-examination and refutation, with eristic – quite literally, "verbal strife" – exposed as the sophistic image of dialectic.[19] In short, simple mastery of a technique, skill, or method of inquiry does not mean that one is philosophizing, because both the sophist and the philosopher might be masters of such things. Therefore, to "teach philosophy" as though it were a method is, at best, to teach something of ambiguous value for the pursuit of wisdom.

If philosophizing were simply a matter of learning a method, there would be no difference between the philosopher and the sophist. The figures of the sophist and the philosopher are most often conflated with one another precisely because they are seen using the same "methods." For example, the sophists ("the Wreckers") in Augustine's *Confessions* use *elenchus* to tear down and "destroy" the arguments of their opponents[20]; so too does Socrates lead his interlocutors (as well as himself) into a state of perplexity (*aporia*) in which they recognize that they do not know what they presumed to know previously. The methods employed by philosophers and sophists are the same; however, the objectives of the sophist and the philosopher are quite different. In contrast to the sophist, the philosopher or dialectician does not engage in *elenchos* simply to "destroy" every opinion or idea suggested in argument; rather, to pursue wisdom, the philosopher must refine what has been said, discarding what has been found as false and "taking up" what is true toward its "metaphysical first principle."[21]

The dialectic of philosophy – as distinct from the eristic of sophistry – is a means, as Pieper calls it, for knowing "reality as such."[22] The methods used (e.g., *elenchos*) are themselves neutral; that is, they are neither specifically philosophic nor sophistic; they become either sophistic or philosophic depending upon their respective ends, and the goals of the philosopher and the sophist are indeed antithetical. One might say that eristic is the sophistic manifestation of *elenchos* that satisfies itself with the acquisition of finite ends either unrelated or unconcerned with the relation of these ends to their ultimate goals (*telos*). By contrast, dialectic is the philosophic manifestation of *elenchus*: it is intellection or *noesis* expressing itself in speech as it seeks beyond all individual manifestations of the truth, goodness, or beauty for the whole of reality in which one participates (*metalepsis*). Whereas the sophist vies for power and glory through eristic, the philosopher undermines all selfish ends[23] and desires as well as all pretense to knowledge, not out of nihilistic destructiveness, but rather as a means of engaging in intellection or *noesis* – that form of thought that "takes up" everything toward the truest vision of reality (*theoria*).

Philosophy Has No Teacher, Not Itself being a Teachable Subject

It is the nature of philosophy to be aporetic, and in a philosophic discussion about the pursuit of wisdom in education, one should not avoid the uncomfortable perplexity of philosophizing. Perhaps one of the most widely accepted assumptions about philosophy – particularly among teachers of philosophy – is that philosophy is itself a teachable subject. Indeed, how could one design to introduce philosophy into schools if it were not a teachable subject? How could one call oneself a "teacher of philosophy," develop a "philosophy curriculum," or organize courses in philosophy if philosophy were not teachable? Even worse, to question such a basic assumption while at the same time attempting to make a case for wisdom's pursuit in schools seems counter-productive and preposterous. Nevertheless, we must allow ourselves to be unsettled by the figure of Socrates, who, standing before his accusers and his judges on the capital charges of corrupting the youth and teaching falsehoods about the gods, insists: "I have never been anyone's teacher."[24]

Here, Socrates was not lying or being ironic. He was telling the truth. One must first know a subject to teach it: math teachers know and teach the subject of mathematics, as do physics teachers know about physics and its methods. Each teacher works very hard to pass on knowledge of his or her respective field to students. And yet the thing that is famously said to have made Socrates "wiser" than others – referred to in the *Apology* as his "human wisdom" (*anthropine sophia*) – is not any purported knowledge of some subject, field, methodology, or "parent discipline" that might be taught to others, but a rather low thing "worth little or nothing"[25]: namely, his awareness of his own ignorance.[26] However, being aware of his ignorance, Socrates would never deign to teach that of which he is ignorant; and philosophy, as the genuine love of wisdom, is necessarily an acknowledgment of one's own deficiency in that after which one seeks: namely, that divine wisdom which is referred to by Pythagoras when he says, "Only the god is wise."

Philosophy is evidently not something one could learn by acquiring a specific knowledge, by methodological practice, repetition, or by any of the modes we commonly associate with teaching the subjects that students must study in school. Writing about the future role of philosophy in mass education systems, Winstanley expresses concerns that as a subject, philosophy will either be "relegated to an after-school, extra-curricular option add-on," or else the "infusion approach" will be taken wherein philosophy will be incorporated into all existing subjects; she instead rallies for teaching philosophy as a core or "full curriculum subject."[27] However, although philosophy most certainly ought to be a "core" concern in education, it can never be a "core subject." Philosophy is not a subject at all because each of the subjects sets itself apart from the others by being concerned with a particular aspect of what is, whereas philosophy is concerned with the "totality" of what is; or, as Pieper writes, "[the philosopher] is interested in the world as a totality and in wisdom in its entirety."[28]

Indeed, philosophizing and studying philosophy are two different things, "so much so that one may even stand in the way of the other."[29] A study is something that we can pick up and put down at our own pleasure. However, philosophy is not an attitude or a subject that we may pick up and leave at any doorpost; rather, to be genuine, it must be a way of life. As Pieper writes, "All philosophy rather flows from man's basic existential disposition toward the world, an attitude largely beyond any willful determination and decision."[30]

But if philosophy is not a subject that may be taught, if philosophy is potentially impeded by the vigorous sort of study that regularly brings with it success and accolades, how then are we to follow Socrates in pursuing wisdom at school? A few simple remarks may be reasonably made here in response.[31] First, to begin practicing the pursuit of wisdom as a society, it will be necessary to curb our current fixation with improved modes of assessment, on the one hand, and with standardized testing, on the other. These concerns certainly have their place in terms of measuring student proficiencies; but they can hinder teachers, students, administrators, and parents from ever developing any awareness of what it means to exercise one's *schole*, or leisure – the root meaning of our word, "school," and a term intimately related to wisdom's pursuit.

Second, along with our excessive penchant for assessment, the totalitarian[32] fixation with work and accountability in education must also be curtailed. A genuine "wisdom environment" must be carved out somewhere within the school day in which both students and teachers might begin to explore what it means to "leisurize," to contemplate, or to practice *schole*. The prime directive here ought to be the cultivation of *noesis* (intellection) as opposed to mere *dianoesis* (thinking); not rigorous application of the reason necessarily, but rather an attitude of openness and receptivity must be made of paramount significance. Love of what is – whether students find themselves attracted by bodily beauty or the beauties of soul, whether they are drawn toward beautiful ideas or enthused (literally "filled with spirit") by music or art, mathematics or literature, any thoughts, seeings (*theoria*), or cognitions of any sorts related to these beauties – must be "taken up" in such an environment.

This "taking up" (*anaireseis*) of the love of what is should not be thought of as the sole prerogative of "the philosopher"; quite the contrary: it is our true and shared heritage as human beings who may, like Aristotle says, come to know ourselves through "immortalizing"[33]; similarly, Plato would have us understand that people of all sorts and interests may engage in noetic behavior. In the *Phaedrus*,

Socrates speaks about the "lover of wisdom" (*philosophos*) and the "lover of beauty" (*philokalos*) as equals alongside "one of a musical or loving nature" (*mousikou tinos kai erotikou*).[34] Aristotle likewise speaks of the philosopher alongside the "lover of myth" (*philomythos*).[35] Clearly there are as many routes toward wisdom as there are a myriad of things that might be "taken up" toward their true Beginning (*Arche*).

Philosophy has neither Guru nor Disciple

When I contend above that philosophy is neither a subject having a teacher nor a method of inquiry, this may suggest to some readers that I am saying philosophy is somehow exclusionary – perhaps available only to a special, gifted, or at least predisposed few, and even then, only where an appropriate spiritual guide or "guru" exists. And speaking honestly, I think that there is some truth to this viewpoint. Experientially (and writing as a teacher), it rings true to me that only a few (maybe up to half) of the students one meets are open to philosophizing. The rest are not, and they will occasionally let you know rather aggressively about it.[36]

Similarly, I suspect that those of us who have found some deep interest in and connection with philosophizing or with the writings of philosophers do, in fact, relate to these philosophic men and women, whether long dead or still alive, somehow as our spiritual guides. They occupy a special place in our lives, in our hearts, and minds. Philosophy can draw us into closer relation with a smaller cadre of spirits, although the pursuit of wisdom is not truly exclusionary. Indeed, philosophy is the sacred birthright of all human beings by dint of our nature: we are all beings who, as Aristotle tells us, "seek to know" what is.[37] Although we are mortal beings (*thanatoi*) or "creatures of a day," we also participate by nature in what is immortal (*athanatoi*). We therefore have some share in the eternal that we might come to know during our precious time alive. One such route for our "immortalizing" is philosophy.

I say that experientially it seems to those of us who have fallen in love with philosophy and who are drawn toward it that the guru–disciple relation has been a key part of our learning to live and to practice philosophy in its original, ancient sense as a "way of life," for as Hadot has adeptly shown, philosophy-proper is most certainly a "way of life."[38] However, it also remains true in a deeper sense that with philosophy and philosophizing, there is neither guru nor disciple. In terms of our mortal, egoic, finite, and fluctuating nature, there is no one who philosophizes, let alone one who achieves contemplative insights, or who brings about contemplative insights into others.

The ego-self, in all cases, remains an obstacle. As the anonymous author of *The Cloud of Unknowing* says, it is the last impediment between you and your god,[39] the font of all the wisdom for which you yearn; hence, the ego must be left behind wherever genuine philosophizing manifests itself. This is because the "correct" (*orthos*) study of philosophy, being the manner of our "immortalizing," and following the words of Socrates in the *Phaedo*, one must simultaneously always remain "nothing other than the practice of dying and being dead."[40] In other words, the ego-self that thinks, feels, and does is an illusory "I" – not the contemplative event wherein there can be no distinction in that union between seer and seen. Here, the mortal aspect has died away, leaving only whatever it is that is immortal, this being the locus point of philosophy-proper.

The strange fact of there being no guru, no student, no teacher, no teaching or subject, and no method in genuine philosophizing obviously problematizes all our academic fixations with assessment and school-as-usual, for how could even the best formative or summative assessment practices be used to evaluate student "progress" in noetic cognition when, strictly speaking, *noesis* only arises to the extent that the self is allowed to disappear? When there is no one who might receive either accolades or censure for attaining or for failing to attain to a knowledge of what is? The pursuit of wisdom demands the cultivation of absolute humility, and leaving behind all self-regard to know is what Pieper calls the "totality." Indeed, Pieper has written poignantly about how this lack of self-regard is the distinguishing characteristic of a genuine philosopher:

> [T]he true philosopher, thoroughly oblivious of his own importance, and "totally discarding all pretentiousness," approaches his unfathomable object [namely, wisdom] unselfishly and with an open mind. The contemplation of this object, in turn, transports the subject beyond mere self-centered satisfaction and indeed releases him from the fixation on selfish needs, no matter how "intellectual" or sublime.[41]

In Pieper's view, wherever selfishness dominates the existential arena, "there we should not expect true philosophy to flourish, if it can come about at all."[42]

Conclusion

Philosophy, when it is understood properly and in a manner akin to Socrates' "the art of dying," is at the core of any true liberal education, where "liberal" means "to be free, especially to be free of oneself, to be free of those passions and habits within us that might deflect us from grasping what is there."[43] As the most liberating of all the arts, philosophy must also entail the freedom to pursue the highest objects of existence. But this necessarily means that all lower aims and all lower sights, i.e., all those aims or ends not commensurate with knowing "reality as such" or with "absolute freedom" (*moksa*), must be put aside. Time and time again, contemplatives therefore warn against engaging in wisdom's pursuit for money,[44] or in meditative and contemplative practices for the various powers that one might acquire.[45] Philosophy cannot be put to work in the service of worldly attainments and ambitions without bringing about its own destruction, or without turning into sophistry.

The sophist Protagoras once proclaimed that the purpose of pursuing wisdom – something he claimed for himself – is to teach others how to deal successfully with the world; in his view, it is the business of the wise to teach others how to take proper care of their personal affairs.[46] In this regard, Protagoras' attitude toward wisdom's pursuit coincides with the views of most modern-day education reformers. However, as Pieper remarks, philosophic inquiry into "the totality of things" cannot properly be made commensurate with the world of work and its finite aims: "Whoever seeks to eliminate the fundamental incommensurability between philosophy and the world of work only serves to make the philosophical act improbable of achievement or even impossible."[47]

We can now see clearly the wrong-headedness of so much that is being undertaken in the name of philosophy in schools today. For instance, one cannot properly engage in philosophizing as a means to improve critical thinking, to enhance academic performance, or to boost test scores. Indeed, where Winstanley demands that philosophy be "presented as a useful and relevant subject" that offers children "benefits" which may be demonstrated by "fair empirical assessment,"[48] it would seem to me to be most dangerous for philosophy that it be associated with any grades at all: not only do grades serve as rewards and punishments that very often deflect students – particularly the keen, ambitious, and competitive ones – from learning what they are learning for its own sake. Aquinas writes about the "circular movement" of the soul that is engaged in contemplation, "there is no error," just as there is no error in the knowledge of first principles which we know by simple intuition (*simplici intuiti*)[49]; and certainly, without the possibility of error, how could grades make any sense at all? Consequently, in a true wisdom-seeking environment, students and teachers must be liberated from the widespread and all-consuming concern with grades and the assessment of student work to make "space" for the possibility of philosophy.

Notes

1. Parts of this chapter have appeared in Sean Steel, *The Pursuit of Wisdom and Happiness in Education: Historical Sources and Contemplative Practices* (Albany: SUNY Press, 2014a).
2. Van Morrison, "In the Garden," in *No Guru, No Method, No Teacher*. Mercury Records, 1986.
3. Joanna Haynes, *Children as Philosophers: Learning Through Enquiry and Dialogue in the Primary Classroom* (London: Routledge, 2002), 40.
4. Haynes, *Children as Philosophers*, 44.
5. *Ibid.*, 129; see Michael Bonnett, "Teaching Thinking, and the Sanctity of Content," *Journal of Philosophy of Education* 29/3 (1995): 307.
6. See volume 1 of Diogenes Laertius, *Lives of Eminent Philosophers*, R.D. Hicks, trans. (Cambridge: Loeb Classical Library and Harvard University Press, 1925), II.12–14.
7. See Adler's discussion of "maieutic" or "Socratic questioning" as the "means" of teaching every student in "the third column" of his vision for education. Mortimer J. Adler, *The Paideia Proposal* (New York: MacMillan, 1982); see Haroutunian-Gordon's use of the Platonic notion of education as *periagoge* in Sophie Haroutunian-Gordon, *Turning the Soul: Teaching through Conversation in High School* (Chicago: University of Chicago Press, 1991).
8. Douglas Carmichael, "I'm Sick of Socrates," *Improving College and University Teaching* 23/4 (1975): 252.
9. See Anthony G. Rud, "The Use and Abuse of Socrates in Present Day Teaching," *Education Policy Analysis Archives* 5/20 (1997): 7; see Carrie-Ann Biondi, "Socratic Teaching: Beyond *The Paper Chase*," *Teaching Philosophy* 31/2 (June 2008): 119–40.
10. This point is also affirmed by Benson, who remarks that no one is aware of his ignorance after his discussion with Socrates: Laches, Callicles, Hippias, Euthyphro, Protagoras, and Cephalus. Hugh Benson, "The Aims of Socratic Elenchos," in *Knowledge, Teaching, and Wisdom*, Keith Lehrer, B. Jeannie Lum, Beverly A. Slichta and Nicholas D. Smith, eds. (London: Kluwer Academic Publishers, 1996), 29.
11. See Rud, "The Use and Abuse of Socrates in Present Day Teaching," 4.
12. Haroutunian-Gordon writes that Socrates "does not follow his stated method because he is in an ill-structured teaching situation – a situation where one cannot proceed by following predetermined methods or asking others to do so." See Sophie Haroutunian-Gordon, "Teaching in an Ill-Structured Situation: The Case of Socrates," *Educational Theory* 38/2 (1988): 231.
13. Sebastian Mitchell, "Socratic Dialogue, the Humanities, and the Art of the Question," *Arts and Humanities in Higher Education* 5/2 (2006): 181; cf. Leonard Nelson, *Socratic Method and Critical Philosophy: Selected Essays*, T.K. Brown, trans. (New York: Dover Press, 1949).
14. Apart from his "method of question-and-answer," Socrates is thought to employ "synthetic hypothesis," as well as "collection and division." See Carmichael, "I'm Sick of Socrates," 252.
15. See David H. Calhoun, "Which 'Socratic Method'? Models of Education in Plato's Dialogues," in *Knowledge, Teaching, and Wisdom*, 49–70.
16. Michael Hand, "Can Children Be Taught Philosophy?" in *Philosophy in Schools*, Michael Hand and Carrie Winstanley, eds. (London: Continuum, 2008), 5.
17. See any number of myths Plato has Socrates tell in his dialogs; compare these stories with, for instance, the Promethean myth as told by the sophist Protagoras in Plato's *Protagoras*, in *The Collected Dialogues*, Edith Hamilton and Huntington Cairns, eds. (Princeton: Princeton University Press, 1961), 320c–28d.
18. See the speech in John Dillon and Tania Gengel, trans. *The Greek Sophists* (London: Penguin Classics, 2003). The similarities between the speeches are remarkable and easy to see; for useful analyses of the rhetorical devices used in each of the speeches, see Gerald J. Biesecker-Mast, "Forensic Rhetoric and the Constitution of the Subject: Innocence, Truth, and Wisdom in Gorgias' 'Palamedes' and Plato's 'Apology'," *Rhetoric Society Quarterly* 24.3/4 (1994): 148–66; James A. Coulter, "The Relation of the Apology of Socrates to Gorgias' Defense of Palamedes and Plato's Critique of Gorgianic Rhetoric," *Harvard Studies in Classical Philology* 68 (1964): 269–303; Thomas J. Lewis, "Parody and the Argument from Probability in the 'Apology,'" *Philosophy and Literature* 14/2 (1990): 359–66; also see Thomas J. Lewis, "Identifying Rhetoric in the Apology: Does Socrates Use the Appeal for Pity?" *Interpretation* 21/2 (1993): 105–14; Kenneth Seeskin, "Is the Apology of Socrates a Parody?" *Philosophy and Literature* 6/1–2 (1982): 94–105.
19. Thomas Chance has written an excellent commentary on Plato's *Euthydemus*. His thesis is that "eristic appears similar to, but is really different from, dialectic" (18). In his view, "eristic is the antithesis to dialectic, in fact, as the very paradigm of otherness" (19). Although the methods of *elenchos* are outwardly the same, the inward disposition of the sophist that makes use of them is quite different from that of the

philosopher. See Thomas H. Chance, *Plato's Euthydemus: Analysis of What Is and Is Not Philosophy* (Berkeley: University of California Press, 1992).
20 See Augustine, *The Confessions*, R.S. Pinecoffin, trans. (London: Penguin, 1961), III.3.6. Sophistic debate is commonly called "eristic" because of its association with Eris, the Greek goddess of strife. Eristic speech is quarrelsome or contentious debate; it is a form of verbal battle in which rivals in a contest (*agon*) compete for victory.
21 R.G. Collingwood, *An Essay on Philosophic Method* (Oxford: Clarendon Press, 2005), 13, 14.
22 Josef Pieper, *In Defense of Philosophy: Classical Wisdom Stands up to Modern Challenges*, Lothar Krauth, trans. (San Francisco: Ignatius Press, 1966), 41.
23 Pieper views the selfishness of the sophist and the selflessness of the philosopher as the best way of truly distinguishing between their two characters. The Sophist looks exactly like a philosopher. He speaks exactly like a philosopher. In fact, it could be said he resembles a true philosopher much more than the philosopher himself. In other words: it has been made extremely easy not to recognize the decisive difference. The difference consists in this: the true philosopher, thoroughly oblivious of his own importance, and "totally discarding all pretentiousness," approaches his unfathomable object unselfishly and with an open mind. The contemplation of this object, in turn, transports the subject beyond mere self-centered satisfaction and indeed releases him from the fixation on selfish needs, no matter how "intellectual" or sublime. The Sophist, in contrast, despite his emancipation from the norms of "objective" truth and the resulting claims to be "free," remains nevertheless imprisoned within the narrow scope of what is "useable.' See Pieper, *In Defense of Philosophy*, 38–9.
24 *Ego de didaskalos men oudenos popot' egenomen*. Plato, *Apology*, 33a.
25 *hoti he anthropine sophia oligou tinos axia estin kai oudenos*. Ibid., 23a.
26 Ibid., 21d.
27 Carrie Winstanley, "Philosophy and the Development of Critical Thinking," in *Philosophy in Schools*, 94–5.
28 Josef Pieper, "On the Platonic Idea of Philosophy," in *For the Love of Wisdom: Essays on the Nature of Philosophy*, Roger Wasserman, trans. (San Francisco: Ignatius Press, 1995), 161.
29 Pieper, "A Plea for Philosophy," in *For the Love of Wisdom*, 91; cf. Pieper, *In Defense of Philosophy*, 23.
30 Pieper, *In Defense of Philosophy*, 23.
31 For more details, refer to Steel, *The Pursuit of Wisdom and Happiness in Education*; see Sean Steel, "Oil and Water: Assessment and the Pursuit of Wisdom," in *The Good, The Bad, and The Ugly: Developing Teacher's Assessment Literacy within Cross-Cultural Contexts*, Kim Koh, Cecile DePass, and Sean Steel eds. (Rotterdam: Sense Publishers, forthcoming).
32 I use the word "totalitarian" here purposefully. Pieper writes about our culture as one of "total work"; that is, it is one that overvalues work and is adamantly opposed to (and in fact, set upon the destruction of) leisure. His discussion of the Soviet "five-year plans" and their attempts to "order everything" along with their claim to "provide the exclusive value standards for all aspects of life" strikes me as remarkably similar to the way that school boards and the government envision "accountability" in education. For an excellent discussion in which the totalitarian urge manifests itself in liberal democratic societies, see Josef Pieper, "Leisure and its Threefold Opposition," in *Josef Pieper: An Anthology* (San Francisco: Ignatius Press, 1981), 137–43.
33 Aristotle, *Nicomachean Ethics*, in *The Basic Works*, Richard McKeon, ed. (New York: Modern Library, 2001), X.vii.8. In the *Symposium*, Socrates recounts Diotima saying much the same thing: "it is in contemplating (*theomenoi*) the Beautiful Itself (*auto to kalon*)" that "human life is to be lived," for only "when a human being looks (*blepontos*) there and contemplates (*theomenou*) that with that by which one must contemplate it, and be with it" that true virtue is begotten in him, making him "dear to god" (*theophilei*), and "if any other among men is immortal (*athanato*), he is too." Plato, *Symposium*, 212a.
34 Plato, *Phaedrus*, 248d.
35 Aristotle, *Metaphysics*, I.ii.10; 982b18.
36 As a positive side note, I can say with equal, experiential, and anecdotal confidence that students in high school are generally more open to philosophy and philosophizing than are pre-service teachers. For more, see Sean Steel, "On the High School Education of a Pithecanthropus Erectus," *The High School Journal* 98/1 (2014b): 5–21; see Sean Steel, "Shamanic Daughters, Three-Minute Records, and 'Deaducation' in Schools," *Interchange* 45/1 (2014c): 1–17.
37 Aristotle, *Metaphysics*, 980a22.
38 Pierre Hadot, *Philosophy as a Way of Life: Spiritual Exercises from Socrates to Foucault*, Arnold I. Davidson, ed., Michael Chase, trans. (Oxford: Blackwell Publishing, 1995); see Pierre Hadot, *What is Ancient Philosophy?* Michael Chase, trans. (Cambridge: The Belknap Press of Harvard University Press, 2002).
39 Anonymous, *The Cloud of Unknowing*, James Walsh, ed. (Ramsey, NJ: Paulist Press, 1981), XLII.

40 Plato, *Phaedo*, 64a.
41 Pieper, *In Defense of Philosophy*, 38.
42 *Ibid.*, 39.
43 James V. Schall, "Liberal Education," *Liberal Education* 92/4 (2006): 46.
44 One is reminded here of the ancient sophists who charged a fee for their instruction versus the philosopher Socrates who spoke with anyone at no charge. Indeed, the reason Socrates was so poor was because he knew that there was something beyond riches. Schall writes helpfully about the relation between the genuine teacher-philosopher and his pocketbook: "Properly speaking.... teachers cannot be paid for what they teach. For what they teach, if it is true, is not theirs. They do not own it. They did not make it or make it to be true. This fact is why any financial arrangement with a true teacher... is not a salary or a wage but an 'honorarium,' something offered merely to keep the teacher alive, not to 'pay' him for ownership of a segment of 'truth' said to be exclusively his. What he who teaches knows, then, is known for its own sake, not for his sake – even when the knowing is, as it should be, his. Truth is not like private property, something we should own and cherish. Rather it is something that, when passed from teacher to pupil, makes both something more and neither any less.... The motivation of the teacher has to be something intrinsic, some 'love of wisdom' for itself.... Besides, teachers do not need much in the way of material goods, as their delight is really not to be found in financial rewards; if a teacher does seek wealth, his teaching is suspect." See James V. Schall, "On the Mystery of Teachers I Never Met," in *On the Unseriousness of Human Affairs: Teaching, Writing, Playing, Believing, Lecturing, Philosophizing, Singing, Dancing* (Wilmington: ISI Books, 2001), 64.
45 St. John of the Cross, *The Ascent of Mount Carmel*, E. Allison Peers, trans. (Mineola: Dover Publications, 2008).
46 Plato, *Protagoras*, 318e.
47 Pieper, "A Plea for Philosophy," 97.
48 Winstanley, "Philosophy and the Development of Critical Thinking," 95.
49 Thomas Aquinas, *Summa Theologica*, Jordan Aumann, trans. (London: Blackfriars, 1966), 2a2ae.180.6. Whereas the discursive movements of the *ratio* may be evaluated for their aptitude, the circular movement calms these learning priorities, seeking their effective cessation. Whereas reasoning and typical classroom thinking involves the measurement and "progression" of rational capacities to certain skill sets in thinking and cognitive development, the circular movement of the soul cannot be so evaluated, because by its nature it is separate from all discursive thought and therefore "free of error." Indeed, the circular movement has no measure other than that in which it participates by pursuing wisdom in contemplative gazing.

Bibliography

Adler, Mortimer J. 1982. *The Paideia Proposal*. New York: MacMillan.
Anonymous. 1981. "XLII." In *The Cloud of Unknowing*. James Walsh ed. Ramsey: Paulist Press: 200–1.
Aquinas, Thomas. 1966. "Action and Contemplation." In *Summa Theologica*. Vol. 46. Jordan Aumann trans. London: Blackfriars: 179–82.
Aristotle. 2001. "Nichomachean Ethics." In *The Basic Works*. Richard McKeon ed. New York: Modern Library.
Augustine. 1961. *The Confessions*. R.S. Pinecoffin trans. London: Penguin.
Benson, Hugh. 1996. "The Aims of Socratic Elenchos." In *Knowledge, Teaching, and Wisdom*. Keith Lehrer, B. Jeannie Lum, Beverly A. Slichta and Nicholas D. Smith eds. London: Kluwer Academic Publishers: 21–33.
Biesecker-Mast, Gerald J. 1994. "Forensic Rhetoric and the Constitution of the Subject: Innocence, Truth, and Wisdom in Gorgias' 'Palamedes' and Plato's 'Apology.'" *Rhetoric Society Quarterly* 24.3/4: 148–66.
Biondi, Carrie-Ann. 2008. "Socratic Teaching: Beyond *The Paper Chase*." *Teaching Philosophy* 31/2: 119–40.
Bonnett, Michael. 1995. "Teaching Thinking, and the Sanctity of Content." *Journal of Philosophy of Education* 29/3: 295–309.
Calhoun, David H. 1996. "Which 'Socratic Method'? Models of Education in Plato's Dialogues." In *Knowledge, Teaching, and Wisdom*. Keith Lehrer, B. Jeannie Lum, Beverly A. Slichta and Nicholas D. Smith eds. London: Kluwer Academic Publishers: 49–70.
Carmichael, Douglas. 1975. "I'm Sick of Socrates." *Improving College and University Teaching* 23/4: 252.
Chance, Thomas H. 1992. *Plato's Euthydemus: Analysis of What Is and Is Not Philosophy*. Berkeley: University of California Press.

Collingwood, R.G. 2005. *An Essay on Philosophic Method*. Oxford: Clarendon Press.

Coulter, James A. 1964. "The Relation of the Apology of Socrates to Gorgias' Defense of Palamedes and Plato's Critique of Gorgianic Rhetoric." *Harvard Studies in Classical Philology* 68: 269–303.

Dillon, John and Tania Gengel trans. 2003. *The Greek Sophists*. London: Penguin Classics.

Hadot, Pierre. 1995. *Philosophy as a Way of Life: Spiritual Exercises from Socrates to Foucault*. Arnold I. Davidson ed. Michael Chase trans. Oxford: Blackwell Publishing.

———. 2002. *What is Ancient Philosophy?* Michael Chase trans. Cambridge: The Belknap Press.

Hand, Michael. 2008. "Can Children Be Taught Philosophy?" In *Philosophy in Schools*. Michael Hand and Carrie Winstanley eds. London: Continuum: 3–17.

Haroutunian-Gordon, Sophie. 1988. "Teaching in an Ill-Structured Situation: The Case of Socrates." *Educational Theory* 38/2: 225–37.

———. 1991. *Turning the Soul: Teaching through Conversation in High School*. Chicago: University of Chicago Press.

Haynes, Joanna. 2002. *Children as Philosophers: Learning through Enquiry and Dialogue in the Primary Classroom*. London: Routledge.

John of the Cross. 2008. *Ascent of Mount Carmel*. E. Allison Peers trans. Mineola: Dover Publications.

Laertius, Diogenes. 1925. *Lives of Eminent Philosophers*. R.D. Hicks trans. Vols. 1 and 2. Cambridge: Loeb Classical Library and Harvard University Press.

Lewis, Thomas J. 1990. "Parody and the Argument from Probability in the 'Apology.'" *Philosophy and Literature* 14/2: 359–66.

———.1993. "Identifying Rhetoric in the Apology: Does Socrates Use the Appeal for Pity?" *Interpretation* 21/2: 105–14.

Mitchell, Sebastian. 2006. "Socratic Dialogue, the Humanities, and the Art of the Question." *Arts and Humanities in Higher Education* 5/2: 181–97.

Morrison, Van. 1986. "In the Garden." *No Guru, No Method, No Teacher*. Mercury Records.

Nelson, Leonard. 1949. *Socratic Method and Critical Philosophy: Selected Essays*. T.K. Brown trans. New York: Dover Press.

Pieper, Josef. 1966. *In Defense of Philosophy: Classical Wisdom Stands up to Modern Challenges*. Lothar Krauth trans. San Francisco: Ignatius Press.

———. 1981. *Josef Pieper: An Anthology*. San Francisco: Ignatius Press.

———. 1995. *For the Love of Wisdom: Essays on the Nature of Philosophy*. Roger Wasserman trans. San Francisco: Ignatius Press.

Plato. 1961. "Protagoras." In *The Collected Dialogues*. Edith Hamilton and Huntington Cairns eds. Princeton: Princeton University Press.

———. 1968. *The Republic*. Allan Bloom trans. New York: Basic Books.

Rud, Anthony G. 1997. "The Use and Abuse of Socrates in Present Day Teaching." *Education Policy Analysis Archives* 5/20: 1–14.

Schall, James V. 2001. "On the Mystery of Teachers I Never Met." In *On the Unseriousness of Human Affairs: Teaching, Writing, Playing, Believing, Lecturing, Philosophizing, Singing, Dancing*. Wilmington: ISI Books: 63–82.

———. 2006. "Liberal Education." *Liberal Education* 92/4: 44–7.

Seeskin, Kenneth. 1982. "Is the Apology of Socrates a Parody?" *Philosophy and Literature* 6.1/2: 94–105.

Steel, Sean. 2014a. *The Pursuit of Wisdom and Happiness in Education: Historical Sources and Contemplative Practices*. Albany: SUNY Press.

———. 2014b. "On the High School Education of a Pithecanthropus Erectus." *The High School Journal* 98/1: 5–21.

———. 2014c. "Shamanic Daughters, Three-Minute Records, and 'Deaducation' in Schools." *Interchange* 45/1: 1–17.

———. Forthcoming. "Oil and Water: Assessment and the Pursuit of Wisdom." In *The Good, The Bad, and The Ugly: Developing Teacher's Assessment Literacy within Cross-Cultural Contexts*. Kim Koh, Cecile DePass and Sean Steel eds. Rotterdam: Sense Publishers.

Winstanley, Carrie. 2008. "Philosophy and the Development of Critical Thinking." In *Philosophy in Schools*. Michael Hand and Carrie Winstanley eds. London: Continuum: 85–95.

10 Is Socrates Culturally Imperialistic?

Rebecca LeMoine

Derived from the conversations of classical Greek philosopher Socrates (as depicted largely in Plato's dialogs), the Socratic method is one of the most widely used approaches to teaching. It has long been a staple of law school courses, and is increasingly being used in other educational settings including medical school.[1] Beyond the college classroom, the method has even been adapted for use in psychological counseling.[2] Though scholars and practitioners disagree about what the method entails, the Socratic method arguably involves the use of questioning to expose contradictions within a person's thinking. Unlike the sophists, however, Socrates brings these tensions to light not with the aim of humiliating and conquering his interlocutors; rather, he continually casts himself as a fellow seeker of the truth interested above all in discovering what constitutes a virtuous life and in exhorting himself and others to care for virtue. The Socratic method thus encompasses not merely a set of rhetorical techniques, but, more importantly, the goal of "turning" the entire soul toward what Socrates calls "the Good." Herein lies the crux of the problem I examine in this chapter. If the Socratic method centers on inculcating virtue or producing what might justly be termed a conversion, is it therefore an *exclusionary* approach to teaching, i.e., one hostile to different ways of life? Simply put, is the Socratic method culturally imperialistic?

While myriad manuals exist for training middle school, high school, and college teachers to employ one of Socrates' main techniques – the *elenchus*, an argument of disproof, or refutation – few advocates of the Socratic method stop to ask if the Socratic method is suitable for classes with students from differing cultural backgrounds. Given the increasingly diverse composition of student populations in both secondary and higher education, it is crucial to examine the appropriateness of using the Socratic method in culturally diverse contexts. As a teacher at an officially designated Hispanic-serving institution with a large international student body, this question is of deep personal importance in crafting my own pedagogy. Like many, I believe educators have a responsibility to ensure that the teaching methods they employ are just. If the Socratic method blindly privileges and imposes one set of cultural values on an audience of students hailing from various regions of the world, then to my mind it is not just. Even those who do not share this conception of justice will at least likely agree that good educators are committed to discovering the most effective means of promoting student learning. If the Socratic method does not translate well beyond an audience of Western students, then using it in a multicultural context may be counterproductive. For these reasons, criticisms of the Socratic method as being culturally imperialistic must be taken seriously.

Twenty years ago, Martha Nussbaum attempted to address this criticism in *Cultivating Humanity: A Classical Defense of Reform in Liberal Education*. Nussbaum presents her approach to education as avoiding two extremes. On the one hand, she confronts more conservative thinkers like Allan Bloom, who famously argues in *The Closing of the American Mind* that contemporary American universities have failed students by promoting skepticism of absolute truth and openness to all cultural beliefs, i.e., cultural relativism.[3] In Nussbaum's view, Bloom's solution – the "Great Books" approach to education, which tends to focus exclusively on texts within the Western tradition – ignores the openness that Plato's Socrates shows toward learning from other cultures. It also defies the very purpose of the Socratic method, which is to encourage self-examination:

> There is no more effective way to wake pupils up than to confront them with difference in an area where they had previously thought their own ways neutral, necessary, and natural.... In our complex world, Socratic inquiry mandates pluralism.[4]

For Nussbaum, the Socratic method works best in multicultural contexts. Nussbaum's rejection of the "Great Books" approach does not lead her to adopt the postmodern alternative Bloom attacks, however. Drawing largely on Derridean deconstruction, left-wing opponents malign the Socratic method, Nussbaum argues, on the grounds that "logic itself is patriarchal or a tool of colonial oppression."[5] Nussbaum finds such criticism insulting to non-Western cultures. Logic, she contends, is not the exclusive legacy of the Western tradition.

Whereas Nussbaum should be commended for attending to a significant critique of the Socratic method that other advocates of the Socratic method generally neglect, her defense does not go far enough. This is apparent from subsequent scholarly reviews of *Cultivating Humanity*. For instance, in his review of the book for the *Harvard Educational Review*, Burbules criticizes Nussbaum for dismissing the view of the Committee on Blacks in the American Philosophical Association that "black students do not feel comfortable with required courses in formal logic":

> Nussbaum takes any doubts along these lines as expressing the racist idea that "black students cannot think logically" (p. 177). But perhaps the onus of the debate over why African-American students are underrepresented in the field of philosophy is not on the students themselves, but on what philosophers think it means to "think logically," or on the assumption that this method represents the only valid basis for arguing and adjudicating different views about truth and value, or on the possibility that the putatively universal truths explored in philosophy departments may not in fact speak to the concerns of many individuals and groups. One need not be a relativist to think that.[6]

In my estimation, Burbules is correct in his assessment that Nussbaum's defense of the Socratic method against the charge of cultural imperialism is too shallow. Though a valuable beginning, attending to this criticism necessitates more than a few pages of argumentation. It also requires a more sympathetic and complete presentation of the views of critics than Nussbaum gives.

In this chapter, I consider at greater depth critiques of the Socratic method as culturally imperialistic. These critiques fall, I argue, into three general categories: the "linguistic imperialism" critique, the "normative imperialism" critique, and the "philosophic imperialism" critique. The first critique maintains that the Socratic method is culturally imperialistic because it typically takes place within one language – in Socrates' case, Greek; in contemporary American universities, usually English – and therefore privileges certain participants and a particular framework of thought. The second critique argues that as a mode of education that values critical thinking and the input of students, the Socratic method implicitly devalues the norm of respect for tradition and authority figures embraced in other cultures' educational approaches, such as in the Confucian tradition. Moreover, by emphasizing the primacy of discourse, the Socratic method discounts other means of truth-seeking. Finally, the third critique contends that the Socratic method inherently tries to convert interlocutors to the philosophic way of life and, in doing so, dismisses the value of other ways of life. This critique fits with a more common, general critique of the method: that its practitioners merely manipulate their interlocutors into arriving at a predetermined set of "truths."

While taking these criticisms seriously and hopefully doing them justice, my aim is to show that the Socratic method can be defended against these charges. The general thrust of my argument is that while the Socratic method often takes place within a single language, presupposes the superiority of certain norms, and tries to encourage students to live philosophically, it is one of the few teaching methods that allows for and thrives on difference, and that encourages reflection upon the method itself. Indeed, many of the criticisms leveled at the Socratic method can be applied to any teaching method whatsoever. This is not to say these concerns are trivial; often they reveal deeply important truths about the human condition. Yet, it is noteworthy that in various ways the Socratic method, when properly conducted, tries to overcome some of the problems every teaching method faces. For this reason, as elaborated on in the rest of this chapter, it seems to me that the Socratic method may be an exceptional educational model for culturally diverse classrooms.

The "Linguistic Imperialism" Critique

One criticism leveled at the Socratic method derives from the view that language constrains what humans can express and that the imposition of a particular language therefore functions as an act of domination. Derrida explores the politics of language in *Monolingualism of the Other, Or, The Prosthesis of Origin*. Born into a Jewish family in Algeria during the period of French colonialism, Derrida recounts how he was forced to learn French in school rather than Arabic or Berber. This experience helped him recognize the role of language in constructing power relations. As Derrida explains, "Every culture institutes itself through the unilateral imposition of some 'politics' of language. Mastery begins, as we know, through the power of naming, of imposing and legitimating appellations."[7] Though he could question or challenge the language, he could only do so within the language itself.[8] Hence, French exercised a kind of tyranny over him, an alien language imposed as a result of the particular historical event of colonization. The efforts the French colonizers made to exclude the native languages of Algeria demonstrated their own recognition of the power of language. In another series of lectures, Derrida draws out the implications thusly:

> In the broad sense, the language in which the foreigner is addressed or in which he is heard, if he is, is the ensemble of culture, it is the values, the norms, the meanings that inhabit the language. Speaking the same language is not only a linguistic operation. It's a matter of *ethos* generally.[9]

The "linguistic imperialism" critique thus bleeds into the "normative imperialism" critique examined in the next section. Speaking in a particular vernacular shapes the range of thoughts available for expression; the very structure or grammar of the language limits and influences what is conveyed, privileging certain norms. Language is not, in other words, the neutral tool we often take it to be.

Insofar as the Socratic method is couched within a specific language, it is therefore culturally imperialistic according to this critique. To be sure, the conversations depicted in the Platonic dialogs only take place in Greek. Indeed, when Socrates sets out in the *Meno* to provide concrete evidence of how his method of questioning can help even an uneducated person "recollect" knowledge of mathematics by demonstrating the use of this method on a slave, the first question he asks is if the slave can speak Greek (82b). The ability of teacher and student to speak the same language is a prerequisite for learning, and never do we see Socrates propose the possibility of his speaking in a language other than Greek – though he claims to interrogate "anyone [he] happens to meet, young and old, foreigner and citizen" and lives in one of the most culturally diverse cities in the ancient world (*Apology*, 30a). It would seem, then, that the Socratic method involves the imposition of a particular language on its participants, as well as the framework of values and norms that, as Derrida says, "inhabits" that language.

Modern day uses of the Socratic method may be equally subject to this critique. One scholar, reflecting on his experience as a teacher of Athabascan students in the remote Alaskan village of

Nyotek, found himself reinscribing the colonizer–colonized dynamic often manifested in relations between white settlers and native tribes by using the Socratic method in his classroom. Though he asked the students questions, he did so always looking for particular answers. Moreover, the dialog always took place in English. Looking back, he realized that

> [i]n such a classroom the subaltern may speak, but only insofar as he or she speaks the language of the colonizer, which is not so much a form of speech as a form of mimicry, even as the haunting laughter of the loon is not to be confused with the imitative notes of a parrot.[10]

For this teacher, the Socratic method comprised part of the process of linguistic imperialism. His questions and ways of phrasing ideas helped to indoctrinate his students into the mindset the white colonizers wished to impose on these subjugated peoples.

One possible defense of the Socratic method against the linguistic imperialism critique is that for dialog of any kind to take place, a common language is necessary. It is simply a matter of necessity and convenience, one might contend, that this language is Greek for Socrates, and typically English for teachers in the United States. Nothing precludes one from using the Socratic method in Spanish, Chinese, or any other language. That is, there is nothing inherently language-bound in the nature of the Socratic method. If there were, it could not be used in English-speaking classrooms in the contemporary world because the original use of the method occurred in ancient Greek. Moreover, it is feasible to imagine a bilingual or multilingual conversation involving the Socratic method. In short, nothing within the Socratic method itself is linguistically imperialistic. Any teaching method employed within the dominant culture's language could be subject to the same critique – even a method drawn from the most foreign of cultures to one's own.

One is justified in wanting a better defense than this, however. Beyond the universality of the Socratic method in terms of the language(s) in which it can be conducted, it might be noted that, by insisting interlocutors express their honest opinions, the method – at least when properly conducted – allows students to control the direction the inquiry takes. This means it is possible for a student to introduce the class to words from her native language. Throughout the dialogs, Socrates requests that his interlocutors only put forth their true opinions; at times, he even asks twice or more if the interlocutor truly holds the opinion he has expressed. Though we have no example of Socrates engaged in dialog with a non-Greek speaking interlocutor, given that Socrates' questions often involve obtaining from his interlocutor a definition of the term under consideration, it is not unfathomable that foreign students could respond by redirecting the inquiry toward an examination of an equivalent word in their native language, or even by explaining that no such term exists where they come from and thus they do not understand the importance of the inquiry. One of the defining features of the Socratic method is that it works *with* the opinions of interlocutors. For instance, when Cephalus and Polemarchus in the *Republic* put forth understandings of justice derived from prominent Greek poets, Socrates does not dismiss them by arguing that the poets are not good sources of authority on what justice is (although eventually he leads Glaucon and Adeimantus, who are more suspicious of the Greek poets, to consider this point). Rather, he acknowledges the poets as sources of authority and suggests we must be careful to make sure we have interpreted them correctly.[11] In other words, he allows the interlocutors' responses to dictate the general direction of the investigation. This, in large part, accounts for the difficulty of carrying out a Socratic discourse. As most instruction manuals on using the Socratic method in class warn, the conversation can literally go anywhere. One might walk in with a series of planned questions, only to find that the student responses lead the discussion down a completely unexpected path.[12] This does not mean the Socratic method is a free-for-all; a good Socratic teacher is able to think "on the fly" and ask meaningful questions that lead to deeper understanding and examination. Nonetheless, the heavy emphasis on student input means that the conversation could begin with a discussion of an English word and transform into a discussion of a word from any language.

In my own experience using the Socratic method in culturally diverse classes, this is an uncommon, but not unprecedented occurrence. On at least a few occasions, I have pushed students to think about what, say, "justice" means and in response received a lesson on an equivalent term in a student's native language and what they think it means. When encouraged to bring to the conversation what they know, students will often do precisely that. Practitioners of the Socratic method might better elicit such responses by inviting the non-native English speakers in the room to share equivalent words in their language. In fact, in a culturally diverse classroom, this is arguably what a Socratic teacher should do, for this kind of input can greatly enhance the discussion. When students start to see that a word they take for granted means something different or perhaps has no place in another culture, this pushes students to grapple with the universality of experiences they often take for granted as universal. By contrast, sometimes a convergence of opinions on a particular concept across different cultures can lead to significant insights.[13] Here we might remember that the *Cratylus*, a dialog concerned explicitly with language, ends by concluding that the study of the words used to describe a thing is inferior to the study of the things themselves. The dialog as a whole, however, provokes readers to wonder why different names for the same object develop and why foreign words sometimes become part of the lexicon of one's own culture. In raising these questions, the dialog suggests that comparing different languages can be helpful in inspiring deeper examination of the naturalness of the understandings of phenomena that the words we use to describe them convey.

Even without provoking students to bring other languages into the conversation, the Socratic method arguably encourages significant self-reflectivity on the language in which it takes place. Evidence of this emerges in numerous dialogs, whether in the *Republic* when Socrates pushes his interlocutors to consider more deeply the meaning of "justice," or in the *Euthyphro* when he examines the meaning of "piety," or in *Hippias Major* when he and Hippias try to determine what the "beautiful" is. In each of these dialogs and many others, Socrates submits to examination conventional understandings of the term at hand. Oftentimes, this results in *aporia* or perplexity about what the concept under consideration truly means, showing that even within a single society or person conflicting conceptions of a term often exist. The emphasis the Socratic method places on ascending beyond localized understandings of a particular phenomenon and instead searching for a definition that applies universally makes this self-reflectiveness possible. Additionally, Socrates' frequent movements outside the conventions of Greek language help to present the language in a different, strange light. In *Hippias Major*, for instance, Socrates repeatedly uses language that Hippias finds "ugly" or improper, such as mentioning pots and ladles in the context of a serious inquiry. This move itself invites deeper examination of what "the beautiful" is. Likewise, near the beginning of his defense speech in Plato's *Apology*, Socrates asks the jury to sympathize with him just as if he were a "foreigner" being asked to speak in another dialect. For he will not, he says, speak the language they are accustomed to hearing in the courts, but rather will speak as he always does in the marketplace or elsewhere. Socrates' own form of speech, then, is not traditionally Greek – and this is true even when he converses in places more typically open to philosophic dialog. Conducted properly, the Socratic method challenges the conventions of the language in which it takes place. Hence, even when occurring within the bounds of a single language, the Socratic method works significantly against linguistic imperialism by providing opportunities for refashioning the language.

The "Normative Imperialism" Critique

A second critique leveled at the Socratic method extends deeper, highlighting how the method intrinsically promotes certain values over others and, in doing so, disadvantages students from certain cultural backgrounds. One common example cited in the scholarly literature is the use of the Socratic method in classrooms with students from areas immersed in the Confucian tradition of learning, such as China. Whereas the Socratic method privileges questioning and self-generated knowledge, the Confucian tradition emphasizes acquiring essential information from respected authority figures.[14] Though some Western instructors believe Chinese students take a passive or shallow approach to learning – merely repeating through rote memorization the authoritative dictates of their teachers – from the Chinese perspective, memorization allows for deeper processing of ideas, as each new repetition brings greater clarification.[15] Moreover, the point of Confucian learning is not to absorb uncritically whatever one's teacher or textbook says, but rather to become steeped in existing knowledge before daring to make one's own contributions. From a Confucian perspective, "the fervor with which Western students are exhorted to question and to challenge, especially early on in the learning about a topic, is foolish."[16] Confucian learning also takes a more pragmatic orientation to learning. One does not learn for the sake of learning, but to develop the virtues and skills needed to fulfill one's role in society and in the civil service. Hence, one scholar asks,

> What are we trying to accomplish by exposing students from Japan and other non-Western cultures to Socratic notions of education, which differ significantly from their expectations of teaching and learning and from the expectations they will return to when they go home?[17]

In sum, the Socratic method can be seen as culturally imperialistic in that it presupposes the superiority of a particular set of normative values generally identified as distinctly "Western": the priority of the individual over the collective, the equality of teacher and student as mutual learners rather than a more hierarchical teacher–student relationship, and the importance of truth-seeking above the need for a more practical education designed to safeguard social harmony.

Not only does the Socratic method operate within a particular normative framework that privileges certain cultural values over others, but in using the Socratic method teachers may also unwittingly penalize students unaccustomed to or unaccepting of these values. Numerous studies show that students from non-Western cultures often struggle with participating in Socratic discussions or even understanding the purpose of such discussions.[18] Unlike their Western peers, who are often taught at a young age the value of critical thinking and of classroom participation, students from a Confucian learning background tend to exhibit reluctance toward stating their own opinions in class or challenging the ideas of their teacher or other classmates. Again, this is because their native cultural framework of education emphasizes hearing what the teacher has to say, not singling oneself out in class, and engaging in cooperative rather than more individualized learning. Teachers who use the Socratic method in classrooms with students from diverse cultural backgrounds need to be aware of this when calling on students or assigning grades based on classroom participation. As Gorry puts it, "The student sins by failing to follow the rules of the game, but what if the student is failed because s/he cannot comprehend that the rules are different to those that s/he are used to?"[19] Another study reports that "using the Socratic method beyond the United States can yield similar pedagogical benefits but requires modifications to honor different cultural norms."[20] In this case, the teachers – all professors or lecturers of legal studies – took the traditional law school model of subjecting individual students to rigorous questioning about the case at hand and made important alterations to fit the Chinese context, such as beginning with small group discussions to help students gain greater comfort and confidence in their own reasoning rather than finding themselves thrown into the humiliating experience of being "on the spot" in front of the entire class. Without these modifications, the students would have felt intimidated – a critique of the Socratic method that echoes concerns about its potential to marginalize female and minority students.[21]

Some scholars take this critique even further, contending that the very expectation of dialog between members of different cultures constitutes an act of cultural imperialism, however benign it may seem. Comparative political theorist Jenco, for instance, points out that the privileging of speech excludes cultural traditions that place greater value on other means of communication:

> Practices that capture what cannot be expressed adequately in words – whether because too sublime (as are some religious truths), too complicated, or because so instantiated in practice that it is not comprehensible through language to begin with – can be acknowledged only with difficulty.... Practices that complement text-based interpretative traditions, or that constitute traditions of their own – practices like imitation, ritual, dance, or other forms of non-verbal expression – are rendered silent, passed over in favor of text-based reconstructions of individual utterances.[22]

In merely assuming the priority of dialog over other modes of communication, the Socratic method, on this view, favors a single set of cultural norms. It presumes that truth-seeking must take place within a dialogic form. This critique likely owes its origins to works like *The Birth of Tragedy from the Spirit of Music*, in which Nietzsche blames Socrates and Plato for initiating a corrosive shift away from the Dionysian, life-giving art of tragedy to the rigidly intellectual activity of philosophy. By implying the supremacy of giving an account of one's reasons, the Socratic method allegedly denies the validity of truths that cannot be thusly communicated.

It would be impossible to deny that the very structure of the Socratic method favors questioning, individual thinking, and discourse. By using the Socratic method in the classroom, teachers therefore may be justly accused of privileging certain normative values over others. Yet, as with the linguistic imperialism critique, this critique seems inescapable no matter which teaching method one employs. A Confucian teacher imposes the ideals of authority, tradition, and conformity for the sake of social harmony. A teacher whose courses heavily involve ritual dance privileges non-verbal discourse over verbal discourse. No teaching method can be neutral; no teaching method develops within a normative vacuum. Insofar as the Western philosophical tradition is implicated in a long history of imperial conquest (although some prominent Western philosophers resisted this movement), perhaps one ought to be more concerned about using teaching methods from this tradition than from others. Yet, in Plato's dialogs Socrates often exposes the contradictions inherent in imperialism.[23] To implicate the Socratic method in Western imperialism simply because it is of Western origin therefore seems problematic. Though scholars often regard Western political thought as having originated with Socrates and Plato, this does not mean their philosophies bear responsibility for every injustice Westerners have committed. To be sure, critics perform a valuable service by calling our attention to the norms underlying the Socratic method – stripping practitioners of the false notion that the Socratic method, or any teaching method, acts as a "neutral" tool. This in itself does not, however, constitute a legitimate reason for abandoning the Socratic method. If it does, then any teacher who does not use teaching methods from the cultures of the various students in her classroom is behaving in an exclusionary, oppressive manner.

Additionally, one advantage of the Socratic method, as previously argued, is that it works with the logic of the specific interlocutors at hand. Though the method favors discourse and the use of the intellect, Socrates not infrequently appeals to his interlocutors by evoking images and myths. In the *Republic*, Socrates claims he can only provide what "appears to be a child of the good" – i.e., the image of the sun – because the "opinions" he himself now holds about it remain beyond the range of the present discussion (506e). This implies both that Socrates cannot always convey the greatest truths through dialectic conversation, and that he himself does not entirely grasp these truths. Hence, contrary to Nietzsche's criticism of Plato, the dialogs depict Socratic teaching as reliant upon rather than simply dismissive of artistic or non-rational modes of knowing. At the same time, the dialogs demonstrate the value of reason and dialog, out of which the criticism under consideration itself emerges.

Even when an interlocutor's viewpoint unfolds within the strictures of discourse and reasoning, the specific nature of the rules of logic through which Socratic examination takes place derives from the interlocutors themselves. As discussed in the previous section, if an interlocutor treats a given text as a source of unquestionable authority, the Socratic teacher works within this framework to show why the interlocutor's interpretation, or perhaps the text itself, may be contradictory. As Meckstroth puts it,

> The authority by which the interlocutor finds himself convicted of incoherence, then, is always in the final instance his own, never that of Socrates or of some impersonal set of logical rules that might confront him as an alien law.[24]

Interestingly, one study in which researchers used an almost literal adaptation of Socrates' questioning of Meno's slave to teach native Argentinians the same mathematical lesson found that "the Socratic dialogue is built on a strong intuition of human knowledge and reasoning which persists in more than 24 centuries after its conception, providing one of the most striking demonstrations of universality across time and cultures."[25] Though the Argentinian students failed to arrive at the same understanding as Meno's slave, the vast majority responded exactly as Meno's slave did – reproducing his correct responses and errors. This suggests that even if people from different cultures begin with different premises, there may be some universality to the reasoning process. Whatever the case may be, by working within the interlocutors' framework of thinking, the Socratic method to a significant degree escapes the normative imperialism critique.

It is also to the great credit of the Socratic method that it allows for questioning of the very norms it inherently propagates. Evidence of this appears no more clearly than in Plato's *Republic*. Though, as we have seen, the Socratic method is associated with critical thinking, self-generated knowledge, and learning for the sake of learning, in the *Republic* the method leads to the apparent advocacy of precisely the opposite principles. After all, scholars have often criticized Plato for allegedly promoting a totalitarian regime in which all but the "gold-souled" are taught to accept the dictates and "noble lies" perpetrated by the philosopher-kings and not to engage in independent thinking. Whereas many challenge this interpretation, it must be admitted that Socratic questioning enables the construction of such a city in speech, forcing readers to approach Socratic education itself from a more questioning position. Is there some danger in exposing citizens to this form of education? What sacrifices or trade-offs might it involve? These are some of the questions the dialog raises, whatever indications one thinks Plato gives of how we should resolve them.

Finally, it is worthwhile to recognize that Western students themselves often struggle with the Socratic method. Though they may be more accustomed to participating in class and engaging in critical thinking, for many the experience of subjecting their dearest ideas to questioning never becomes easier. Many others begin with a certain level of intimidation until they become comfortable with their instructor and classmates, even with prior exposure to the Socratic method. Moreover, certain aspects of Western education and culture incline some Western students not to understand the value of the Socratic method. Though widely used, the Socratic method is by far not the most prevalent model of education in the Western school system. Some may therefore enter the classroom equally as accustomed to lecture-style learning as their Confucian peers. In the age of the Internet and instantaneous answers, Western students often display their own resistance to Socratic education, preferring a more Confucian model of education in which the teacher imparts knowledge to them. Hence, while teachers should be aware of how differences in cultural background may affect the performance of students in classrooms where the Socratic method is used, it may be safer to assume that all students will struggle with the method and that few will enter with an appreciation of it. It is then incumbent on the Socratic teacher to provide the proper conditions for a fruitful Socratic conversation and to help students understand the benefits of such conversation.

The "Philosophic Imperialism" Critique

Thus far, I have adopted a view of "culture" centered on horizons or constellations of beliefs, habits, and languages roughly corresponding with particular peoples. It is also possible, however, to critique the Socratic method on the grounds that it attempts to convert participants to what one might call "philosophic" culture. Similar to the normative imperialism critique, this critique charges Socratic teachers with manipulating students into conforming to a particular way of life – although, in this case, these values are not so much "Greek" or "Western" as philosophic. That is, whereas Socratic education may significantly call into question the values of any existing culture, it is nevertheless imperialistic, according to this critique, in that it tries to impose the values of an "otherworldly" philosophic culture. Put simply, Socrates has in mind what a virtuous person looks like; he may pretend as though he does not know what virtue is and as though he and his interlocutors are equals in the dialog taking place, but in actuality he is a cunning manipulator coercing them into accepting predetermined answers about the good life.

To my mind, two substantial responses can be given to this critique. First, as the *Republic* shows, the final power always rests with Socrates' interlocutors. Cephalus is not persuaded by Socrates' refutation of his notion of justice, and he excuses himself from the conversation with no objection on Socrates' part. Admittedly, participation in Socratic conversation may not be so voluntary in contemporary classrooms where students' grades depend on it, but this suggests students can "take or leave" the revelations of the conversation. This point is well illustrated throughout Plato's dialogs. Though some of Socrates' interlocutors amount to little more than "yes men," interlocutors like Thrasymachus or Callicles from the *Gorgias* exhibit substantial resistance to assenting to the conclusions to which the *elenchus* draws them. Furthermore, even more acquiescent interlocutors often give the impression of not having been fully "converted" by Socrates' arguments. After all, in the *Republic*, Socrates raises serious questions about the notion of justice as doing good to one's friends and harm to one's enemies, yet this conception of justice later becomes foundational to the city in speech without so much as a reminder from his interlocutors of the potential problems with it. This suggests that Socrates' refutation of this definition of justice was not as effective as it initially seemed. In other words, even if Socratic teachers aim to convert their students to the philosophic way of life, their ability to do so is limited. Only teachings that truly resonate with the soul can have the desired effect.

Second, there is substantial evidence that when Plato's Socrates claims not to know the answers to the questions he raises, he is telling the truth. To be sure, he makes clear that he holds particular "opinions" about questions such as what the Good is, and that he sees his opinions on some matters as more advanced than those of his interlocutors (*Republic*, 506e). Using these insights, he tries to guide his interlocutors toward the opinions he holds. At the same time, the dialogs repeatedly stress the importance of submitting to examination even the ideas of which one is most sure.[26] As Bickford explains, for Plato the claims arrived at through dialectic "are only as strong as continued argumentation makes them .... Socrates must at once get his interlocutors to question their own knowingness, while at the same time urging them to question his own."[27] A good Socratic teacher does not remain content, then, with leading her students toward the truths her own investigations have uncovered. Rather, a good Socratic teacher will push further, encouraging the students to examine even these opinions. This is perhaps why so often Socrates' inquiries end in *aporia*. It is also perhaps why Plato himself wrote dialogs rather than treatises, for dialogs reproduce the Socratic pedagogical practice of inducing perplexity by leaving ideas open to discussion instead of unambiguously advocating a particular set of beliefs.[28]

If the Socratic method entails submitting one's ideas to continuous examination, then, as Nussbaum proclaimed, Socratic education may very well thrive in pluralistic learning environments. As Meckstroth argues,

> Past a certain threshold of precision, rigor will benefit more by expanding the range of competing views one explicitly refutes and by increasing the sensitivity and imagination with which one enters into each of those views' internal logics in order to be as certain as possible that one's supposed proofs do not rely on any tendentious assumptions one's interlocutors could coherently reject.[29]

A culturally diverse classroom may thus be the ideal environment for a Socratic discussion. By including a range of participants, such a class offers greater potential for exposing an idea to multiple forms of critique. While this may not result in the idea being overturned, the process of submitting a truth to scrutiny from various angles makes it more likely that any ideas that endure this test will contain at least some element of truth. No wonder, then, that Socrates engaged foreigners and that Plato himself traveled widely and welcomed foreigners into his Academy. Of course, one might still accuse Socratic teachers of being philosophic imperialists if by philosophic culture one means practicing self-examination. But, again, if this is a form of imperialism, it is one completely dependent on the willingness of students to take up the provocation to self-examination.

Conclusion

In defending the Socratic method against the three critiques discussed in this chapter – the "linguistic imperialism," "normative imperialism," and "philosophic imperialism" critiques – I do not mean to downplay the concerns they raise. Certainly these are serious concerns and just as a good Socratic teacher will submit his ideas to examination, so should he submit the Socratic method itself to examination. Nonetheless, even a good critique deserves to be examined. That is what this chapter set out to do. Though I hope to have persuaded that the Socratic method is not merely a defensible teaching method for culturally diverse contexts, but in fact a method that is well-suited for such contexts, Socratic teachers or those considering using the Socratic method in their classrooms should give thought to the potential problems that the cultural imperialism critique illuminates. Even if Socrates himself cannot be justly accused of acting imperialistically, is it possible that other teachers could misuse the Socratic method to pursue, consciously or unconsciously, imperialistic aims? This question is well worth asking of ourselves before and as we use the Socratic method in our own classrooms.

Notes

1 See, e.g., Evan Peterson, "Teaching to Think: Applying the Socratic Method Outside the Law School Setting," *Journal of College Teaching & Learning* 6/5 (2009): 83–8; and Douglas R. Oyler and Frank Romanelli, "The Fact of Ignorance: Revisiting the Socratic Method as a Tool for Teaching Critical Thinking," *American Journal of Pharmaceutical Education* 78/7 (2014): 1–9.
2 See, e.g., James C. Overholser, "Guided Discovery: Problem-Solving Therapy Integrated Within the Socratic Method," *Journal of Contemporary Psychotherapy* 43/2 (2013): 73–82; James C. Overholser, "Positive Psychotherapy According to the Socratic Method," *Journal of Contemporary Psychotherapy* 45/2 (2015): 137–42; and Gavin I. Clark and Sarah J. Egan, "The Socratic Method in Cognitive Behavioural Therapy: A Narrative Review," *Cognitive Therapy and Research* 39/6 (2015): 863–79.
3 Allan Bloom, *The Closing of the American Mind: How Higher Education Has Failed Democracy and Impoverished the Souls of Today's Students* (New York: Simon & Schuster, 1987).
4 Martha C. Nussbaum, *Cultivating Humanity: A Classical Defense of Reform in Liberal Education* (Cambridge: Harvard University Press, 1997), 33.

5 Nussbaum, *Cultivating Humanity*, 38.
6 Nicholas C. Burbules, "Book Review – *Cultivating Humanity: A Classical Defense of Reform in Liberal Education* by Martha C. Nussbaum," *Harvard Educational Review* 69/4 (1999), http://hepg.org/her-home/issues/harvard-educational-review-volume-69-issue-4/herarticle/_150.
7 Jacques Derrida, *Monolingualism of the Other, or, The Prosthesis of Origin*, Patrick Mensah, trans. (Stanford: Stanford University Press, 1998), 39.
8 Derrida, *Monolingualism*, 14.
9 Jacques Derrida, *Of Hospitality: Anne Dufourmantelle Invites Jacques Derrida to Respond*, Rachel Bowlby, trans. (Stanford: Stanford University Press, 2000), 133.
10 Stephen Gilbert Brown, *Words in the Wilderness: Critical Literacy in the Borderlands* (Albany: SUNY Press, 2000), 95. For more on the phenomenon of the mimicry of colonial subjects, see Homi K. Bhabha, *The Location of Culture* (London: Routledge, 1994).
11 As Frank argues, Socrates' approach shifts poetic authority from the poets to their auditors and interpreters. Jill Frank, *Poetic Justice: Rereading Plato's* Republic (Chicago: University of Chicago Press, 2018), 50–80.
12 This difficulty is discussed, e.g., in Matt Copeland, *Socratic Circles: Fostering Critical and Creative Thinking in Middle and High School* (Portland: Stenhouse Publishers, 2005), 65–7.
13 On "equivalences of experience," see Eric Voegelin, "Equivalences of Experience and Symbolization in History," in *The Collected Works of Eric Voegelin, Vol. 12: Published Essays, 1966–1985*, Ellis Sandoz, ed. (Columbia: University of Missouri Press, 1990), 115–33.
14 For a more comprehensive comparison of the two traditions of learning/teaching, see Roger G. Tweed and Darrin R. Lehman, "Learning Considered within a Cultural Context: Confucian and Socratic Approaches," *American Psychologist* 57/2 (2002): 89–99.
15 Ference Marton, Gloria Dall'Alba and Tse Lai Kun, "Memorizing and Understanding: The Keys to the Paradox?" in *The Chinese Learner: Cultural, Psychological, and Contextual Influences*, David A. Watkins and John B. Biggs, eds. (Hong Kong: Comparative Education Research Centre; and Melbourne: Australian Council for Educational Research, 1996), 69–84.
16 Joe Greenholtz, "Socratic Teachers and Confucian Learners: Examining the Benefits and Pitfalls of a Year Abroad," *Language and Intercultural Communication* 3/2 (2003): 124. To be clear, this characterization of Western learning may speak more to the contemporary emphasis on individualism and inclusivity than to the Socratic context, in which interlocutors are encouraged not to express their opinions mindlessly but rather to submit them to rigorous examination.
17 Greenholtz, "Socratic Teachers," 123.
18 Interestingly, one study finds this is true not only of non-European students, but also of Eastern European students. Even though Eastern European students share the Socratic cultural heritage of their Western European peers, the legacy of communist rule in Eastern European school systems has made a significant mark on how Eastern European students approach education, making them less comfortable with questioning and stating their own views in the classroom. Ulrich Kühnen *et al.*, "Challenge Me! Communicating in Multicultural Classrooms," *Social Psychological Education* 15 (2012): 59–76.
19 Jonathan Gorry, "Cultures of Learning and Learning Culture: Socratic and Confucian Approaches to teaching and Learning," *Learning and Teaching: The International Journal of Higher Education in the Social Sciences* 4/3 (2011): 15.
20 Erin Ryan *et al.*, "When Socrates Meets Confucius: Teaching Creative and Critical Thinking Across Cultures Through Multilevel Socratic Method," *Nebraska Law Review* 92 (2013): 289–348.
21 For an overview of these critiques and a response, see Jennifer L. Rosato, "The Socratic Method and Women Law Students: Humanize, Don't Feminize," *Southern California Review of Law and Women's Studies* 7 (1997): 37–62.
22 Leigh Kathryn Jenco, "'What Does Heaven Ever Say?' A Methods-Centered Approach to Cross-Cultural Engagement," *American Political Science Review* 101/4 (2007): 744.
23 In numerous dialogs, Plato depicts Socrates objecting to Athens' imperial ambitions and the appetites it unleashes. This is clearest, e.g., in *Gorgias* 515e–517a, 519a–b, and in the silence on Athens' empire in the funeral oration of Plato's *Menexenus*. Also see Mary P. Nichols, "Philosophy and Empire: On Socrates and Alcibiades in Plato's *Symposium*," *Polity* 39/4 (2007): 502–21.
24 Christopher Meckstroth, "Socratic Method and Political Science," *American Political Science Review* 106/3 (2012): 648.
25 Andrea P. Goldin *et al.*, "From Ancient Greece to Modern Education: Universality and Lack of Generalization of the Socratic Dialogue," *Mind, Brain, and Education* 5/4 (2011): 180–85.
26 Here I am challenging standard postmodernist accounts of Plato that present him as an absolutist thinker. On my interpretation (which I cannot fully defend here), though Plato does not share the postmodernist

rejection of the possibility of absolute truth, he agrees that due to the limitations of human understanding we must always hold our "truths" in question.
27 Susan Bickford, "Enduring Uncertainty: Political Courage in Plato" (paper presented at the American Political Science Association Annual Meeting, Philadelphia, PA, September 4, 2016), 22.
28 See, e.g., Ruby Blondell, *The Play of Character in Plato's Dialogues* (Cambridge: Cambridge University Press, 2002); Diskin Clay, *Platonic Questions: Dialogues with the Silent Philosopher* (University Park: Pennsylvania State University Press, 2000); and J. Peter Euben, *The Tragedy of Political Theory: The Road Not Taken* (Princeton: Princeton University Press, 1990).
29 Meckstroth, "Socratic Method," 649.

Bibliography

Bhabha, Homi K. 1994. *The Location of Culture*. London: Routledge.
Bickford, Susan. "Enduring Uncertainty: Political Courage in Plato." Paper presented at the American Political Science Association Annual Meeting, Philadelphia, PA, September 4, 2016.
Blondell, Ruby. 2002. *The Play of Character in Plato's Dialogues*. Cambridge: Cambridge University Press.
Bloom, Allan. 1987. *The Closing of the American Mind: How Higher Education Has Failed Democracy and Impoverished the Souls of Today's Students*. New York: Simon & Schuster.
Brown, Stephen Gilbert. 2000. *Words in the Wilderness: Critical Literacy in the Borderlands*. Albany: SUNY Press.
Burbules, Nicholas C. 1999. "Book Review – *Cultivating Humanity: A Classical Defense of Reform in Liberal Education* by Martha C. Nussbaum." *Harvard Educational Review* 69/4. http://hepg.org/her-home/issues/harvard-educational-review-volume-69-issue-4/herarticle/_150.
Clark, Gavin I. and Sarah J. Egan. 2015. "The Socratic Method in Cognitive Behavioural Therapy: A Narrative Review." *Cognitive Therapy and Research* 39/6: 863–79.
Clay, Diskin. 2000. *Platonic Questions: Dialogues with the Silent Philosopher*. University Park: Pennsylvania State University Press.
Copeland, Matt. 2005. *Socratic Circles: Fostering Critical and Creative Thinking in Middle and High School*. Portland: Stenhouse Publishers.
Derrida, Jacques. 2000. *Of Hospitality: Anne Dufourmantelle Invites Jacques Derrida to Respond*. Rachel Bowlby trans. Stanford: Stanford University Press.
———. 1998. *Monolingualism of the Other, or, The Prosthesis of Origin*. Patrick Mensah trans. Stanford: Stanford University Press.
Euben, J. Peter. 1990. *The Tragedy of Political Theory: The Road Not Taken*. Princeton: Princeton University Press.
Frank, Jill. 2018. *Poetic Justice: Rereading Plato's Republic*. Chicago: University of Chicago Press.
Goldin, Andrea P., Laura Pezzatti, Antonio M. Battro and Mariano Sigman. 2011. "From Ancient Greece to Modern Education: Universality and Lack of Generalization of the Socratic Dialogue." *Mind, Brain, and Education* 5/4: 180–85.
Gorry, Jonathan. 2011. "Cultures of Learning and Learning Culture: Socratic and Confucian Approaches to Teaching and Learning." *Learning and Teaching: The International Journal of Higher Education in the Social Sciences* 4/3: 4–18.
Greenholtz, Joe. 2003. "Socratic Teachers and Confucian Learners: Examining the Benefits and Pitfalls of a Year Abroad." *Language and Intercultural Communication* 3/2: 122–30.
Jenco, Leigh Kathryn. 2007. "'What Does Heaven Ever Say?' A Methods-Centered Approach to Cross-Cultural Engagement." *American Political Science Review* 101/4: 741–55.
Kühnen, Ulrich, Marieke C. van Egmond, Frank Haber, Stefanie Kuschel, Amina Özelsel, Alexis L. Rossi and Youlia Spivak. 2012. "Challenge Me! Communicating in Multicultural Classrooms." *Social Psychological Education* 15: 59–76.
Marton, Ference, Gloria Dall'Alba and Tse Lai Kun. 1996. "Memorizing and Understanding: The Keys to the Paradox?" In *The Chinese Learner: Cultural, Psychological, and Contextual Influences*. David A. Watkins and John B. Biggs eds. Hong Kong: Comparative Education Research Centre; and Melbourne: Australian Council for Educational Research: 69–84.

Meckstroth, Christopher. 2012. "Socratic Method and Political Science." *American Political Science Review* 106/3: 644–60.

Nichols, Mary P. 2007. "Philosophy and Empire: On Socrates and Alcibiades in Plato's *Symposium*." *Polity* 39/4: 502–21.

Nussbaum, Martha C. 1997. *Cultivating Humanity: A Classical Defense of Reform in Liberal Education*. Cambridge: Harvard University Press.

Overholser, James C. 2013. "Guided Discovery: Problem-Solving Therapy Integrated Within the Socratic Method." *Journal of Contemporary Psychotherapy* 43/2: 73–82.

——— 2015. "Positive Psychotherapy According to the Socratic Method." *Journal of Contemporary Psychotherapy* 45/2: 137–42.

Oyler, Douglas R. and Frank Romanelli. 2014. "The Fact of Ignorance: Revisiting the Socratic Method as a Tool for Teaching Critical Thinking." *American Journal of Pharmaceutical Education* 78/7: 1–9.

Peterson, Evan. 2009. "Teaching to Think: Applying the Socratic Method Outside the Law School Setting." *Journal of College Teaching & Learning* 6/5: 83–8.

Rosato, Jennifer L. 1997. "The Socratic Method and Women Law Students: Humanize, Don't Feminize." *Southern California Review of Law and Women's Studies* 7: 37–62.

Ryan, Erin, Xin Shuai, Yuan Ye, You Ran and Li Haomei. 2013. "When Socrates Meets Confucius: Teaching Creative and Critical Thinking Across Cultures Through Multilevel Socratic Method." *Nebraska Law Review* 92: 289–348.

Tweed, Roger G. and Darrin R. Lehman. 2002. "Learning Considered Within a Cultural Context: Confucian and Socratic Approaches." *American Psychologist* 57/2: 89–99.

Voegelin, Eric. 1990. "Equivalences of Experience and Symbolization in History." In *The Collected Works of Eric Voegelin, Vol. 12: Published Essays, 1966–1985*. Ellis Sandoz ed. Columbia: University of Missouri Press, 115–33.

11 The Socratic Method in Today's University

Paul Corey

The Socratic Method, the Liberal Arts, and Illiberal Threats

Liberal arts education in North America is in decline. The humanities have been especially hit hard, with declining student enrollment, cutbacks to programs, and fewer full-time job opportunities for professors.[1] However, there is another reality today: both the institutions and the culture of liberal democracy are under threat from illiberal forces within Western society. We see this particularly on the political right and the rise of demagogic politicians such as Trump who appeal to populist anger; but we also see it on the left, especially on university campuses roiled by identity and sexual politics, and students making stringent demands. A question arises: is the decay of liberal democratic culture linked with the decline of liberal arts education?[2]

It is against this background that this chapter will consider challenges to the Socratic method in today's university classrooms. The method has long been considered an essential feature of liberal education, primarily taught in introductory philosophy classes but applicable to other disciplines. It stands as the first and perhaps most exemplary model of open, free, and critical thinking in a liberal society. Though Socrates is presented in Plato's dialogs as being critical of democracy (*Republic*, 557a–565c), he nevertheless recognized and appreciated how the democratic city of Athens tolerated his philosophizing (*Apology*, 37 c–d; *Crito*, 52a–53a). Of course, even Athenian patience ran out: after years of cultural decline during the Peloponnesian War, the city executed Socrates in 399 BCE for impiety and corrupting the youth. Notwithstanding the official charges against Socrates, he was essentially executed for shaming his contemporaries because he revealed that they did not know what they claimed to know. The method is therefore perilous for practitioners who live in democracies gravitating toward decadence and illiberality.

Though there is no universally agreed upon definition of the "Socratic method," a number of features stand out in Socrates' approach to pedagogy as depicted in Plato's dialogs. First, the method is a *dialectical* form of argumentation, proceeding as a discussion between two or more people, not as a lecture or sermon. Second, in the dialog an "interlocutor" states an opinion/hypothesis, which is then submitted to a series of questions asked by someone else, to determine whether the opinion is implicitly true or riddled with contradictions and weaknesses. This is *elenchus* and is what most people understand as the "Socratic method." If a position is refuted, the interlocutor experiences perplexity (*aporia*); however, the primary purpose of the method is not for the questioner to get pleasure out of this. Though Plato often depicts Socratic discussions ending in *aporia*, true dialectic goes further; indeed, Socrates warns against "misology" – the radical skepticism of all arguments (*Phaedo*, 88c–91c). Hopefully the interlocutor, once his argument has been shown lacking, will be motivated to find a better argument and, with prompting, articulate something true. The dialectical philosopher, in Socrates' words, is like a "midwife," helping a soul give birth to wisdom (*Theaetetus*, 149a–151d). This means that a dialectician must employ the rules of logic, a well-known feature of the method. But Plato's Socrates also uses images, myths, and poetic references to enhance certain arguments, or to make points that cannot be made through *elenchus* alone.[3] The most famous image is "the cave" in *Republic*, which Socrates uses to describe education (514a–517c).

There is also an ethical aspect to the Socratic approach which is less recognized, one intimately tied to education. True education does not give students intelligence. Students' souls are not blank slates, as they already possess intelligence (*nous*) and some vague awareness of truth, of which they need to be reminded (*anamnesis*). Nor is Socratic education a matter of filling an empty soul with skills and information. Rather, Socratic pedagogy is primarily a task of turning a soul (*Republic*, 518b–d) and guiding it along an ascending "pathway" that leads to the love (*eros*) and intellection of higher forms of truth, justice, beauty, and goodness; it also cultivates excellence (*arête* or "virtue") in the soul of the student as a consequence of seeing these higher forms.[4]

This chapter will consider five student mentalities which collectively challenge Socratic pedagogy in today's classroom:

1. *Online Mentality*: feeling the need to be connected to digital networks;
2. *Job-Seeking Mentality*: understanding university education solely as a path to employment;
3. *Relativist Mentality*: thinking that all values or truth claims are relative to the culture or individual;
4. *Safe Space Mentality*: thinking that all students, particularly those from traditionally victimized identities, must be kept "safe" in the classroom from ideas, words, or images that offend and traumatize;
5. *Troll Mentality*: saying deliberately provocative or offensive things, often from a far-right perspective, to elicit an emotional response and encourage confrontation.

These mentalities are not mutually exclusive: two or more of these may, and usually do, exist within a single student. It is best to understand these mentalities as various directions in which students' souls gravitate. Today's Socratic professor must adjust her speech and pedagogic strategies to the combination of mentalities she is engaging. What may work in one class or with one student may not work in another class or with another student.

Each of the five mentalities, and their respective responses, requires more thorough scholarly examination than will be provided by this chapter. What is offered here is sweeping and provisional. There is also an overarching institutional issue that will not be addressed: the need of universities to recognize the centrality of the liberal arts and the importance of the Socratic method in educating fully democratic citizens. Furthermore, other institutional issues, such as expanding class sizes, the growth of university administrations, and the decline of full-time tenured faculty, also need addressing since they affect the class environment. But institutional change is not the focus of this chapter. Rather, it considers what the professor can do herself to keep Socratic pedagogy alive in her classes. This is not for the faint-hearted; not only does creating a Socratic classroom require constant energy and diligence, it comes with considerable risks of offending certain students or putting the professor at odds with her institution.

Mentalities and Socratic Responses

The Online Mentality and Use of Technology in the Classroom

All students today possess online mentalities. They feel compelled to be "plugged-in" to their computers, phones, and tablets. This mentality has emerged out of a society saturated with digital technology. These electronic devices are no longer a luxury but a necessity for students, and they cause distraction once they are brought into the classroom. Many students will be on at least one device during class, connecting with others or accessing content unrelated to the course material. Students often pride themselves on being multitaskers.[5] However, studies have demonstrated that when students multitask with devices in class – taking notes on computers, Facebooking, shopping, texting – it results in more distraction, less retention, and poorer academic performance.[6] Furthermore, when a student is on a device, she is not only distracting herself, but also those around her.[7]

There are larger issues at play. First, the omnipresence of information technology creates the impression that "wisdom" is attained through the gathering and spread of information, not through critical thinking, which is why the online mentality feels that it must always be plugged-in. Second, the speed at which information technology and social media operate seems to be having an impact on human consciousness. The online mentality expects things to happen faster and has less patience for lulls or gaps, feeling compelled to fill every second with information and distraction. The slow, nuanced, and occasionally boring slog of Socratic reasoning cannot compete with the dynamo of digital media, which allows a "surfer" to skim the surface of everything without diving deeply into anything.[8] Third, devices impact our ability to interact face-to-face, which is central to the Socratic method.[9] With texts and emails, students do not see facial reactions. The Internet also allows a person to sink into a solipsistic echo chamber (*via* a "chat room" or online group), in which his own opinions and tastes are repeated back to him. In this way, the Internet reinforces silos of like-minded people, sheltered from actual face-to-face dialog, who become sensitive and outright angry when they encounter opposing opinions in offline public spaces.

Some educational theorists have argued that truly innovative professors should accept the "culture of hyper attention" that comes with the predominance of digital media; the only way students will learn in the new environment is if professors embrace and integrate these technologies into their pedagogies, providing constant online stimulation and activities in the classroom.[10] But as Turkle argues, it is doubtful that this approach, even if successfully applied, would result in anything more than fragmented learning and ill-formed thoughts; when students are simultaneously using different electronic gadgets and programs, there is no sustained focus. Students will only partially digest small bits of information and form "tweet"-sized thoughts rather than fully coherent arguments. Professors should establish a different approach that students may resist at first, but which, in the long term, is more conducive to deep learning – one that cultivates what Turkle calls "unitasking," encouraging students to focus on one point at a time by listening carefully, reading deeply, and responding critically.[11]

The true Socratic classroom therefore needs to be, for the most part, a device- and computer-free environment, with exceptions for in-class written assignments and students who need technology for accessibility. In such a class, students are encouraged to handwrite notes summarizing classroom discussion, rather than to transcribe verbatim on a computer. At least one major study has demonstrated that even when computers are used exclusively for note-taking, it results in "shallower processing" of class content than if notes are taken longhand.[12] With the decline of cursive writing, students may be less able to write longhand. Nevertheless, the Socratic classroom should shift from an environment where students are basically stenographers and toward a space of face-to-face dialog with minimal note-taking. For example, in small-to-medium sized courses, it may be possible to conduct what Copeland calls "Socratic Circles," where a group of three to six students forms a circle in the center of the class to discuss a specific issue. The remaining students form an outer circle, listening and assessing. When the inner circle dialog is finished, students in the outer circle can participate. The professor acts as a moderator, intervening at key points.[13] Obviously, Socratic Circles are easier to conduct in smaller classes, but there are opportunities for more dialog even in large classes. And because the Socratic method is a "face-to-face" pedagogy, it cannot be fully practiced in an online course. Though some online courses may be well designed and allow for dialog through discussion boards and video links, they simply cannot recreate the full experience of a living Socratic classroom.

Technology can actually assist the Socratic professor who wants to lead a device-free class. Termed the "flipped classroom," course materials and pre-taped lectures can be posted on the course website, which students are required to digest before coming to class, allowing the professor to transform her "lectures" into critical discussions. A substantial participation grade needs to be required so that students attend, assessed by a clear rubric (to avoid charges of "subjective" grading) that possibly includes in-class written assignments, where students reflect on class discussions. The flipped classroom holds potential for the Socratic professor, provided class is not a simple "review" for tests and assignments.[14]

This shift away from the digital classroom should not be understood as nostalgia for the old-fashioned "talk and chalk" class; rather, it should be considered "innovatively analog," comparable to, say, the resurgence of analog vinyl records in an age of digital music streaming. The analog classroom, as with an analog recording, is not seeking to destroy the digital world, but to offer a singular, richer, more nuanced experience in the midst of omnipresent digitalization with its binary codes.

The Job-Seeking Mentality and the Demand for Employable Skills

The job-seeking mentality emerges out of the societal and corporate demand for skilled workers who can contribute to the economy. This has led to parental and student focus on receiving hireable skills through enrollment in STEM disciplines (science, technology, engineering, mathematics) and business programs, rather than liberal arts. Most students expect that a university degree provides opportunity for more lucrative employment. Student recruitment representatives from universities are constantly faced with the same question from potential students and their parents: will this degree provide a pathway to employment? The question is not unreasonable; students and parents hope that the investment required for post-secondary education is worth it. Over the past few decades, universities have directed energy and resources toward STEM and business programs, which attract students and private donors. This has led to what Nussbaum disparagingly calls "education for economic growth": education that provides skills for jobs that contribute to technological advancement and GDP growth in a globalized economy.[15] When education is understood as simply training for future employment, the liberal arts appear to be useless at best, or an enemy of economic growth at worst. As Nussbaum points out, educators for economic growth not only ignore the arts, they "fear them" and "campaign against the humanities and arts as ingredients of basic education. This assault is currently taking place all over the world."[16] Thus the Socratic professor, who teaches general electives to STEM and business students, will face the ire of practically minded students who ask: why do I need to take this course? How can I possibly benefit from it?

Turning universities into, essentially, vocational institutes leads to a number of problems. First, it produces graduates who may have technical skills, but who often lack advanced communication skills and abilities to think critically and creatively in the workplace. Second, there is no guarantee that technical skills which are in demand today will not be obsolete within a few years. Third, this ethos encourages students to view everything instrumentally, including other people; students are thus more inclined to assess other people on whether they are useful for monetary success. Such students may be more inclined to treat others disrespectfully if these others are perceived as either competition or as having no utilitarian value – an ethos reinforced in popular "reality television" programs, where it is dog-eat-dog on the path to success. Finally, all of this means that students are being groomed to be employees and consumers, not proper democratic citizens who are capable of true self-examination, social criticism, and prudential action. Students who lack the so-called "soft skills" of communication and critical thinking are less likely to think independently, and more likely to become "yes-men," performing the instrumental tasks they are hired to do, even when these tasks need to be rethought. In their social/political lives they are more prone to be swayed by large groups, compelling demagogues, and bad arguments.[17]

Nussbaum argues that universities need to cultivate critical and creative thinking, and encourage students' empathic imagination, to stop this slide into ignorance and inhumanity. For Nussbaum, Socratic pedagogy is central to such an education. She writes: "critical thinking should be infused into the pedagogy of classes of many types, as students learn to probe, to evaluate evidence, to write papers with well-structured arguments, and to analyze the arguments presented to them in other texts." In this way, students not only learn the art of self-examination, but also how "Socratic thinking is important for democracy," with the potential to shape social and political institutions.[18]

With this in mind, the Socratic professor must convince students that her liberal arts course is worthwhile. Best to begin with some practical, vocationally focused arguments. The Socratic professor can point out that the "jobs of today" are not necessarily the "jobs of tomorrow"; students must become economically adaptable by acquiring the "transferable" skills of oral and written communication, as well as critical and creative thinking, best learned through liberal arts courses.[19] The professor can point to studies that demonstrate how people with liberal arts degrees are gainfully employed over the long term.[20] She can also direct students to articles showing that employers do not just want employees with technical skills, but also those who can communicate, problem-solve, and create.[21]

After using these arguments, the Socratic professor can then lead the discussion toward more philosophical considerations. Phillips offers practical tips on how to burst through students' obsession with practicality. In his introductory philosophy classes, he asks students early in the course why they are in university. Phillips writes:

> Invariably they say something like, "to get a degree" ... I ask why they want a degree ... "to get a job." Why a job? "To make money." Why do you want money? "So that I can buy stuff and support my family." Why do you want to do that? And this is where we hit a roadblock. After a pregnant pause, I get a few tentative answers. "Because that's what you're supposed to do." Or, "Buying stuff is fun."

Students have trouble responding to this last question because they have not spent enough time thinking about their life goals. Phillips admits that this "first-day pedagogical approach" is not exactly "unique or cutting edge," but it is entirely Socratic: it questions students about topics of immediate concern (their university education, future employment) and gets them to reflect critically.[22] Hopefully some practically minded students will take this as an invitation to philosophical reflection.

The Relativist Mindset and the Pursuit of Pleasure

The Socratic professor faces a large segment of the student population indifferent to the types of questions Socrates examined: what is justice? Love? The good life? This indifference is due, in large part, to the prevailing dominance of value relativism as the self-evident moral position for generations of students. All values and truth claims are "relative" to the culture or individual, and therefore completely "subjective."

Relativism has been around for several decades on university campuses. In 1987 it was the main target of Bloom's controversial critique of higher education, *The Closing of the American Mind*. For the Relativist, the Socratic method of examining others' opinions is fruitless because all opinions and "lifestyles" are equally valuable. Most students possess an easy-going relativist mentality: don't get upset! It's all good! The democratic soul is attracted to relativism because it seems to promote tolerance of different viewpoints and ways of life. A Socratic professor is accustomed to hearing certain refrains: "Everyone has the right to their opinion."; "Different strokes for different folks."; "Judge not, lest ye be judged!" However, such sentiments may neuter critical thinking, leading to permissive attitudes toward illiberal, intolerant, and destructive worldviews.

The general sense among many students, especially those born and raised in the West, is that the Socratic questions have already been answered: good is whatever gives you pleasure, as long as you do not harm others. If you point out to students that such a position asserts universal values about what is good (good is pleasure, good is not harming others), most do not seem bothered. As Myers argues, professors today are faced with a "compound skepticism": if professors criticize their students' relativism ("Nazis are bad, so surely you would condemn what they did?"), the students revert to their principles of "no harm" and "seek pleasure" ("The Nazis harmed others, so do not harm in your pursuit of pleasure"); if professors criticize their students' hedonism ("Some pleasures are bad for you"), the students revert back to relativism ("You do not have the right to criticize what other people find pleasurable, even if in *your opinion* it is bad for them").[23] The point of university, in such students' minds, is to get skills, in order to get a job, make money, buy what gives you pleasure, and contribute to an economy that gives people access to these multiple pleasures. The job-seeking mentality and hedonistic relativism are thus mutually reinforcing.

A number of arguments can be employed in a Socratic classroom with Relativists. A few examples: 1) if you state categorically "All truth is relative," then you have contradicted yourself because you have just asserted an objective truth that is not relative; 2) if you say without qualification "Do not judge others" you have contradicted yourself again because you are judging those who judge; 3) if you say "All values are relative," then you cannot criticize or condemn any act, even an atrocity or sadistic crime; 4) if you say, "You must be tolerant of everyone," then that means tolerating those who are intolerant, which is self-defeating; 5) if you say "I do not have the right to criticize anyone else for what they believe, say, or do," then that means no one has the right to criticize *you* for what you believe, say, or do, which is self-defensive; 6) and lastly, relativism implies that we are all locked within our own absolutist worldviews, and hence no one is truly open to persuasion or considering other ways of thinking that might be better, leading to solipsism.

Rather than using these arguments to reprimand students for their shallowness, they can be stated in a manner that is patient, friendly, and open. Rhodes advises professors to concede the "legitimacy of relativism provisionally" with her students, and then start the "philosophic enterprise of careful, open-minded inquiry from scratch with every student who responds." Because students' relativism is "received rather than systematically deduced," and thus "soft rather than hard," it is possible, with the right approach, to get students excited about reconsidering their own relativism.[24] A similar approach can be taken with regard to students' unreflective hedonism, in which happiness is reduced to pleasure. A professor can provisionally concede this position, and even point out that some philosophers have thought this. However, she can get students to recognize a difference between pleasure and happiness, perhaps by demonstrating that not all people in the throes of pleasure (i.e., drug addicts) are necessarily "happy." A better term for "happiness" might be "flourishing," in the Aristotelean sense of *eudaimonia*, which is an activity, not just a feeling. To flourish, a person must do things that are not always immediately pleasurable (i.e., the pain of physical exercise, the arduousness of intellectual inquiry). If students insist on identifying happiness with pleasure (i.e., "A philosopher is happy because he finds philosophy pleasurable"), then the discussion can turn to higher and lower pleasures. This, in turn, leads to questions about the good life, human excellence, and so on.

There is no guarantee that these strategies will persuade, but headway can be made with at least some students if the arguments are targeted and the environment is right.

The Safe Space Mentality and Identity Politics

In recent years, university campuses have been rocked by student demands to be shielded from ideas, texts, or images that are potentially offensive, traumatizing, or just different, particularly those bearing on race, gender, sexuality, and identity, or dealing with sensitive topics such as abortion, Israel, Islam, animal welfare, and climate change. Hence, we see the recent demand by some students to turn classrooms into "safe spaces."[25] It is perfectly reasonable for students to expect campus safety measures to be in place to protect them from physical assault and harassment, and for action to be taken if such things occur; it is also reasonable to expect that certain campus organizations be confidential safe spaces, especially student support groups. There are real cases of assault, harassment, and hate on campus, and universities are obliged to respond. But the safe space mentality goes further, embracing what O'Neill calls an "ideology of safety," where even expressing an idea in class could be considered an act of violence against someone who is offended by it.[26] With the increasing support of activist administrators and some professors, Safe Spacers mobilize to turn the entire campus into an intellectual safe space, issuing demands such as: placing "trigger warnings" on course syllabi to identify potentially traumatizing materials; censoring certain materials altogether from courses if deemed too offensive; reprimanding/firing professors who do not espouse progressive ideas regarding race, sexuality, gender, etc.; and disinviting provocative guest speakers who challenge the reigning political orthodoxies on campus.

Lukianoff and Haidt point out that this new movement of "political correctness" is

> largely about emotional well-being.... [I]t presumes an extraordinary fragility of the collegiate psyche, and therefore elevates the goal of protecting students from psychological harm....[T]his movement seeks to punish anyone who interferes with that aim, even accidentally. You might call this impulse *vindictive protectiveness*.

One of the main pathologies fostered by vindictive protectiveness is "emotional reasoning," where students let feelings guide their interpretation of reality and thereby express themselves emotionally rather than reasonably.[27] The emotion that gets the most license is anger, because people who express anger, especially if they are from a traditionally marginalized identity, feel empowered, righteous, and authentic.[28] Consequently, many universities have been challenged by groups with an aggrieved sense of victimhood, which often manifests itself in the call for intellectual safe spaces.

Lukianoff and Haidt argue that the Socratic method opposes the safe space mentality because the method "fosters critical thinking, in part by encouraging students to question their own unexamined beliefs, as well as the received wisdom of those around them. Such questioning sometimes leads to discomfort, and even to anger, on the way to understanding."[29] Thus, the Socratic professor is in a difficult situation when trying to engage the safe space mentality, because she may cause offense with her critical approach. This chills free speech and academic freedom. For the safe space mentality, a higher principle than academic freedom is "academic justice," which occurs when an academic community stops any teacher, researcher, or guest speaker whose ideas (supposedly) justify the continued oppression of traditionally oppressed groups.[30] This could mean that a professor receives official charges against her, and potentially loses her job, because of ideas she has stated or published.[31]

At first glance, and contrary to the Relativist, it may seem that Safe Spacers possess an absolutist mentality. However, the absolutism of safety and academic justice intermingles with relativism, particularly when it comes to identity politics, and this compounds the problem faced by the Socratic professor. Identity politics occurs when one's political positions are based on the interests of the group (i.e., "lesbian") or the intersectional groups (i.e., "Muslim, black, female") with which you identify, particularly if those groups have been historically victimized. Within such politics, "critical thinking" amounts to deconstructing the oppressive white, patriarchal, heteronormative, colonial, and capitalistic structures of the West. More important than critical thinking in identity politics is "allyship": for example, a white male cannot know what it is like to be an indigenous female, but he can *ally* himself with her by deferring to her experiences and supporting her political demands.[32] Instead of a critically engaged pluralism, allyship espouses a deferential relativism.

The Socratic method is generally not perceived as a pedagogy of the oppressed (ironic given that Socrates was executed). It is viewed, rather, as the pedagogy of ancient Greek white males, and therefore as a biased and culturally imperialistic method of teaching. By appealing to so-called "universal" concerns about justice and the good life, the Socratic method seeks to crush identities and subjective experiences in pursuit of "truths" that favor white, male, European privilege. Therefore, Socratic pedagogy is rejected, but at a cost: rather than students critically engaging each other's positions, and perhaps learning from each other and modifying their own viewpoints, they retreat into their identities, which are absolutist islands immune from external criticism, and simultaneously ally themselves with other victimized identities. But "allyship" reaches a breaking point when marginalized identities find they cannot be allied on certain issues – for example, a Jewish lesbian feminist and a Muslim male of Arab descent may disagree about polygamy, sexual orientation, or the State of Israel.[33] The Socratic professor thereby is caught in this relativistic sea of identities and intersections, each demanding safety and absolute deference but not critical engagement.

A delicate approach must be taken. The goal is to move a safe space mentality from a place of vindictive protectiveness and self-righteous anger, to another place where the student is able to discuss his experiences and opinions rationally, in dialog with others. Socratic reasoning, contrary to how it is often perceived, is not just abstract cold logic; it is tied to lived-experience, including victimization and injustice. Again, it is about establishing the right atmosphere in class. Hyman provides this piece of advice:

> The trick is to find a way to get [students] open and receptive rather than defensive . . . I have sometimes done things as earnest as walk around the room saying, "I am now creating a magic circle inside this space. In here, we're going to act with as much openness and curiosity as we can, and give each other permission to think out loud." That goes a long way.[34]

This specific technique may not suit everyone; other strategies can be used to set the right tone. Regarding "trigger warnings," it is probably reasonable to give a common-sense warning to students if certain materials are particularly violent, sexual, grotesque, or racist, and for most this is probably sufficient. If the university mandates trigger warnings on syllabi, the professor can use these as a source of Socratic questioning: why trigger warnings? Are they necessary? Is it good to be protected from ideas you do not like? From such questions, a thoughtful, carefully moderated dialog can ensue.

The Socratic professor should be upfront about her approach at the start of a course: that she is creating a "safe space" that permits students from different backgrounds and identities to express their experiences and viewpoints without fear of harassment, but which also allows for critical inquiry (not personal attacks) of those experiences and viewpoints. Furthermore, the professor should also say that the Socratic approach used in the class is itself provisional, and that it too can be subjected to critical inquiry. She is in no way attempting to demean students' experiences or backgrounds, nor is she attempting to offend for "shock value." The hope is that Socratic questioning can direct students from different identities to areas of shared concern, and enter into a critically engaged pluralism rather than an uncritical, deferential allyship with others. This previous sentence, however, is problematic from the standpoint of radical identity politics, and might even be interpreted as a "micro aggression" – yet another imposition of a Western male model of pedagogy on oppressed minorities and women. But as LeMoine argues in her chapter "Is Socrates Culturally Imperialistic?" which appears in this volume, Socratic education can flourish in pluralistic learning environments, and, indeed, the culturally diverse classroom is the ideal setting for Socratic dialog. Though the method requires that interlocutors follow the basic rules of discourse and reasoning, LeMoine argues it works within the logic of an argument presented by an interlocutor; it does not impose a framework on that person. This allows for numerous "frameworks of thinking" to be offered in class and investigated.

The Socratic professor is not looking to homogenize the world with a pronouncement of absolute truth; rather, pluralism (rather than relativism) is a basic fact of human life. There are multiple ways of flourishing in, and conceptualizing the world, but not all ways are equal or equally conducive to flourishing. Socratic questioning explores all of this, serving as an alternative model for students who may think of justice solely in terms of identity. Furthermore, those enraptured by identity politics should be shown that it also leads to right-wing populism. This brings us to the Troll.

The Troll Mentality and the New Political Demagoguery

The Socratic professor must be conscious of the right-wing "troll" mentality, which is relatively new to university campuses, but will likely become more noticeable and vocal in the years ahead. Inspired by the rhetoric and behavior of right-wing populist politicians and media personalities, the classroom troll, like his online brethren, deliberately provokes or offends to cause a reaction. Though "left-wing" trolls exist, this terrain has been mostly been taken over by the right. It is part of a cultural shift in democratic societies where a sizable minority is gravitating toward far-right demagogic rule – the most dramatic example being the triumph of Trump in the 2016 U.S. presidential election. Trump's approach to politics, and his outrageous statements, have enabled some of Trump's supporters to employ similar tactics when confronting people with whom they disagree.[35] The campus troll seeks to unsettle liberal opinions on race, gender, feminism, sexuality, the environment, the economy, etc., not to inspire critical thinking, but to elicit an emotional reaction and create confrontation. Ironically, this new breed of right-wing populism has actually embraced aspects of left-wing identity politics, insofar as it is a reactionary assertion of "white identity," fueled by a self-righteous sense of victimization. It also uses emotional reasoning to assert its own view of reality against all contrary evidence and attack those who are perceived to be elites – those who have thrived in the globalized technological economy with its cosmopolitan liberalism, at the expense of white populations in industrial and rural areas with more conservative values.

A new type of demagogic politics has been unleashed in the West – one which goes beyond Trump and his supporters, and will likely endure, regardless of the fate of the Trump administration. Trump succeeded not only because he could exploit white resentments, but because he operated within what has been called a "post-truth" environment. No matter how many falsehoods, outrageous claims, and offensive statements were made during his campaign and the early part of his presidency, and no matter how many times these statements were identified by the mainstream media, it had little impact on a certain portion of the public; indeed, it only seemed to reinforce Trump's hardcore supporters.[36] As such, the "truth" no longer seemed to matter. Consequently, the Oxford Dictionary chose "post-truth" as its 2016 word of the year, defining it as "relating to or denoting circumstances in which objective facts are less influential in shaping public opinion than appeals to emotion and personal belief."[37] Higgins argues that both liberals and conservatives display symptoms of living in a post-truth condition.[38] Much of this is exacerbated by the Internet and social media, which facilitate the distribution of falsehoods and conspiracy theories. But whereas the left-wing embrace of post-truth relativism has a long history, and is the child of postmodern intellectuals, the conservative embrace of post-truth "Trumpism" is a more recent phenomenon, and is proudly anti-intellectual, leading to what Higgins calls "conservative postmodernism."[39] It is as if post-truth conservatives, in a moment of honesty, have said to left-wing Relativists:

> You are right! Everything *is* just opinion. Truths and moral standards cannot be rationally discussed. All that matters is power. It is best to assert your own identity and political demands aggressively, and deny all contrary positions, even if those positions are supported by research, evidence, and rational arguments.

It is unclear, as of 2017, how many students from this disaffected post-truth demographic will enter college classrooms and employ populist tactics.[40] If they become more prominent, the Socratic professor will be faced with new problems. She might not identify with the intellectual elite that is the target of populist anger, but she will be perceived that way by some students. She can try to reason, but the troll mentality may have little patience for Socratic dialectics; indeed, to even speak about "critical thinking" will be perceived as a sign of elitism.

To respond to this mentality, the Socratic professor should take some preliminary steps. Talen noticed that his class discussions were becoming confrontational in the immediate aftermath of Trump's election. He had his students develop a code of conduct: recognize the difference between genuine "critical thinking" and just "being critical"; avoid personal attacks on other people for their opinions, but encourage critical engagement with those opinions; insist that students identify the mediums and sources on which their opinions are based.[41] These guidelines may cut down on trolling, and may make it easier for a Socratic professor to distinguish between a genuine Troll and a student with conservative opinions who is open to critical debate.

A Troll requires different strategies than a thoughtful conservative or liberal. If a Troll is threatening or insulting, disciplinary action is required. But if a Troll is simply stating opinions, then he must be engaged, no matter how outrageous his opinions. Trolls may be partially helpful from a Socratic perspective as they will at least question left-wing platitudes. However, given the "post-truth" nature of contemporary demagoguery, with its anti-intellectual belligerence, it is more likely that a Troll's comments will need to be qualified or rejected. Add to this the tendency of Trolls to propagate outrageous conspiracy theories and the Socratic professor may find her class descend into chaos.

When a Troll says something intended to outrage, it is incumbent upon the professor to momentarily suspend comments from other students (to avoid a shouting match), and confront the student directly in front of the whole class. Rather than saying to the Troll that his opinions are beneath consideration and will not be discussed (which will only encourage the student's belief that universities are citadels of left-wing "group-think"), it is likely best, no matter how ridiculous or unsavory, to examine the student's statements head-on. If the professor does not feel equipped to respond to the Troll in the moment, she can bring the conversation temporarily to a close, indicating that the matter will be revisited in a future class. This way the Troll knows that he is not off the hook, while giving the Socratic professor time to explore the student's claims and respond accurately.

By seriously considering certain outrageous opinions and giving the Troll a classroom platform, the Socratic professor may raise the ire of Safe Spacers, who might accuse the professor of creating a "hostile learning environment." Nevertheless, this is a risk that should be taken. The Safe Spacers may learn to respect the Socratic approach, because the intent, ultimately, is to shame the Troll, not by personally attacking him but by cross-examining him. Post-truth conservativism cultivates resistance to shame. Doubling-down, rather than admitting error, seems to be a winning strategy for right-wing populists, and it may increasingly serve as a model for those who support such public figures. This means that the Socratic professor must use shame strategically, in much the same way that Socrates made Thrasymachus and Callicles feel shame for their "might makes right" arguments (*Gorgias*, 481b–527e; *Republic*, 336b–354a, especially 350d). Rather than getting emotional, insulting, or censorious – exactly what a Troll wants – the Socratic professor demonstrates, through logical cross-examination and consideration of sources, how the student's opinions may be false or contradictory and how the student's entire approach is unproductive. Trolls, as opposed to Safe Spacers, are more likely to respond positively to "tough-talk," but the toughness is in the argument and in the professor's composure. This will, hopefully, lead to a productive form of shame in the mind of the Troll. There is no guarantee that this will happen. Feelings of shame did not stop Socrates' student Alcibiades from becoming a lecherous demagogue (*Symposium*, 216b), nor did Socrates' shaming of his accusers stop the Athenian jury from sentencing him to death. To be sure, the use of shame is perilous. But with the Troll, it is likely the best strategy.

In the current educational environment, it is unpopular to argue that a professor should ever make a student feel shame. There is plenty of research demonstrating the deleterious effects of shame on students.[42] Undoubtedly, shame can become pathological, and it is not the right strategy to employ with all students, especially not Safe Spacers or those who are naturally shy. At the same time, shame has a positive role in the development of a healthy psyche. Shamelessness leads to antisocial tendencies, lack of respect for others, unrealistic self-appraisal, megalomania, and various types of personality disorders. As Johnson writes, "it is probably impossible to eliminate shame from the classroom. Nor would we wish to. Shame is an intrinsic part of effective socialization."[43] The effective use of shame in the classroom is something worthy of more scholarly attention, especially in the age of right-wing Trolls.

Conclusion

Two general pieces of advice: first, be open with students about your Socratic approach at the start of a course; second, be attentive to the various types of souls in your class, responding to each in kind, and thereby establishing a classroom environment in which students can become open, or at least not openly hostile, to Socratic teaching. On the one hand, the environment cannot become hostile, where students exchange angry barbs with each other and with the professor; on the other, the professor should not, out of fear or intellectual laziness, become obsequious, simply catering to her students and avoiding controversial topics so as to be "popular" and curry favor. This is a difficult balance to strike, and any educator who truly employs the Socratic method takes risks, both philosophical and professional.

These are challenging times to be a Socratic professor, but Socratic pedagogy is needed as much as ever. The goal is to recruit students into Socratic dialectics without alienating or unnecessarily offending. There is no guarantee that any of the strategies suggested above will work; you could end up running afoul of your students and institution, potentially facing (contradictory) charges of being an impractical Luddite, a bigoted conservative, or a left-wing propagandist. But for the Socratic professor, there is no other choice than to continue trying to create the space in which the method can be practiced. After all, the unexamined life is not worth living, and it is in the name of that life that the Socratic professor must dive in and take risks.

Notes

1 For American statistics on the decline of humanities bachelors, see "Bachelor's Degrees in the Humanities," *Humanities Indicators: A Project of the American Academy of Arts and Sciences*, May 2017, www.humanitiesindicators.org/content/indicatordoc.aspx?i=34. Accessed June 28, 2017. For Canadian statistics, see "The Future of Liberal Arts: Report," *Universities Canada*, 2016, https://www.univcan.ca/the-future-of-the-liberal-arts-report. Accessed July 31, 2017.
2 Martha Nussbaum, *Not for Profit: Why Democracy Needs the Humanities* (Princeton: Princeton University Press, 2010); Fareed Zakaria, *In Defense of a Liberal Education* (New York: W.W. Norton & Co., 2015). For Canadian perspectives, see David Livingstone, ed., *Liberal Education, Civic Education, and the Canadian Regime: Past Principles and Present Challenges* (Montreal and Kingston: McGill-Queen's University Press, 2015).
3 See Sokolon's "Poetic Questions in the Socratic Method" in this volume.
4 This is discussed at greater length in chapters by Jansche, LeMoine, and Sokolon in this volume.
5 Sherry Turkle, *Reclaiming Conversation: The Power of Talk in a Digital Age* (New York: Penguin Books, 2015), 213–17.
6 Michael Grace-Martin and Geri Gay, "Web Browsing, Mobile Computing, and Academic Performance," *Educational Technology and Society* 4/3 (2001): 95–107; Carrie B. Fried, "In-Class Laptop Use and its Effects on Student Learning," *Computers and Education*, 50/3 (2008): 906–14; James M. Kraushaar and David C. Novak, "Examining the Affects of Student Multitasking With Laptops During the Lecture," *Journal of Information Systems Education* 21/2 (2010): 241–51.

7. Faria Sana, Tina Weston and Nicholas J. Cepeda, "Laptop Multitasking Hinders Classroom Learning for Both Users and Nearby Peers," *Computers and Education* 62 (March 2013): 24–31.
8. Nicholas Carr, *The Shallows: What the Internet is Doing to Our Brains* (New York: W.W. Norton and Company, 2010), 3–7.
9. See Turkle, *Reclaiming Conversation*.
10. N. Katherine Hayles, "Hyper and Deep Attention: The Generational Divide in Cognitive Modes," *Profession* (2007): 187–99.
11. Turkle, *Reclaiming Conversation*, 216–21.
12. Pam A. Mueller and Daniel M. Oppenheimer, "The Pen Is Mightier Than the Keyboard: Advantages of Longhand Over Laptop Note Taking," *Psychological Science* 25/6 (2014): 1159–68.
13. Matt Copeland, *Socratic Circles: Fostering Critical and Creative Thinking in Middle and High School* (Portland, ME: Stenhouse Publishers, 2005).
14. For problems with the "flipped classroom," see Turkle, *Reclaiming Conversation*, 231.
15. Nussbaum, *Not for Profit*, 13–26.
16. *Ibid.*, 23–24.
17. *Ibid.*, 13–77.
18. *Ibid.*, 54–55.
19. See Zakaria, *In Defense of a Liberal Education*.
20. See "Future of Liberal Arts: Report," *Universities Canada*; Nikki Wiart, "Revenge of the Arts: Why a Liberal Arts Education Pays Off," *Macleans*, July 26, 2016, www.macleans.ca/education/revenge-of-the-arts-why-a-liberal-arts-education-pays-off. Accessed July 28, 2017.
21. See David Helfand, "Liberal Arts is the Future of Work, So Why is Canada Pushing 'Job Ready' Skills?," *Globe and Mail*, May 12, 2014, https://www.theglobeandmail.com/news/national/education/education-lab/as-canada-pushes-job-ready-skills-the-rest-of-the-world-embraces-liberal-arts/article18492798/. Accessed July 28, 2017; "Future of Liberal Arts: Report," *Universities Canada*; Jessica Wynne Lockhart, "Liberal Arts Degrees are Here to Stay," *Toronto Star*, March 13, 2017, https://www.thestar.com/life/coursesforcareers/2017/03/13/liberal-arts-degrees-are-here-to-stay.html. Accessed July 28, 2017; Scott Stirrett, "Why Liberal Arts Degrees are More Valuable Than You Might Think," *Globe and Mail*, March 7, 2017, https://www.theglobeandmail.com/report-on-business/small-business/talent/why-liberal-arts-degrees-are-more-valuable-than-you-might-think/article34031330. Accessed July 28, 2017.
22. Kristopher G. Phillips, "Is Philosophy Practical? Yes and No, but that's Precisely Why We Need It," in *Why the Humanities Matter: In Defense of Liberal Education*, Lee Trepanier, ed. (Lanham: Lexington Books, 2017), 51–2.
23. Richard Myers, "Liberal Education and the Democratic Soul: Lessons from Alexis de Tocqueville," in *Liberal Education, Civic Education*, 188–89.
24. James Rhodes, *Eros, Wisdom and Silence: Plato's Erotic Dialogues* (Columbia: University of Missouri Press, 2003), 8.
25. For a general account of the safe space phenomenon, see the essays in *Unsafe Space: The Crisis of Free Speech on Campus*, Tom Slater, ed. (London: Palgrave Macmillan, 2016).
26. Brendan O'Neill, "From No Platform to Safe Space: A Crisis of Enlightenment," in *Ibid.*, 17.
27. Greg Lukianoff and Jonathan Haidt, "The Coddling of the American Mind," *The Atlantic*, September 2015, www.theatlantic.com/magazine/archive/2015/09/the-coddling-f-the-american-mind/399356. Accessed July 28, 2017.
28. See Peter Wood, "A Climate of Censorship: Eco-Orthodoxy on Campus," in *Unsafe Space*, Slater, ed., 99.
29. Lukianoff and Haidt, "Coddling of American Mind."
30. See Sandra Y.L. Korn, "The Doctrine of Academic Freedom: Let's Give Up on Academic Freedom in Favor of Justice," *Harvard Crimson*, February 18, 2014, www.thecrimson.com/column/the-red-line/article/2014/2/18/academic-freedom-justice. Accessed July 28, 2017.
31. Laura Kipnis, *Unwanted Advances: Sexual Paranoia Comes to Campus* (New York: Harper, 2017).
32. See Nathan Heller, "The Big Uneasy," *The New Yorker*, May 30, 2016, www.newyorker.com/magazine/2016/05/30/the-new-activism-of-liberal-arts-colleges. Accessed July 28, 2017.
33. *Ibid.* for an account of the limits of allyship, and how identity/intersectional politics has divided the political left.
34. *Ibid.*
35. Peter Hessler, "How Trump is Transforming Rural America," *The New Yorker*, July 24, 2017, www.newyorker.com/magazine/2017/07/24/how-trump-is-transforming-rural-america. Accessed July 28, 2017.
36. *Ibid.*
37. "Oxford Dictionaries Word of the Year," *English Oxford Living Dictionaries*, 2016, https://en.oxforddictionaries.com/word-of-the-year/word-of-the-year-2016. Accessed January 24, 2017.

38 Kathleen Higgins, "Post-Truth: A Guide for the Perplexed," *Nature,* November 28, 2016, https://www.nature.com/news/post-truth-a-guide-for-the-perplexed-1.21054. Accessed July 28, 2017; "Post-Truth Pluralism: The Unlikely Political Wisdom of Nietzsche," *The Breakthrough,* September 2013, http://thebreakthrough.org/index.php/journal/past-issues/issue-3/post-truth-pluralism. Accessed July 28, 2017.

39 Higgins, "Post-Truth Pluralism."

40 Regarding Trump supporters on campus, see Katie J.M. Baker, "College Trump Supporters: 'We're the New Counterculture,'" *BuzzFeed News,* November 21, 2016, https://www.buzzfeed.com/katiejmbaker/college-trump-supporters-the-new-counterculture?utm_term=.rp0q2R5jAa#.nnDJr0kpaA. Accessed July 29, 2017; Anemonia Hartocollis, "On Campus, Trump Fans Say They Need 'Safe Spaces,'" *New York Times,* December 8, 2016, https://www.nytimes.com/2016/12/08/us/politics/political-divide-on-campuses-hardens-after-trumps-victory.html. Accessed July 29, 2017; Philip Vogel, "The Hidden Trump Supporters at America's Most Liberal Colleges," *Student Voices,* January 25, 2017, https://mystudentvoices.com/the-hidden-trump-supporters-at-americas-most-liberal-college-f0b6892a6fe7. Accessed July 29, 2017.

41 Colleen Flaherty, "Talking Trump in Class," *Inside Higher Ed,* March 14, 2017, https://www.insidehighered.com/news/2017/03/14/communication-professor-establishes-rules-his-students-talking-about-trump-class. Accessed July 28, 2017.

42 Ted Thompson, Rachel Altmann and John Davidson "Shame-Proneness and Achievement Behaviour," *Personality and Individual Differences* 36/3 (2004): 613–27; Jeannine E. Turner and Jenefer Husman, "Emotional and Cognitive Self-Regulation Following Academic Shame," *Journal of Advanced Academics* 20/1 (2008): 138–73.

43 Diane Elizabeth Johnson, "Considering Shame and Its Implications for Student Learning," *College Student Journal* 46/1 (2012): 5.

Bibliography

Universities Canada. 2016. "The Future of Liberal Arts: Report." Universities Canada. Available at https://www.univcan.ca/the-future-of-the-liberal-arts-report.

———. 2016. "Oxford Dictionaries Word of the Year: Post-Truth." English Oxford Living Dictionaries. Available at https://en.oxforddictionaries.com/word-of-the-year/word-of-the-year-2016.

———. May 2017. "Bachelor's Degrees in the Humanities." *Humanities Indicators: A Project of the American Academy of Arts and Sciences.* Available at www.humanitiesindicators.org/content/indicatordoc.aspx?i=34.

Baker, Katie J.M. November 21, 2016. "College Trump Supporters: 'We're the New Counterculture.'" *BuzzFeed News.* Available at https://www.buzzfeed.com/katiejmbaker/college-trump-supporters-the-new-counterculture?utm_term=.rp0q2R5jAa#.nnDJr0kpaA.

Bloom, Allen. 1987. *The Closing of the American Mind: How Higher Education Has Failed Democracy and Impoverished the Souls of Today's Students.* New York: Simon & Schuster.

Carr, Nicholas. 2010. *The Shallows: What the Internet is Doing to Our Brains.* New York: W.W. Norton and Company.

Cooper, John M. ed. 1997. *Plato: Complete Works.* Indianapolis: Hackett Publishing Co.

Copeland, Matt. 2005. *Socratic Circles: Fostering Critical and Creative Thinking in Middle and High School.* Portland, ME: Stenhouse Publishers.

Flaherty, Colleen. March 14, 2017. "Talking Trump in Class." *Inside Higher Ed.* Available at https://www.insidehighered.com/news/2017/03/14/communication-professor-establishes-rules-his-students-talking-about-trump-class.

Fried, Carrie B. 2008. "In-Class Laptop Use and its Effects on Student Learning." *Computers and Education* 50/3: 906–14.

Grace-Martin, Michael and Geri Gay. 2001. "Web Browsing, Mobile Computing, and Academic Performance." *Educational Technology and Society* 4/3: 95–107.

Hartocollis, Anemonia. December 8, 2016. "On Campus, Trump Fans Say They Need 'Safe Spaces.'" *New York Times.* Available at https://www.nytimes.com/2016/12/08/us/politics/political-divide-on-campuses-hardens-after-trumps-victory.html.

Hayles, N. Katherine. 2007. "Hyper and Deep Attention: The Generational Divide in Cognitive Modes." *Profession*: 187–99.

Helfand, David. May 12, 2014. "Liberal Arts is the Future of Work, So Why is Canada Pushing 'Job Ready' Skills?" *Globe and Mail*. Available at https://www.theglobeandmail.com/news/national/education/education-lab/as-canada-pushes-job-ready-skills-the-rest-of-the-world-embraces-liberal-arts/article18492798/.

Heller, Nathan. May 30, 2016. "The Big Uneasy." *The New Yorker*. Available at www.newyorker.com/magazine/2016/05/30/the-new-activism-of-liberal-arts-colleges.

Hessler, Peter. July 24, 2017. "How Trump is Transforming Rural America." *The New Yorker*. Available at www.newyorker.com/magazine/2017/07/24/how-trump-is-transforming-rural-america.

Higgins, Kathleen. September 2013. "Post-Truth Pluralism: The Unlikely Political Wisdom of Nietzsche." *The Breakthrough*. Available at http://thebreakthrough.org/index.php/journal/past-issues/issue-3/post-truth-pluralism.

———. November 28, 2016. "Post-Truth: A Guide for the Perplexed." *Nature*. Available at https://www.nature.com/news/post-truth-a-guide-for-the-perplexed-1.21054.

Johnson, Diane E. 2012. "Considering Shame and Its Implications for Student Learning." *College Student Journal* 46/1: 3–17.

Kipnis, Laura. 2017. *Unwanted Advances: Sexual Paranoia Comes to Campus*. New York: Harper.

Korn, Sandra Y.L. February 18, 2014. "The Doctrine of Academic Freedom: Let's Give Up on Academic Freedom in Favor of Justice." *Harvard Crimson*. Available at www.thecrimson.com/column/the-red-line/article/2014/2/18/academic-freedom-justice.

Kraushaar, James M. and David C. Novak. 2010. "Examining the Affects of Student Multitasking With Laptops During the Lecture." *Journal of Information Systems Education* 21/2: 241–51.

Livingstone, David ed. 2015. *Liberal Education, Civic Education, and the Canadian Regime: Past Principles and Present Challenges*. Montreal: McGill-Queen's University Press.

Lukianoff, Greg and Jonathan Haidt. September 2015. "The Coddling of the American Mind." *The Atlantic*. Available at www.theatlantic.com/magazine/archive/2015/09/the-coddling-of-the-american-mind/399356.

Mueller, Pam A. and Daniel M. Oppenheimer. 2014. "The Pen Is Mightier Than the Keyboard: Advantages of Longhand Over Laptop Note Taking." *Psychological Science* 25/6: 1159–68.

Nussbaum, Martha. 2010. *Not for Profit: Why Democracy Needs the Humanities*. Princeton: Princeton University Press.

Phillips, Kristopher G. 2017. "Is Philosophy Practical? Yes and No, but That's Precisely Why We Need It." In *Why the Humanities Matter: In Defense of Liberal Education*. Lee Trepanier ed. Lanham: Lexington Books: 37–64.

Rhodes, James. 2003. *Eros, Wisdom and Silence: Plato's Erotic Dialogues*. Columbia: University of Missouri Press.

Sana, Faria, Tina Weston and Nicholas J. Cepeda. March 2013. "Laptop Multitasking Hinders Classroom Learning for Both Users and Nearby Peers." *Computers and Education* 62: 24–31.

Slater, Tom ed. 2016. *Unsafe Space: The Crisis of Free Speech on Campus*. London: Palgrave Macmillan.

Stirrett, Scott. March 7, 2017. "Why Liberal Arts Degrees are More Valuable Than You Might Think." *Globe and Mail*. Available at https://www.theglobeandmail.com/report-on-business/small-business/talent/why-liberal-arts-degrees-are-more-valuable-than-you-might-think/article34031330.

Thompson, Ted, Rachel Altmann and John Davidson. 2004. "Shame-Proneness and Achievement Behaviour." *Personality and Individual Differences* 36/3: 613–27.

Turkle, Sherry. 2015. *Reclaiming Conversation: The Power of Talk in a Digital Age*. New York: Penguin Books.

Turner, Jeannine E. and Jenefer Husman. 2008. "Emotional and Cognitive Self-Regulation Following Academic Shame." *Journal of Advanced Academics* 20/1: 138–73.

Vogel, Philip. January 25, 2017. "The Hidden Trump Supporters at America's Most Liberal Colleges." *Student Voices*. Available at https://mystudentvoices.com/the-hidden-trump-supporters-at-americas-most-liberal-college-f0b6892a6fe7.

Wiart, Nikki. July 26, 2016. "Revenge of the Arts: Why a Liberal Arts Education Pays Off." *Macleans*. Available at www.macleans.ca/education/revenge-of-the-arts-why-a-liberal-arts-education-pays-off.

Wynne Lockhart, Jessica. March 13, 2017. "Liberal Arts Degrees are Here to Stay." *Toronto Star*. Available at https://www.thestar.com/life/coursesforcareers/2017/03/13/liberal-arts-degrees-are-here-to-stay.html.

Zakaria, Fareed. 2015. *In Defense of a Liberal Education*. New York: W.W. Norton & Co.

12 The Socratic Method's Search for Standards

Ramona June Grey

Most of us who use a Socratic method in our political theory courses aim not merely to familiarize our students with canonical texts, but to engage them in a "search for standards." And when we think about political theory as a search for standards, it is the normative approach that comes to mind. Questions such as "what makes a just individual or a society just?" distinguish this approach, which is often associated with *classical* political theory. Although we may disagree on what specific theorists have to offer, we routinely draw upon the classical works of political theory, beginning with Plato's *Republic*, for the purpose of providing students with greater insights into what is "truly" political, which inevitably requires a discussion of justice and other fundamental values. Studying classical political philosophy – as we remind students – enables us not only to understand the ideas and ideals associated with the Greek *polis*, but, more importantly, sets before us criteria by which to judge political choices in terms of standards of right and wrong, justice, and injustice.

Not everyone, however, shares this view of the strengths of the classical tradition. There are those theorists who believe that they have found a better approach. Political theory in their opinion can move forward only if it draws upon the tools of scientific inquiry, which means uncovering the underlying causes of political behavior: why and for what purpose(s), for instance, do rulers and ruled claim that their constitutions align with principles of justice. For these *modern* theorists, who trace their lineage back to Aristotle, only by formulating scientific hypotheses based on the facts of human nature can political theory advance our knowledge. Or they prefer an historical approach to the study of political thought seeking to explain when and why a particular idea (or ideal) of justice appears, how it changes over time, and why (or whether) it continues to influence the present. Still another group of political theorists prefers a critical or analytic approach that involves dissecting, but not necessarily improving upon, the theories of others.

Today, political thinkers, Laslett proclaims, "do not preach." On the contrary, they (and we) are "plain, honest men (and women) who tidy up muddles" in our thinking, "and have no axe to grind."[1] Those who agree with Laslett attribute *contemporary* political theory's contribution to normative inquiry – and perhaps its maturity – to the rise of twentieth-century analytical philosophy and twenty-first-century postmodernism. And, indeed, is this not the approach we practice, and our graduate and undergraduate students are encouraged to emulate? Instead of engaging in metaphysical speculation or entirely trusting that history and science can guide knowledge of human nature and society, students are taught to critically analyze the claims of canonical theorists – including other contemporary thinkers, while paying close attention to how the use (and abuse) of language influences an understanding of politics and values.

Notwithstanding major disagreements advocates of these approaches to theorizing and studying canonical texts have with each other, they all agree on the shortcomings of "classical" political theory and its stress on justice-seeking, which, they complain, not only teaches us little about politics, but will defeat the ends that the theorist, like Plato, hopes to achieve. For even if we could agree on what a truly "just" society would look like, there still remains the question of what we are prepared to do to achieve it (assuming, of course, that we will want it when we see it). And for theorists who prefer an analytic approach, this raises another question: whether a "just" society is logically consistent or compatible with other political values like freedom or fairness.

But does this mean that the classical approach of justice-seeking is no longer of any value, or that there is only one viable approach to posing and answering questions concerning justice, freedom, fairness, and other political values? No, actually. Practitioners and teachers of political theory, including those thinkers associated with the *classical normative tradition* have never totally confined their inquiry to universal political truths transcending time and circumstances with a view to only prescribing how human beings ought to live. For that matter, *modern* political theorists have not entirely limited their inquiry to describing what ends or purposes, in fact, guide social institutions and public life. Nor have *contemporary* thinkers confined themselves to pointing out conflicting values, incongruities in the use of political concepts, or logical and empirical fallacies in canonical texts.[2]

Nevertheless, many textbooks routinely (and often unquestioningly) treat the canonical works of classical, modern, and contemporary political theory as historical traditions largely distinguished by these distinct approaches to theorizing about politics.[3] How a particular theorist, or a political theory, may subtly (or not so subtly) combine normative, empirical, and analytical inquiry is overlooked or, at best, marginally considered. By way of illustrating this, I wish to offer an alternative analytical framework for introducing students to canonical texts: one that examines more carefully the differences between *justice-seeking* (asking us to aspire to a standard of what we ought to be), *knowledge-seeking* (requiring that we adjust our standards of justice to the empirical and/or historical facts of human nature, institutions, and social conditions), and the *analytic or critical critic approach* (requiring our standards of justice be clearly expressed and thought out). While it is important to note that these three approaches are somewhat arbitrary, each approach on closer examination is distinct in the types of questions it allows the theorist to raise and what he or she considers the purpose of theory. As "ideal types," each of these approaches provides a lens through which students may better appreciate what it is that the political theorist is trying to do. These different approaches to theory may also suggest why we – as teachers of political thought – do not necessarily agree on the purpose and uses of the Socratic method.

This need not, however, lead to the conclusion that political theorists (or teachers), based upon the approach they seemingly prefer, can be slotted into boxes. As already noted, political thinkers often without meaning to, seldom remain wedded to one approach. Any discussion of these approaches will, undoubtedly, (and should) draw students' attention to crossovers. Put another way, insofar as these three approaches correspond to Hume's classic distinction between value, fact, and reason, few thinkers avoid mixing (and sometimes confusing) them. My intention when using this conceptual framework is not to reduce political theory to a few, fixed categories of inquiry or to attach new labels to canonical thinkers, but instead consider how the complex interplay between justice-seeking, knowledge-seeking, and critical analysis animates a Socratic dialog, broadly conceived, and what some might call the vocation of political theory. Furthermore, if political theory can be viewed as a search for standards, then each approach – justice-seeking, knowledge-seeking, and critical analysis – may offer a distinctive contribution to what, for the theorist, is the real or potential value of political inquiry. Before suggesting how this analytical framework may be used as part of a Socratic method for engaging students in a contemporary classroom setting, let us consider what each approach – justice-seeking, knowledge-seeking, and critical analysis – generally contributes to the political theorist's search for standards.

The Normative Approach: The Political Theorist as Moralist and Justice-Seeker

Typically, when we think of political theory as a search for standards, it is the normative thinker or "justice-seeker" who comes to mind and, especially, "the prototypical political theorist: Plato."[4]

Other thinkers associated with this approach include Augustine, Aquinas, Rousseau, and, partly, Marx. Contrary to those who insist that this approach is no longer useful, one can also find any number of justice-seekers among contemporary theorists, including Strauss, Arendt, Rawls, Sandel, and Barry.[5] In fact, one can find some form of a justice-seeking approach in virtually every treatise or tract penned by a political theorist.

I do not mean to suggest, however, that every theorist engaged in normative political inquiry is exclusively preoccupied with justice *per se*. Theorists who adopt a normative approach to politics frequently seek out other political "goods" or principles besides justice, including happiness, liberty, equality of rights, duty, economic security, fairness, etc. We should also note that some "justice-seekers" take issue with reducing all political values or virtues down to one principle: justice. Justice is one, but only one, of many equally valuable political values or goods. Nor should justice, they remind us, be confused with morality. That said, however, the meaning of justice, like the meaning of a good life, is fungible enough to accommodate many political values and, no doubt, many theorists have associated "justice" with what they value. All justice-seekers, despite their vastly different interpretations of what exactly ails modern society, are convinced that the thrashing out of ultimate political choices, while in a very real sense is the concern of all human beings, is the social function of political theory.

Still, does not "the thrashing out of ultimate political choices," a student will inevitably ask, result in disagreement on what makes an individual or a society just? Consensus among justice-seekers indeed may be more apparent than real. They do not always agree among themselves as to what makes a society just or whether justice for individuals is always the same as justice for their society – a problem Plato wrestled with in the *Republic*. Marx, for example, regarded Plato's *Republic* "as an Athenian idealization of the Egyptian caste system."[6] Not only is there disagreement among justice-seekers over what constitutes justice, but there is even less consensus over how exactly we achieve justice or other political goods that are, or can be, identified with it.

While the differences among justice-seeking theorists should not be minimized, they nevertheless "bear certain family resemblances,"[7] and these resemblances are most discernible in their treatment of experiences and facts, which, for them, are not meaningful unless they can be tied to a moral standard whose source may be natural or divine – and sometimes both. For those who embrace the normative approach, all political inquiry is, and ought to be, value-laden. Theirs is a statement of what ought to be, of values forcefully articulated, or opposed. What matters are that the values we choose (or that they choose for us) be right. For a justice-seeking thinker values are not reducible to personal judgments. They are better understood as principles that must be valued if people are to live as they should. "True politics," justice-seeking theorists are convinced, "must first do homage to morals."[8] These justice-seeking theorists would, if they could, introduce a morality into the world that was not there before, or if it was, has been lost.[9] The purpose of a justice-seeker's inquiry, as initiated by Plato, is to identify genuine political virtue, justice, and the good life as opposed to the conventional imitations of them.

Implicit and, often explicit, is the contention that the present conduct of human beings leaves much to be desired, which brings us to another shared characteristic among justice-seeking theorists. The fact is that political theorists who adopt this approach, even those with conservative proclivities, find little comfort in things as they are. Looking at the world around them, these political theorists usually begin their tracts with a vision of "the human predicament."[10] The seminal works of theory have been a response to political crisis, or are, as Hobbes put it, "occasioned by the disorders of the present time." Athens' "unquiet times" in the fifth century BC, Italian disunity during the fifteenth century, the great schism within the Catholic Church in the sixteenth century, the English civil wars of the seventeenth century, the "critical period" following the American Revolution and the Reign of Terror after the French Revolution in the late eighteenth century, the farm-labor unrest throughout the nineteenth century, the fall of kings and czars, economic collapse, and the rise of dictators in the last century (with more to come) are often, for the justice-seekers, symptoms of "a deeper malady in society."[11]

From this awareness of a dire or impending crisis, they draw up an indictment against their society or those who threaten the foundations of their society. As a result, the justice-seeking theorist appears to be battling against convention, ignorance, stupidity, cowardliness, even human nature – all that keeps us from drawing closer to "justice," as he or she defines it. Indeed, there are times when it seems for them there is never enough justice, let alone the right kind of justice, to be found anywhere in the world. Undoubtedly influenced by the Athenian trail and execution of his teacher Socrates, Plato concluded that every actual or existing political regime is a hopelessly flawed replica of the just regime, every system of governing, including his own practical regime set out in the *Laws*, is an imperfect copy of the ideal *polis*.

That something has gone terribly wrong further demands for the justice-seeking theorist that we take stock of who (or what) is responsible for our plight; hence, another family resemblance in justice-seeking theory is the *identification of villains and, potentially, unrecognized heroes*. And here again, political theorists do not uniformly agree on who or what is responsible for our plight (and, conversely, who or what will redeem us.) Their villains sometimes appear *among us*: the sophists, the inept princes, the bourgeois, the tyrannical majority, or radicalized students (like Plato) *and* their teachers; at other times, the evil appears *outside* of us: a weak Leviathan or one that is too strong, imperial powers, an alien church or creed, absentee landlords, global corporations, and so forth. Sometimes they will point to the devil *within* us – the human propensity for selfishness, glory, envy, power (or worshiping those with power), hubris, or failing to appreciate the limits of human reason. Whether they are seeking a justice that will tame us or liberate us, theorists will move between both types of villains, within and without.

To have any chance of success (even a partial success) a "just" regime will need to be imposed by an uncorrupted or "knowledgeable" few. Ordinary folk cannot be trusted to do the right thing, either because the theorist (for example, Burke) fears that they will abandon the civilizing values and practices they are familiar with to pursue an idealized world of "abstract" justice, or will accept the existing world of injustice and may even (as Rousseau feared) prefer servitude over deliverance. Either way, the "crisis" that the theorist uncovers results not so much from flawed institutional arrangements, badly executed public policies, or faulty reasoning, but from fundamental errors in moral reasoning. Exposing such errors is, however, only a necessary but hardly sufficient beginning.

A path to redemption or "glimpse of a deliverance" is what gives political theory both a timely and timeless quality. Central to normative or justice-seeking approach in theory is:

> an estimation of importance (in public and private life), not in the sense of what is likely to happen, but of what ought to happen, the discrimination of a better from a worse way, the conviction that some courses of action are morally obligatory, and the expression of choice or preference growing from an attitude of desire, of fear, or confidence toward what the present holds and what the future may bring forth.[12]

It is not unusual for our "deliverance" from social maladies to take place in an ideal society where everyone, as Reeve says of Plato's *Republic*, "comes as close to being fully virtuous, and so to pursuing and achieving genuine happiness, as he can."[13]

This seems to imply that all justice-seekers are utopian, which is false, particularly if "utopian" presupposes the total restructuring of public and private life. So conceived, utopia, as some theorists insist, is an illusion – at best, unreal and at worse, dangerous. Whereas some normative theorists focus on the good society, others – today we usually think of them as liberal justice-seekers – are content with exploring paths to *a* better society. Consequently, if these theorists find a place for utopia in their world, it is envisioned as a goal (or an aspiration) instead of an actual place, and change, when it comes, will likely be piecemeal rather than total, prosaic rather than dramatic, evolutionary rather than revolutionary. They are able to take into account a world where equally legitimate values collide and vie with each other without being overly fearful that the bonds that make civil society possible will unravel.

Still, it is sometimes said against justice-seeking theorists that they are more concerned with having the world reflect their theory than with having their theory reflect the world. According to critics, a justice-seeking approach in theory elevates persuasion above explanation. Not everyone considers this a vice however. One who did not agree was John Stuart Mill, for whom, having "ascertained the form of government which combines the greatest amount of good with the least of evil," thought it was necessary "to obtain the *concurrence* of (his) countrymen, or those from whom the institutions are intended, in the opinion which we have previously arrived at."[14] Simply stated, for justice-seeking theorists the aim of political inquiry is not merely to predict the future, but to influence it. "Up to now," Marx declared, "philosophy has concerned itself with understanding the world; henceforth, it will be concerned with transforming it" (a task he assigns to scientific socialists.) Hence, what makes justice-seeking theories influential is not a mere matter of whether they are true, but whether they are believed.

In the end, what matters most when considering the justice-seeking approach with students is whether the values a political theorist champions really are moral or just. Unless one believes that society, as it is presently conceived and organized, is good enough, or we need not bother examining moral standards in public and private life, there still is value in this approach to theory. If "we make our world significant by the courage of our questions and the depth of our answers,"[15] then justice-seeking will retain a place in political inquiry, including for those who gravitate to the other approaches. Few political theorists, including those who prefer a more empirical or analytic approach to political theory, completely avoid engaging in some form of justice-seeking.

Historical and Scientific Approaches: The Political Theorist as Knowledge-Seeker

If justice-seeking presupposes a standard that human beings ought to embrace – but, unfortunately, seldom do – the main emphasis in a *knowledge-seeking* approach centers on constructing a political theory based upon the world as it is and men and women as they are. Rather than pondering abstract standards of justice and right rule, theorists who adopt this approach are determined to make use of the materials at hand. They seek to unearth, figuratively and literally, the nature of political authority and legitimacy, its sources and uses. Like the justice-seeker, they too are interested in political ends or moral standards, as well as people's beliefs about them. Unlike those primarily engaged in justice-seeking, however, the theorist preoccupied with knowledge-seeking appears more concerned with *understanding* than with *judging* the values rulers and ruled embrace. For them an understanding of political principles must take into account, rather than ignoring what people want, what they value, and how they actually behave. Whereas the justice-seeking theorist hopes to uncover political truths that will enable us to make value judgments about facts, the knowledge-seeking theorist aspires to begin with the empirical world, including the worlds others posit.

For the theorist engaged in a knowledge-seeking approach, values – including justice, happiness, equality, etc. – reflect human interests and desires as well as the social, economic, and/or historical circumstances people find themselves confronting. To discover the nature of politics, the knowledge-seeking theorist is intent on examining the forces that shape us, including "circumstances directly found, given and transmitted from the past."[16] In other words, knowledge-seeking theorists wish to derive their standards or principles of right rule (or justice) from a scientific and/or an historical investigation of human nature and the polity, moving from what is to what ought to be instead of the other way around.

Many, if not most, of the political theorists we study adopt this knowledge-seeking approach, at least some of the time, or would like us to think that this is their approach. Aristotle, Machiavelli, Hobbes, and Marx, all thought that they, in contrast to their contemporaries, were providing a "scientific" and/or historical account not only of their world and its values, but of their own values as well. They aim to demonstrate that the world of human activity, including political principles and social norms, can be "objectively" examined in precisely the same manner as studying any other phenomena of nature. These theorists presuppose the social world is both comprehensible and susceptible to control (or manipulation) by knowledge or the rational faculties of human beings. To acquire such knowledge does not consist in conceptualizing the best society or the best ruler, but, first and foremost, in having scrutinized social institutions, the rise and fall of regimes, and, more generally, human nature.

However, canonical thinkers who adopt an empirical approach to political inquiry do not necessarily agree on how, (much less what), we can learn either from science or history and, consequently, their methods for seeking knowledge and insight into the human condition vary widely. Some political theorists aim to emulate the natural sciences in classifying various kinds of constitutional regimes or, like Hobbes, they may invoke "the natural condition of mankind" – a thought experiment for identifying the human character traits that give rise to commonwealths, while still others look to history for clues into what makes a Prince (and a princely loving people) exceptional.

Regardless of whether they draw upon a science of human behavior or historical inquiry, the political thinkers engaged in knowledge-seeking often appear more concerned about predicting what lies ahead than in changing it. They are seeking to uncover the laws of nature (fact) rather than natural law (value), although few theorists – including Aristotle, Hobbes, Machiavelli, or Marx – avoid mixing the two. Theirs is a search for predictable patterns in the behavior of rulers and ruled, bourgeois and proletariat, along with the causal laws that will bring about a greater understanding of human beings, which will bring about a lasting reform or transformation of society.

Implicitly, and often explicitly, in the knowledge-seeking theorists' inquiry is the notion that to achieve political ends, e.g., civic virtue, justice, freedom, a glorious republic, requires a clear-eyed account of human desires and interests. It is not, as Kant held, that "all politics must bend its knee before the Right," instead for the knowledge-seeking political theorist it is the right that must bend its knee before Politics. For these thinkers "the politics which will succeed will be politics adjusted to human nature and especially to the permanent (but not exclusive) egoism of human behavior."[17]

Without judging human desires, the knowledge-seeking political theorist is not only willing to accept a world of self-interested and selfish individuals, but may even view competing interests as a positive aspect of social life. Alternatively, a knowledge-seeking theorist will insist that the nature of human beings is completely, or mostly, malleable, an empty vessel that can accommodate an infinite variety of social customs, rules, or norms. Paradoxically, then, what is human nature is not there, and, as a result, "it" can be molded into anything the theorist (or society) values. However human nature is conceived, these theorists accept that political standards, including justice, are meaningful only to the extent they are relevant to the world – as we know it. For these thinkers it is only after having identified "the laws of nature" governing society that the possibilities (and limitations) of finding a noble prince, instituting an effective Leviathan, or carrying out a proletariat revolution, will become evident.

The mixing of fact and value is not confined to classical political theory, usually associated with Plato's justice-seeking. Underlying the (debatable) empirical findings of an Aristotle, a Machiavelli, or a Marx is the unfolding of a great struggle between legitimate and perverted constitutions, glorious and failed states, oppression and salvation. Only by understanding the natural origins of political life, history, or economic development will human beings, paradoxically, be empowered to choose the right kind of constitution, prince, or justice, and thus arrive at their 'inevitable' future." "Perhaps no one in the history of Western thought was as explicitly enthusiastic about facts as was Karl Marx." And yet, Thorson continues:

> when he postulated his fundamental premise that the means of production is the controlling force of history, he was not stating a fact (as such). . . . What Marx is really telling us is that this

is the way we *should* look at the world if we are to be saved. It is no accident nor, as is sometimes said, is it inconsistent with his views that Marx should have proclaimed, "the philosophers have only interpreted the world; the point however is to *change* it."[18]

Many knowledge-seeking theorists share the conviction that a more scientific or historical inquiry into politics (or a synthesis of both) will get us closer to realizing what human beings value, and ought to value. Facts and hope will somehow coincide.

All of this illustrates that the distinction between these two approaches in political theory, the normative and the empirical, is never that sharp. Spitz was quite right to point out that just as "few if any normative theories are devoid of empirical statements and historical assessments," it is also true that "few if any empirical theories can avoid normative assumptions and value statements." Spitz then added, "what is crucial in all these endeavors is not the approach the theorist takes but the enlightenment his theory yields."[19] Nor is the third approach in political theory, the analytic approach, bereft of value judgments or void of empirical statements. And like the other two approaches to political inquiry, it too should be judged by the enlightenment its practitioners yield.

The Analytic Approach: The Political Theorist As Critic

Today it is not the justice-seeking or knowledge-seeking approach associated with Plato, Aristotle, Machiavelli, Hobbes, Marx and other canonical thinkers, but rather the analytic or critical approach that has become synonymous with *contemporary* political theory. The analytical approach is frequently associated with "the styles, methods and purposes of Anglo-American analytical moral philosophy which developed from the works of Hume, Russell and Wittgenstein."[20] Many notable political thinkers – including Isaiah Berlin, Hannah Pitkin, John Gunnell – employ some variation of this approach. Although each brings to the discipline of political theory a distinct perspective, these political theorists are primarily interested in critically examining foundational theories based upon universal rationality, divine will, utility, or natural law. They focus attention not only on the ways in which political theorists have reified notions of "self-interest" and "rationality," but also on commentators who routinely associate the use of these particular concepts with another reified, analytical construct: "the modern tradition" of political theory.[21] Rather than exploring the real meaning of justice or truth, these analytical thinkers prefer to dissect the forms of reasoning, methods of inquiry, and conclusions found in political theories, including the self-evident moral assertions or universal prescriptions often cloaked in the garb of "realism."

Of particular interest to the analytical thinker is the nature of the questions political theorists have raised and attempted to answer. From an analytical perspective, the questions posed by political thinkers, e.g., what is justice, what is freedom, what constitutes rational conduct and a meaningful social existence are curious and perplexing because, according to Berlin, they do not appear to have a clear source for finding the answers, "no deductive or observational programme leads at all directly to their solution."[22] He and other analytical thinkers agree with Russell's observation, that political theory – like its cousin philosophy:

> is to be studied, not for the sake of any definite answers to its questions, since no definite answers can, as a rule, be known to be true, but rather for the sake of the questions themselves; because these questions enlarge our conception of what is possible, enrich our intellectual imagination and diminish the dogmatic assurance which closes the mind against speculation...[23]

It is by making us aware of the perplexing nature of such questions as "what is justice?" that gives the study of political thought value and purpose. Consequently, analytical political theory has become nearly synonymous with textual analysis, concerned particularly with the ways in which others (who may or may not claim to be wise) conceptualize and interpret political concepts, including justice, equality, and freedom. Once again, the analytic theorist is not interested in bringing to light any definitive or comprehensive definition. Rather his or her aim is simply to examine how the use of these concepts not only informs our perceptions of social reality, but can also expand or limit our moral sensibilities. This is because "concern with language must be an ultimate concern," Gunnell writes, "since it is through language that a world is gained"[24]; or, as Orwell reminds us, is lost.

Implicit in the works of those thinkers who adopt an analytical approach is a human predicament that can be traced back to careless ways of thinking and speaking about human nature, the good life, freedom, and civil society. Ours is an intellectual and conceptual predicament largely inherited from theorists and philosophers who, throughout the ages, have mistakenly presupposed that political truths and social values can be traced to a natural law or "a science of man," which, coincidentally, is an extension of human reason. Political theorists – classical, modern, and even contemporary, according to the analytical critic, have been besotted with the notion of a transcendent morality, and, thus, overly preoccupied with placing "a template of universalistic rationality (and morality) over the world, which it has to measure up to."[25]

For the analytical thinker the perennial, albeit misguided, search for the essence of human nature, and fundamental truth(s) about social reality not only poses philosophical problems when we think about norms in this way, but raises a practical problem in contemporary political thought too; namely, how can one provide a case for justice and democratic values without drawing upon natural law theory or other metaphysical abstractions? In their search for standards, some analytical thinkers have turned to the writings of Wittgenstein for insight into "how language relates to social plurality and difference"[26] with the expectation that critical language analysis grafted onto political theory can liberate human beings from their craving for definitive meanings and will make way for a new intellectually robust theory of democracy.

Still other analytic theorists remain agnostic, content with pursuing critical thinking as a good for its own sake. Our (analytical) task, Oakeshott proclaimed, "consists, not in persuading others, but in making our own minds clear."[27] These analytical thinkers – distant heirs of Socrates, aim to persuade others of the weaknesses in their arguments – including other analytical thinkers. In fact, it is these critical critics who object to privileging the writings of any thinker to support a preconceived notion of political theory. Admittedly critical inquiry can conceivably be used (e.g., Wittgenstein) to prevent language from going on holiday, and may even provide theory of justice and criteria for democracy. Nonetheless, the analytical thinker aims to prevent political theorizing from lapsing into a tendency to draw hasty conclusions – a perennial weakness of the justice-seeking and knowledge-seeking approaches. "There are," Gunnell acknowledges, "various insights that may be derived from Wittgenstein, as well as any number of philosophers, about both the substance and form of political theory, but this does not absolve political theory of the 'trouble of thinking.'"[28] Pascal best summed up the "credo" of those, like Gunnell, who adopt an analytical approach to political theory: "Thought makes the whole dignity of man; therefore endeavor to think well, that *is* the only morality."[29] Implicit in this enterprise are clearly values that, apparently, the analytical thinker can no more run away from than can the rest of us.

Political Theory and the Socratic Approach

All of these approaches – justice-seeking, knowledge-seeking, and analytical inquiry – are themselves analytical categories. By isolating each approach, the student is better able to understand what is important to political theorists and why they think it important. They can also see and appreciate how these approaches can work in tandem. Students can become aware of how easily theorists move between different kinds of questions, often in ways they (and their readers) may or may not be aware of, and the effect these changes have on his or her argument. For example, the *empirical* or knowledge-seeking question, "does every government serve merely the interest of the stronger?" may be changed to, "is it really in the interest of the stronger to have the government serve only them," which is a *normative* or justice-seeking question, or changed to "what do we mean when we say that an interest is strong?," a question that the *analytical* thinker is likely to ask.

Examining differences between these kinds of questions not only encourages students to become more critical thinkers, it also brings students into the ongoing debate, noted at the outset, over what is (and should be) the purpose of political inquiry. In answering this question, we can consider what it is that the political theorist does that sets him or her apart from the philosopher, the theologian, the historian, or, for that matter, the political scientist. What is the political theorist's particular way of looking at his or her world and responding to it? Another advantage of examining political theory texts in terms of justice-seeking, knowledge-seeking, and critical inquiry is that it provides opportunity to consider the merits and limitations of each approach, and how each may contribute to our understanding of justice, freedom, authority, and politics generally. With regard to a justice-seeking approach, we can raise such questions as: 1) what ails the political philosopher (and us)?; 2) does his or her diagnosis of what is wrong with society or human beings make sense?; 3) is his or her diagnosis relevant to our situation?; 4) how does he propose to improve the human situation?; and 5) will his prescription(s) make his world (let alone, ours) better? And more generally, "should political theory concern itself with establishing standards of human conduct?" If we are skeptical and even apprehensive (as many students are) about a political theorist insistence on challenging the conventional values of others, then we need to ask ourselves what exactly is it about his or her "justice-seeking" that we find disturbing, and why? A justice-seeking approach frequently prompts a thinker to scrutinize conventional values, but does the mere questioning of other people's values mean that a justice-seeker is inherently elitist? Put simply, are "justice-seeking" theorists *ipso facto* presuming themselves to be superior to us? Are all political questions ultimately reducible to ethical questions? And if they are, why study politics?

Whereas the justice-seeking approach poses challenging dilemmas regarding the mixing of morality and politics, a knowledge-seeking approach leads itself to examining the theorist's (including Aristotle's) use of nature and/or history (including Machiavelli's) as a standard by which to evaluate human conduct. As such, the knowledge-seeking approach brings to our attention the "methods" a political theorist employs, and whether their particular "empirical" mode of inquiry is appropriate for understanding human nature and politics.

Specifically, what model(s) of science does the knowledge-seeking theorist – including Aristotle, Bentham, or Marx – strive to emulate in his "science of human behavior" in society? Should (and can) a knowledge-seeking approach in political theory focus exclusively on identifying predictable and observable patterns of human behavior for the purpose of garnering truths about, for instance, the origins of government and authority? What difficulties are involved in making a view of human nature the basis of a political theory?

Conclusion

Critical thinking about justice and the good life was the primary purpose of Socrates' political theory. His method (*elenchus*) entailed a relentless questioning of contemporaries, prodding them to examine (and to reexamine) what exactly they meant when they spoke of things that they professed to value such as justice, courage, and piety.[30] Claiming only knowledge of his ignorance, Socrates referred to himself as the gadfly. He was determined to point out the flaws in the arguments and reasoning of others and, as a consequence, the purpose of his questioning appears more negative than positive, characterized less by the conclusions reached than by demonstrating the difficulties of arriving at satisfactory answers.[31] Nevertheless, if the totality of his mission is merely to critique or deconstruct conventional political ideas and principles, what Socrates leaves us with is not the stuff that dreams are made of (much to the dismay of his students, like Plato).

Others simply saw Socrates as a bit of a pest, who would not or could not leave well enough alone. His persistent questioning made them feel uncomfortable, even angry; no one, after all, likes having their ignorance exposed or their principles questioned. Not that this would have deterred Socrates. For him, to reflect on the things that mattered was itself a virtue, even if this virtue was not practiced by many of his contemporaries. If the questions he posed should make people think a little more about what they value, and why they value it, he would have accomplished his calling. "The unexamined life," he informed the jury that would convict him, "is not worth living." And is not the habit of thinking deeply and expressing ideas clearly what we hope our students will acquire from the study of political thought?

As the astute reader will detect, I adopt the framework outlined above as part of an analytical teaching tool, one that raises questions along lines similar to those Socrates employs. In examining canonical texts, it requires students to consider: 1) what they value (justice-seeking); 2) what they know (knowledge-seeking); 3) and how they go about justifying or defending the answers they give to the first two questions (critical analysis). Whereas Socrates is neither a creator nor a constructor of a "grand" political philosophy, his method of *elenchus* can be used to make students aware of how different approaches to the study of politics influence the questions theorists raise and the answers they give. The Socratic method, which I regard as synonymous with an analytical approach, insists that we critically examine society and ourselves for the purpose of gaining, above all, self-knowledge.[32] What I hope to offer students is a lens that may enable them to examine the complex relationship between value, fact, and reason, but also one that can shed light on the strengths and weaknesses of the political views and values that they, often unwittingly, espouse.

Finally with regard to what should be the purpose of studying political theory, this analytical framework encourages students (and ourselves) to reflect on which approach they (and we) find most interesting, and why. Some students will, undoubtedly, embrace a justice-seeking approach, others a knowledge-seeking approach, focusing on the biographies and historical periods of particular theorists (sometimes as a shortcut for understanding the thinker's ideas), and still others will gravitate toward an analytical approach. Regardless of the approach they prefer, ideally all students of political theory should consider what consequences follow from emphasizing one approach to the exclusion of the other two. In fact, the more a thinker confines his or her inquiry to one approach – a descriptive "scientific" and/or historical analysis of human behavior, a vision of ideal justice, or a critical analysis of the premises and assertions of others – arguably, the less political becomes his or her theory. For this reason, most thinkers rarely adopt one single approach to political theory – normative, empirical, or analytical – entirely at the exclusion of the others. And this is because no single approach to political inquiry would be adequate without the other two. Political theorists have, and will remain, fascinated by questions that cannot be reduced to scientific or historical questions, or, despite efforts of some analytic thinkers, be reduced to philosophical questions of linguistics because, such questions, e.g., what is justice or freedom?, require normative judgments. After all, the more interesting and perhaps significant political theorists are those who adeptly blend all three approaches. This certainly is true of the first political theorist: Plato's Socrates.

Notes

1 Peter Laslett, *Philosophy, Politics and Society* (Oxford: Basil Blackwell, 1967), 24.
2 For more on the debate about the purpose of theorizing about politics see Marc Stears, "The Vocation of Political Theory: Principles, Empirical Inquiry, and the Politics of Opportunity," *European Journal of Political Theory* 4 (October 2005): 325–50.
3 John Gunnell, *Political Theory: Tradition and Interpretation* (Cambridge: Winthrop Press, 1979), 70, who argues that these "traditions" in political theory are "in fact basically a retrospective analytical construction."
4 Gunnell, *Political Theory*, 136.

5 See Hannah Arendt, *The Human Condition* (Chicago: Chicago University Press, 1958); Leo Strauss, *Natural Right and History* (Chicago: University of Chicago Press, 1953); Michael Sandel, *Liberalism and the Limits of Justice* (Cambridge: Cambridge University Press, 1982); Brian Barry, *Why Social Justice Matters* (Cambridge: Polity, 2005).
6 Karl Marx, "Capital," in *The Marx and Engels Reader*, Robert Tucker, ed. (New York: W.W. Norton, 1972), 401.
7 Gunnell refers to "family resemblances" among canonical thinkers in *Political Theory*, 136.
8 See Ernest Barker, *Reflections on Government* (London: Oxford University Press, 1942), 227, who attributes this sentiment to Kant.
9 All political thought (and action), Strauss declared, has "in itself a directedness toward knowledge of the good: of the good life, or the good society," and to find either requires being reacquainted with "natural right" or a higher morality; See Strauss, *What is the Purpose of Political Philosophy* (Chicago: University of Chicago Press, 1959), 10.
10 See Michael Oakeshott, "Introduction," *Leviathan* (Oxford: Basil Blackwell, 1957), x.
11 Gunnell, *Political Theory*, 142.
12 George Sabine, "What is a Political Theory?," *The Journal of Politics* (February 1939): 1–16, 11.
13 See C.D.C. Reeve, "Introduction," *Plato's Republic* (Cambridge: Hackett Publishing, 2004), xv, who finds that the best works of political theory are those that not only sharply scrutinize the present political landscape, but also speculate on future possibilities.
14 See J.S. Mill, *Considerations on Representative Government* (London: Longman, Green and Company, 1926), 1. Italics added.
15 Carl Sagan, *Cosmos* (New York: Random House, 1980), 193.
16 Karl Marx, "The Eighteenth Brumaire of Louis Bonaparte," in *Marx-Engels Reader*, Robert Tucker, ed., 595.
17 Michael Oakeshott, "Scientific Politics," in *Michael Oakeshott: Religion, Politics, and The Moral Life*, Thomas Fuller, ed. (New Haven: Yale University Press, 1993): 97–110. Italics added.
18 Thomas Thorson, *Logic of Democracy*, (New York: Holt, Rinehart, and Winston, 1962), 81.
19 David Spitz, "Introduction," in *Political Theory and Social Change*, David Spitz, ed. (New York: Atherton Press, 1967): ix–xii, xi.
20 Stears, "The Vocation of Political Theory: Principles, Empirical Inquiry, and the Politics of Opportunity," 326.
21 Some analytic thinkers, like Gunnell and Vincent, seek to expose the many layers of preconceived and tacit assumptions about what many call the vocation of political theory that generations of academics take for granted. See Gunnell, *Political Theory* and Andrew Vincent, *The Nature of Political Theory* (Oxford: Oxford University Press, 2004).
22 Isaiah Berlin, *Concepts and Categories*, Henry Hardy, ed. (New Jersey: Princeton University Press, 1978), 5.
23 Bertrand Russell, *The Problems of Philosophy* (London: Oxford University Press, 1964), 167.
24 John Gunnell, *Political Philosophy and Time* (Middletown: Wesleyan University Press, 1968), 10.
25 Vincent, *The Nature of Political Theory*, 322.
26 John Gunnell, "Desperately Seeking Wittgenstein," *European Journal of Political Theory* 3 (January 2004): 77–98, 78.
27 Michael Oakeshott, *Experience and Its Modes* (Cambridge: Cambridge University Press, 1933), 3.
28 Gunnell, "Desperately Seeking Wittgenstein," 96.
29 Pascal quoted by Carl Becker, *Modern Democracy* (New Haven: Yale University Press, 1941), 100. Italics added.
30 For more on the structure of the Socratic method, see Hugh Benson, "Socratic Method," in *The Cambridge Companion To Socrates*, Donald R. Morrison, ed. (Cambridge: Cambridge University Press, 2011): 179–200; and George Klosko, "Rational Persuasion in Plato's Political Theory," *History of Political Thought* 7 (1986): 15–31. However, Thomas C. Brickhouse and Nicholas D. Smith, *Plato's Socrates* (Oxford: Oxford University Press, 1996): 147, insist "that there is no such thing as 'the Socratic (method).'"
31 Socrates never attempted to instill knowledge, says Ernest Barker, after all, he had always disclaimed its possession. "He desired to awaken thought. He was the gadfly who stung men into a sense of truth ... he practiced the art of midwifery, and brought thought to birth," see Ernest Barker, *The Political Thought of Plato and Aristotle* (New York: Dover Publications, 1959), 64.
32 My preference notwithstanding, one finds little consensus (suggested by the essays in this volume) on what exactly is, or should be the purpose of Socratic inquiry and its application in the contemporary classroom, which is not surprising. I view Socrates' method as an analytical tool for interrogating arguments as an end or value in itself; however, others may view his *elenchus* as a means or pathway to achieving higher ends, e.g., true justice, an engaged citizenry, a moral character, etc.

Bibliography

Arendt, H. 1958. *The Human Condition*. Chicago: Chicago University Press.
Barker, Ernest. 1942. *Reflections on Government*. London: Oxford University Press.
———. 1959. *The Political Thought of Plato and Aristotle*. New York: Dover Publications.
Barry, Brian. 2005. *Why Social Justice Matters*. Cambridge: Polity.
Becker, Carl. 1941. *Modern Democracy*. New Haven: Yale University Press.
Benson, Hugh H. 2011. "Socratic Method." In *The Cambridge Companion To Socrates*. Donald R. Morrison ed. Cambridge: Cambridge University Press: 179–200.
Berlin, Isaiah. 1978. *Concepts and Categories*. Henry Hardy ed. New Jersey: Princeton University Press.
Brickhouse, Thomas C. and Nicholas D. Smith. 1996. *Plato's Socrates*. Oxford: Oxford University Press.
Gunnell, John. 1968. *Political Philosophy and Time*. Middletown: Wesleyan University Press.
———. 1979. *Political Theory: Tradition and Interpretation*. Cambridge: Winthrop Prsss.
———. 2004. "Desperately Seeking Wittgenstein." *European Journal of Political Theory* 3/1: 77–98.
Guthrie, W.K.C. 1975. *History of Greek Philosophy*, Vol. IV. Cambridge: Cambridge University Press.
Hobbes, Thomas. 1957. *Leviathan*. Michael Oakeshott ed. Oxford: Basil Blackwell.
Klosko, George. 1986. "Rational Persuasion in Plato's Political Theory." *History of Political Thought* 7: 15–31.
Laslett, Peter. 1967. *Philosophy, Politics and Society*. Oxford: Basil Blackwell.
Mill, John Stuart. 1926. *Considerations on Representative Government*. London: Longman, Green and Company.
Oakeshott, Michael. 1933. *Experience and Its Modes*. Cambridge: Cambridge University Press.
———. 1993. "Scientific Politics." In *Michael Oakeshott: Religion, Politics, and The Moral Life*. Thomas Fuller ed. New Haven: Yale University Press: 97–110.
Reeve, C.D.C. 2004. "Introduction." In *Plato's Republic*. Cambridge: Hackett Publishing.
Russell, Bertrand. 1964. *The Problems of Philosophy*. London: Oxford University Press.
Sabine, George. 1939. "What is a Political Theory?" *The Journal of Politics* 1/2: 1–16.
Sandel, Michael. 1982. *Liberalism and the Limits of Justice*. Cambridge: Cambridge University Press.
Sagan, Carl. 1980. *Cosmos*. New York: Random House.
Spitz, David. 1967. "Introduction." In *Political Theory and Social Change*. David Spitz ed. New York: Atherton Press: ix–xii.
Stears, Marc. 2005. "The Vocation of Political Theory: Principles, Empirical Inquiry, and the Politics of Opportunity." *European Journal of Political Theory* 4/10: 325–50.
Strauss, Leo. 1953. *Natural Right and History*. Chicago: University of Chicago Press.
———. 1959. *What is the Purpose of Political Philosophy*. Chicago: University of Chicago Press.
Thorson, Thomas. 1962. *The Logic of Democracy*. New York: Holt, Rinehart, and Winston.
Tucker, Robert ed. 1972. *Marx-Engels Reader*. New York: W.W. Norton.
Vincent, Andrew. 2004. *The Nature of Political Theory*. Oxford: Oxford University Press.

Appendix to Chapter 8
Discussion Questions for Plato's *Laches*

Part IA (178a–181d)

1. What are Lysimachus and Melesias concerned with? Why are they concerned and why do they appeal to Laches and Nicias?
2. How is Socrates introduced into the proceedings? In what sense is Socrates an authority or an expert? Why does he allow Nicias and Laches to go before him?

Part IB (181e–184d)

3. What argument does Nicias make with regard to fighting in armor? What, if anything, does his argument reveal about a) his character and b) his philosophical dispositions (or lack thereof)?
4. What argument does Laches make with regard to fighting in armor? What, if anything, does his argument reveal about a) his character and b) his philosophical dispositions (or lack thereof)?

Part IC (184d–190e)

5. Unable to reach a common understanding, Lysimachus requests that Socrates settle the matter. How does he want Socrates to do this and why does Socrates refuse to settle things in this way? What effect does this have on the conversation going forward?
6. What is Socrates' understanding of knowledge? What is his understanding of the relationship between means (how one proceeds) and ends (knowledge)? Where do Nicias and Laches stand with regard to the method of Socrates?

Part IIA (190e–199e)

7. What is Laches' first definition of courage and what is wrong with it? How does Socrates move Laches to his second definition of courage? What is his second definition and what becomes of it?
8. Nicias finally enters the conversation. After taking a jab at Laches, Nicias offers a definition of courage. What is this definition of courage and does the definition satisfy what Socrates asks of him?

Part IIB (190e–199e)

9. Unlike the definition of courage provided by Laches, that of Nicias gives knowledge a central role. What type of knowledge does courage consist of according to Nicias? How do Laches and Nicias differ with regard to knowledge? What is the position of Socrates on this topic?

10 What is the significance of connecting Nicias with sophistry? Why is Laches' criticism of Nicias on this front less convincing that that provided by Socrates?

Part IIC (199e–201c)

11 Would you describe the end of the dialog as comic? Why or why not? Might an argument be made that it is tragic? If so, why?
12 Why is the dialog named after Laches and not Nicias?

Index

Academy and College of Philadelphia 73
Achilles 25
Adeimantus 13–15, 61
Aeschylus 28
Agathon 36–7
Alcibiades 35–43, 116, 147
Alfarabi 71
Algeria 127
Allen, R.E. 47–8
America *see* the United States
Anytus 24
Apollo 48
Aquinas, Thomas 120, 154
Arendt, Hannah 154
Aristeides 98
Aristophanes 12, 24, 26, 28, 48–9; *The Clouds* 12, 24, 48–9
Aristotle 28, 59, 63, 118–19, 152, 156–8, 160; *Poetics* 28
Athens 26–8, 37, 39–40, 48–9, 78, 104, 116, 138, 154; Persian Wars 28; Prytaneum 26
Augustine 117, 154; *Confessions* 117

Barkalow, Jordon 2, 94
Bendis 17
Bentham, Jeremy 59, 160
Berlin, Isaiah 158
Bibby, Andrew 2, 70
Bickford, Susan 133
Bloom, Allan 125–6, 142; *The Closing of the American Mind* 125, 142
Boghossian, Peter 10
Boyer, Ernest 81
Brann, Eva T.H. 24, 89
Brickhouse, Thomas C. 22
Burbules, Nicholas C. 126
Burke, Edmund 155

Cain, Rebecca Bensen 1, 13
Calhoun, David H. 116
Callias 49
Callicles 60, 133, 147
Canada 81, 85, 89; Alberta 82, 85; British Columbia (BC) 82

Carao, Daniel H. 83
Carmichael, Douglas 116
Catholic Church 154
Cephalus 128, 133
Chaerophon 24, 48
China 130; Confucian education 126, 130–2
Christianity 65
Christodoulou, Daisy 85
Clark, Richard E. 84
The Cloud of Unknowing 119
colonialism 127
Committee on Blacks in the American Philosophical Association 126
constructivism 82–3
Cooper, Barry 1, 22
Copeland, Matt 1, 140
Corey, Paul 2, 138
Cowboy Plato 9, 15–18
Critias 116

Darwin, Charles 87
David, Jacques-Louis 76; *Death of Socrates* 76
Delphic Oracle 12, 23–4, 27, 29, 48–9
Derrida, Jacques 127; *Monolingualism of the Other, Or, The Prosthesis of Origin* 127
Dewey, John 2, 72, 81, 83, 85–90
Dionysius 36
Diotima 36–8

education *see* university
Eisele, Thomas D. 1
English Civil Wars 154
English language 73, 126, 128–9
Enlightenment 60
Euripides 28
Europe 71–2, 75–6, 145
Euthypro 61

Fordyce, David 71
Fott, David 88
Foucault, Michel 23
France 154; French Revolution 154; Reign of Terror 154

Franklin, Benjamin 70–8; *Autobiography* 73, 75; *Proposals Relating to the Education of Youth in Pensilvania* 73
Fullan, Michael 83

Glaucon 14–16, 61, 85, 128
God, or gods or divine 2, 22–9, 37–8, 48–9, 61, 63–4, 67, 76–7, 102, 116–19, 154, 158
Gorry, Jonathan 130
Gower, Barry S. 1
Great Books 10, 70, 72, 125–6
Greek language 17–18, 128–9
Greek poets 128
Grey, Ramona June 2, 152
Gunnell, John 158–9

Hadot, Pierre 119
Haidt, Jonathan 144
Hand, Michael 116
Haroutinian-Gordon, Sophie 116
Harvard Educational Review 126
Haynes, Joanna 115–16
Hegel, Georg Friedrich Wilhelm 22
Higgins, Kathleen 146
Hirsch, E.D. 84
Hobbes, Thomas 59, 154, 156–8
Homer 101; *Iliad* 25
Hume, David 59, 63, 153, 158

Jansche, Vanessa 1, 35
Jefferson, Thomas 70–2, 76–8
Jenco, Leigh Kathryn 131
Jenks, Rod 1, 12
Jesus 23, 64
Johnson, Diane E. 148

Kant, Immanuel 2, 59–60, 62–8, 157; *Critique of Judgment* 65; *Critique of Pure Reason* 63; *Religion within the Boundaries of Reason Alone* 64
Kirschner, Paul 84–5
Klein, Jacob 47
Krahenbuhl, Kevin 82
Kreeft, Peter 1, 10–11
Kronman, Anthony 83–4
Kyriakides, Leonidas 83

Laches 35, 94, 98–108, 164–5
Laertius, Diogenes 116
Laslett, Peter 152
LeMoine, Rebecca 2, 125
Lenkeit, Jenny 83
Livingstone, David W. 2, 81
Lukianoff, Greg 144
Lycon 24
Lysimachus 98–101, 103

McGuire, Steven F. 5, 59
Machiavelli, Niccolò 156–8, 160

Malcolmson, Patrick 83, 85
Mann, Thomas 28; *Magic Mountain* 28
Marsyas 37
Marx, Karl 154, 156–8, 160
Meckstroth, Christopher 132, 134
Melesias 98–101, 103
Meletus 24–6, 29
Mill, John Stuart 156
Myers, Richard 83, 85, 143

Neatby, Hilda 85–7, 89
Nehamas, Alexander 1
Neisser, Barbara 1, 105
Nelson, Leonard 1, 10–12, 98, 116
Nicias 98–104, 107–8, 164–5
Nietzsche, Friedrich 23, 88, 131; *The Birth of Tragedy from the Spirit of Music* 131
Nussbaum, Martha 85, 89, 125–6, 134, 141–2; *Cultivating Humanity: A Classical Defense of Reform in Liberal Education* 125–6
Nyotek, Alaska 128

Oakeshott, Michael 159
O'Connell, Colin 83
O'Connor, David 12
O'Neill, Brendan 144
Organization for Economic Co-operation and Development (OECD) 82
Oxford Dictionary 146

The Paper Chase 22
Phillips, Kristopher G. 142
philosophy; art of dying 27, 53, 61, 118–20; eros 1, 35–43, 139; *intellectus* 115; *noesis* 16, 117–19; *ratio* 115–16
Pieper, Josef 117–20
Pindar 53, 61
Pitkin, Hannah 158
Plato 1, 9, 11–18, 22, 23, 26–8, 35–39, 47–8, 53, 59–68, 70–1, 73, 76–8, 81, 94, 96–9, 104, 107, 116, 118, 125–7, 129, 131–4, 138, 152–5, 157–61; Academy 22, 28, 73, 134; *Alcibiades I* 1, 35–43; *Apology* 1, 12–13, 22–8, 36, 47–9, 52–4, 77, 96, 100, 116, 118, 127, 129, 138; *Charmides* 35; *Cratylus* 129; *Crito* 50, 138; dialogues 11–18, 66–7, 132; *Euthydemus* 116; *Euthyphro* 1, 22, 29, 129; *Gorgias* 12–13, 24, 28, 77, 96, 116, 133, 147; *Hippias Major* 129; *Laches* 35, 94, 98–108, 164–5; *Laws* 155; *Meno* 1, 12, 35, 47–55, 61–2, 96, 127, 132; *Phaedo* 24, 54, 61, 96, 119, 138; *Phaedrus* 61, 118; *Philebus* 22; *Protagoras* 23, 28, 77, 120; *Republic* 2, 9, 12–13, 16–17, 22, 28, 35, 37–41, 50, 61, 81, 85–8, 96, 98, 128–9, 133; *Sophist* 97; *Symposium* 35–8, 42, 147; *Theaetetus* 35–6, 138
Polemarchus 13, 50, 128

political science 1, 81, 90
political theory 22, 104, 152–61; analytic or critical 158–9; justice-seeking 153–6; knowledge-seeking 156–8
Polus 12, 96
Protagoras 23, 28, 77, 120
Protarchus 22
public schools 81, 83
Pythagoras 118

Ramée, Pierre de la 71
Rawls, John 154
Reeve, C.D.C. 155
religion *see* God
Rhodes, James M. 143
Rorty, Richard 88
Rousseau, Jean-Jacques 60, 154–5
Rud, Anthony G. 116
The Rural Socrates 76

Sandel, Michael 154
Saran, Rene 1
Saxonhouse, Arlene 28
Schall, James 89–90
scholarship of teaching and learning (SoTL) 81
Schlosser, Joel Alden 1
Schneider, Jack 71
science, technology, engineering, and mathematics (STEM) 83
Scott, Gary Alan 1, 39
Scythians 101
Sebell, Dustin 1
Seeskin, Kenneth 1, 13, 96
Sintonen, Matt 1
Smith, Nicholas D. 22
Socrates 1–2; comedy 22–9; contrast with Dewey 81, 85–90; cultural imperialism 125–34; *eros* 35–43; as an example 115–20; modern university 138–48; philosophical standards 155, 159–61; recollection 47–55, 59–62, 66; as a storyteller 9–18; student-center learning 95–108; trial 22–3, 28, 48, 77; in the United States 70–8
Socratic method; active-learning 1–2, 10, 11, 18, 60, 81–90, 94–107; *aidos* 23, 25, 28–9; Americanization 2, 70–8; *anamnesis*, memory, recollection 2, 47–55, 59–68, 139; *aporia*, perplexity 10–12, 35, 47, 52–3, 99, 102, 115, 117, 129, 133, 138, 158; cave analogy 9, 16–18, 22, 62, 86–7, 139; comedy 22–9; dialectics 9, 13, 15, 17, 41–2, 47–8, 54, 61, 71, 77, 85–6, 89, 95, 116–17, 131, 133, 138, 147–8; discussion boards 94, 104–5, 140; effectiveness 1, 71–2, 74, 83–5, 88–9, 125–6, 133, 148; *elenchus* 1, 10, 12–14, 70–1, 74, 77, 94–9, 117, 125, 133, 138–9, 160–1; *epanodo* 22; eristics 89–90, 117; *eros* 1, 35–43, 139; *eudaimonia* 143; existence 22–9; expert on love 35–43; Benjamin Franklin 70–8;
Great Books 10, 70, 72, 125–6; *hodos* 22, 96; ignorance 12, 14, 23, 29, 35–6, 38–43, 47–9, 52–4, 68, 75, 85–6, 96–8, 102, 115, 118, 142, 155, 160–1; images 9, 13–18, 25, 50, 54, 62, 66–7, 75–6, 87, 99, 117, 131, 138–9, 143; irony 12, 17, 23, 29, 53, 97, 99; Thomas Jefferson 70–2, 76–8; job-searching mentality 139, 141–2; Immanuel Kant 2, 59–60, 62–8, 157; *Laches* 35, 94, 98–107, 164–5; law school 61, 70, 75, 83, 125, 130; linguistic imperialism 126–9; *maieutics* 71; no method, 2, 115–20; normative imperialism 126, 129–33; online mentality 139–41; opinion 2, 9–18, 25, 28, 35–6, 40, 48–9, 52, 55, 74, 84, 86–7, 96–8, 100, 102–4, 108, 117, 128–31, 133, 138, 140, 142–3, 145–8, 152, 156; pedagogical debate 1–2, 9–11, 18, 22, 66–8, 70–1, 78, 81–90, 94, 96–7, 116, 125, 130, 133, 138–40, 142, 145, 148, 152–61; philosophical imperialism 2, 125, 133–4; philosophical standards, 2, 152–61; political theory 22, 104, 152–61; reason 10–12, 15, 17, 22, 27, 35, 37–43, 48–9, 51, 59, 67–8, 97, 100, 103–4, 107, 115, 118, 130–2, 140, 145; recollection 2, 47–55, 60–3, 65, 67–8; refutation 35, 40–2, 47–52, 54, 94–7, 117, 125, 133; relativist mentality 126, 139, 142–7; Rural Socrates 76–8; safe space mentality 139, 143–6; self-knowledge 39, 41–3, 48, 70, 77–8, 161; skepticism 10, 47–55, 77, 90, 116, 138, 143; Socratic Circles 1, 11, 140; stories and storytelling 9, 13–18, 29, 48, 60, 62; troll mentality 139, 146–8; turning the soul, conversion 62, 68, 125, 139; university today, 2, 81–90, 125–34, 138–48; virtue 12, 23, 25, 27–9, 37, 39, 42, 47–55, 60–1, 75–7, 94–6, 98, 101, 104, 107–8, 125, 130, 133, 139, 154, 157, 161
Sokolon, Marlene K. 1, 9
sophist, sophistry 12–13, 18, 22, 24, 28, 49, 87, 89–90, 97, 100–5, 107–8, 116–17, 120, 125, 155, 165
Speusippus 22
Spitz, David 158
Sprague, Rosamond K. 99, 101
Steel, Sean 2, 83, 89, 115
Stokes, Michael C. 1
Stokke, Anna 85
Strauss, Leo 22–3, 28, 47, 89, 154; *The City and the Man* 47
Sturm, Johannes 71
Sweller, John 84

Tessitore, Aristide 99, 101
Thorson, Thomas 157
Thrasymachus 9, 14, 133, 147
Thucydides 98
Tigner, Steven S. 47
Tocqueville, Alexis de 72

Trump, Donald 138, 146–7
Turkle, Sherry 140

United States, or America 2, 70–8, 85, 94, 125–6, 128, 130, 154
university 2, 9, 59, 73, 81, 83, 85, 115, 138–48
University of Pennsylvania 73

Van Morrison 115
Vaughan, John 76
Vlastos, Gregory 12, 47–8
Voegelin, Eric 27–8

Ward, Ann 1, 47
Watts, Isaac 71, 73; *The Improvement of the Mind* 73
Whipple Jr., Robert D. 1
Wilberding, Erick 1
Winstanley, Carrie 118, 120
Wittgenstein, Ludwig 158–9

Xenophon 12, 23, 70, 73, 76–8, 85; *Memorabilia* 24, 77, 85

Zeus 23

Taylor & Francis eBooks

Helping you to choose the right eBooks for your Library

Add Routledge titles to your library's digital collection today. Taylor and Francis ebooks contains over 50,000 titles in the Humanities, Social Sciences, Behavioural Sciences, Built Environment and Law.

Choose from a range of subject packages or create your own!

Benefits for you
- Free MARC records
- COUNTER-compliant usage statistics
- Flexible purchase and pricing options
- All titles DRM-free.

Benefits for your user
- Off-site, anytime access via Athens or referring URL
- Print or copy pages or chapters
- Full content search
- Bookmark, highlight and annotate text
- Access to thousands of pages of quality research at the click of a button.

REQUEST YOUR FREE INSTITUTIONAL TRIAL TODAY
Free Trials Available
We offer free trials to qualifying academic, corporate and government customers.

eCollections – Choose from over 30 subject eCollections, including:

Archaeology	Language Learning
Architecture	Law
Asian Studies	Literature
Business & Management	Media & Communication
Classical Studies	Middle East Studies
Construction	Music
Creative & Media Arts	Philosophy
Criminology & Criminal Justice	Planning
Economics	Politics
Education	Psychology & Mental Health
Energy	Religion
Engineering	Security
English Language & Linguistics	Social Work
Environment & Sustainability	Sociology
Geography	Sport
Health Studies	Theatre & Performance
History	Tourism, Hospitality & Events

For more information, pricing enquiries or to order a free trial, please contact your local sales team:
www.tandfebooks.com/page/sales

Routledge — Taylor & Francis Group | The home of Routledge books

www.tandfebooks.com